40 Years with a Whistle

Life Lessons from the Field of Play

40 Years with a Whistle

Life Lessons from the Field of Play

Dan John

Foreword
Chris Long

On Target Publications
Aptos, California

40 Years with a Whistle
Life Lessons from the Field of Play

Dan John

Foreword by Chris Long

Copyright © 2019 Daniel Arthur John
Foreword © 2019 Chris Long
Cover photos © 2019 Don Bailey (discus) and Laree Draper (Highland)

ISBN-13: 978-1-931046-42-8
First printing April 2019

On Target Publications
P O Box 1335
Aptos, California 95001 USA
otpbooks.com

Library of Congress Cataloging-in-Publication Data

Names: John, Dan, author.
Title: 40 years with a whistle : life lessons from the field of play / Dan
   John ; Foreword, Chris Long.
Other titles: Forty years with a whistle
Description: Santa Cruz, CA : On Target Publications, [2019] | Includes
   index.
Identifiers: LCCN 2019002164 (print) | LCCN 2019004619 (ebook) | ISBN
   9781931046411 (ePub) | ISBN 9781931046428 (pbk.)
Subjects: LCSH: Coaching (Athletics)--Philosophy. | Coaches
   (Athletics)--Conduct of life.
Classification: LCC GV711 (ebook) | LCC GV711 .J64 2019 (print) | DDC
   796.07/7--dc23

LC record available at https://lccn.loc.gov/2019002164

Also by Dan John

To Mentor

Mentor was the guide of Telemachus in *The Odyssey*.
Athena used Mentor to insist that Telemachus stand up for his
family and seek his father. Mentor's name comes down to us
today as those fine people who insist we stand up for what is
important and seek what is true and good.

To all of my mentors

Long live the Brotherhood
August 2011

Contents

Part Three: What I Think Now

Appendices

Foreword

Dan John is a renaissance man. He's a poet, an athlete, a teacher, a philosopher, a writer, a coach and a scholar. He is equally at home explaining exactly where to place your feet when throwing a discus, deconstructing Shakespeare or discussing the works of Joseph Campbell. He knows the words to Broadway show tunes; he can explain the ins and outs of ancient Greek battle tactics; tell you why the Battle of Agincourt was crucial to Western Civilization, and detail the advantages and disadvantages of the run-and-shoot offense or the split-back veer. If you play Trivial Pursuits with Dan, you'll probably lose.

If you're thinking of embarking on an ill-advised adventure and need a companion, Dan is your guy. (Almost all of my near-death stories begin with, "So this one time, Dan and I.")

There's a section of the Green River on the Utah–Colorado border that John Wesley Powell called "Hell's Half Mile." Dan and I went down the first part of it in an inflatable kayak…until the kayak suddenly deflated and disappeared. We went down the second half in our life jackets.

Dan had just come back from the Middle East with a strange liver ailment which, among other things, caused him to sleep almost to the point of being comatose. He went to sleep early one morning as we were preparing to start on the river and there was nothing I could do to wake him. So, I tied him to the boat so he wouldn't fall out. If the boat happened to flip over, well, that would be a problem. When he eventually awoke and I explained why he was tied to the boat, he agreed it was the only sensible solution.

During another trip on the Colorado, we were on a boat that flipped over at a spot called Skull Rapid. As we clung to the overturned boat, we realized a young woman who had been on the boat with us was in trouble…unconscious, with her eyes rolled back in her head. I held onto the raft; Dan and I held hands and Dan grabbed her by her hair and pulled her to safety. Always good to have a stupidly strong guy with you.

In Dan's garage gym, there are no machines, no stair steppers, ellipticals or treadmills. Instead, you'll find kettlebells, barbells, Olympic plates and bars and, most importantly, a coach who can teach you how to use them.

Dan John has coached and is on a first-name basis with NFL quarterbacks, major league baseball players, Navy SEALs, United States Army Green Berets and Division I throwers. But at his core, he's just a kid from South San Francisco. Professional athletes, high school kids, the Bishop of the Diocese of Salt Lake City or the waiter at the Landmark Cafe—they are all equal in his eyes. This due to Dan being aware of the many people in his life who were instrumental in shaping who he is. You're going meet some of them in this book.

Dan and I have been friends for over 35 years. As I read through this book, over and over I found myself mentally saying, "Yup" and "Absolutely." If you're a coach, an athletic administrator or the parent of a school-age athlete, you need to read this book. I know my coaching staff will be reading it.

Chris Long
Athletic Director, Juan Diego Catholic High School

In the Beginning...

When I look back at my senior year at Utah State, it remains one of the great times of my life. My home life settled, my dorm roommates played well, my grades rocked and I was having the best season of my athletic career.

As we approached the end of May that year, Coach Ralph Maughan, "The Greatest Aggie," asked me to come to his office. I paused. My teammates sniggered. I reviewed my excuses.

"I swear, Coach, it wasn't me."

"This kind of thing gets blown out of proportion."

"I had no idea she was family."

Oddly, I hadn't done anything wrong.

"Danny, I would like you to come back in the fall. I need help with these guys (he waved toward the locker room). They aren't lifting right."

I was 21. Many of my teammates were older. Next fall, I would be coaching them in the weightroom. I didn't have an official title, save "Assistant Coach."

The title of strength coach might not have even existed at the time.

Coach was worried about this "new kind of lifting;" instead of training like athletes, the Aggies were bodybuilding. Rather than mixing quick lifts with powerlifts, we were seeing the team blitz, boil and bake their biceps into submission.

As always, Coach was proactive about a problem. That fall, I was to plan, program, teach and coach the team to lift "properly."

Forty years later, I'm still doing the same thing.

I've learned a lot over those decades and would like to share these lessons with you. I didn't want a book filled with "Xs" and "Os" or sets and reps. I wanted to share the lessons that apply to life and living.

I begin with what are clearly my 10 best lessons of coaching. Each of these works well for the teacher, student, parent and neighbor too. Following the advice of the 10th lesson, I explore the stories of the people who shaped my career and the gems of advice they shared with me. I finish with my vision of coaching—basically looking at training from the big picture and the toolkit to allow one to succeed.

The lessons are simple.

The application is difficult.

The rewards are worth everything.

Dan John

Part One: Commandments

Chapter 1

40 Years with a Whistle

Go that way, really fast. If something gets in your way, turn.
~ **Charles de Mar,** *Better off Dead* (1985)

I have an odd weakness for 1970s and '80s comedies. They are certainly silly at times and often there are overlapping plots that don't make a lot of sense. *Better off Dead* is an underappreciated film from this era.

You certainly don't need to rush out and see it. And it should come as no surprise that the film didn't receive an Academy Award. The character played by John Cusack wants to impress his ex-girlfriend by skiing down K-12, a dangerous ski course. His advice from his friend, Charles de Mar, played by Curtis Armstrong who was also Booger in *Revenge of the Nerds,* gives us this classic piece of coaching:

Go that way, really fast.
If something gets in your way, turn.

As I've been pondering my experiences—good and bad— from teaching and coaching since 1979, I laughed out loud when I recently revisited this film. It has a Christmas scene; we watch it annually as part of our Christmas movie binge watching. The reason I laughed is simple: Charles de Mar is absolutely right.

If you want to give advice, shout it out!

For investments: *Buy low, sell high!*

For long-term nutrition advice: *Eat like an adult!*

For track athletes: *Run fast, turn left!*

For skiing:

Go that way, really fast. If something gets in your way, turn.

Screamed advice from the grandstands of competition and life is almost always true. I had a parent once get on me from the grandstands because we only had 10 men on the field for a punt. In American football, we are expected to have 11.

I turned to my assistant and said:

"Actually, I think we are doing pretty good. We usually only have nine!"

Now look, coaching and teaching have little to do with screaming out the obvious.

Screaming out the obvious is what ruins social media and social interactions. There is nothing worse than sitting next to some lout who continually yells at the television:

"They need to catch that ball!"

"They need to stay in bounds!"

"They need to X…or Y…or whatever more!"

I'm always shocked when I realize this genius is sitting so close to me when it is obvious the skill set should be rewarded with millions of dollars as a professional coach.

Lucky me to have him here!

If you are willing to invest years in working with someone, you will build the trust and knowledge that a simple cue might be a game-changer:

"Short Two!"

"West Special!

"Short Two" is a technical point in the discus that allowed one of my athletes to improve from eighth place to state champion on one throw. "West Special" spurred 11 teenage boys to realign and score a touchdown.

But, the journey to get to those cues can take a while. Screaming the obvious is one thing, cueing appropriate information is another.

Like John Powell says about the discus: "I said it was simple, not easy."

Life is pretty simple. A few decades ago, Robert Fulghum wrote about this in *All I Really Need to Know I Learned in Kindergarten*. Three of the ideas are the most ignored rules in gyms, training facilities and most public spaces:

> *1. Share everything.*
> *2. CLEAN UP YOUR OWN MESS.*
> *3. Flush!*

All true. All simple.

None done.

To succeed in school, every coach I have ever had has told our team, in some variation, that if we simply go to class, we will be fine.

"Show up!"

"Show up!" is the first of my three "secrets" of success:

> *1. Show up!*
> *2. Don't quit.*
> *3. Ask questions.*

Whenever I give someone these three steps, I feel like I am having my Charles de Mar moment.

These are true.

Absolutely true.

Screaming the obvious is NOT coaching. Coaching is literally carrying someone from here to there. Coaching is taking someone on the path. Sometimes we get there.

Sometimes we don't.

Oddly, getting there is not nearly as important as striving to get there.

It's the hardest lesson of life. Cervantes tells us, "It's the road, not the inn," and it is always fun to quote that line...but difficult to live it.

Dan Millman taught us this in *The Peaceful Warrior:*

> *"The journey...the journey is what brings us happiness... not the destination."*

That's coaching. Let's get there.

Chapter 2
The 10 Commandments of Coaching

Not only have I coached since 1979, I have also taught. I have been in elementary, high school, junior college and university classrooms instructing history, economics, religious education and studies and, obviously, sports and conditioning. (I have friends who tell me I know the *Holy Bible* so well because I knew all the original writers.)

For me, it is not unusual to try to organize complicated concepts in something along the lines of the 10 Commandments. This list, *The 10 Commandments of Coaching,* is not a list of "Thou shalt" or "Thou shalt nots;" rather, it is a series of "Do this" principles.

Here you go:

1. *Constant assessment*

2. *Constant upgrading*

3. *Ignore perfect*

4. *This isn't moral theology.*

5. *Everything works!*

6. *Achieving a goal versus achieving success*

7. *After the peak is the cliff.*

> *8. Self-discipline is a finite resource.*
>
> *9. Fundamentals trump everything else.*
>
> *10. Take a moment to appreciate those who went before you.*

There is nothing new or original about any of these. Some of the "commandments" might be more appropriate at certain times, but as the years and decades pass, all of them will ring true. Some of them, sadly, need to be learned and relearned time and again.

While there may be other absolute truths about coaching, teaching and life in general, these 10 are a nice framework to begin the discussion concerning longevity in any field.

Let's look at each commandment in the following chapters.

Chapter 3
Constant Assessment

I always say "constant assessment" the same way Mad-Eye Moody screamed "constant vigilance" to a young Harry Potter. And, I hope it resonates with my people as much as it did with the students at Hogwarts.

It's hard for me to explain "constant assessment" without wanting to pull out a big piece of paper and draw a continuum. On one end is honest assessment and evaluation. In between, we find a lack of decisiveness. And, on the other, we find the "murmurer."

In every organization, there is always a "murmurer." God complained about these people to Moses in *The Book of Numbers*: "How long will this wicked assembly keep complaining about me? I've heard the complaints of the Israelites that they've been murmuring against me."

If you want to be a leader, you have to know that you WILL be constantly second- and third-guessed.

Murmur. Murmur. Murmur.

If people complained about the way God handled things, you have to realize they might find issues with your mortal wisdom too.

If you want to ruin your life as a coach, just sit in the stands during a meet. You will be surprised how stupid, ill-informed, lost and unfair you are as a coach and a leader.

True assessment is not standing behind Macbeth and whispering suggestions and better ideas. Lady Macbeth's great line, "That I may pour my spirits in thine ear," makes marvelous stage craft, but it is a poor role model for an assistant coach.

What I am trying to say, nicely, is that no matter what you do, someone will find issues, problems and personal insult.

Always.

Let's discuss true and honest assessment.

There is a great cliché from the therapy folks: "If you ain't assessing, you're guessing." I like that and, yes, it is true. This is why I make such a big deal about measurements and standards. If a jumper jumps higher or farther, we know we are on the right track. I don't need to know the score on the various tests, screens or printouts.

But, we don't all work in track and field, swimming or simple weight loss. The standards there are all easy to measure with stopwatches, measuring tapes and weight scales. We'll need to dig deeper into true assessment.

Constant assessment is a pillar of proper coaching.

There are two terms I use a lot when it comes to the ongoing process of assessment:

> *Plan changes*
>
> *Game changers*

I hate plan changes. As I look over my life, I find the most stressful moments came from plan changes.

Before the era of cell phones, I used to carpool with several other parents for a sports league for my daughter. On one day, "we" all agreed I would pick them up. That was the plan—obviously, someone changed the plan or I wouldn't still talk about it.

For about two hours, I drove frantically around Salt Lake Valley from empty house to empty field to empty house trying to find the troop of eight-year-old girls I was responsible for that Saturday morning.

Later, I discovered one mom decided on having a "play day surprise" and took all the girls to the mall to go shopping and eat lunch.

I didn't know. Nor, for the record, did my wife.

That was a classic plan change.

As a coach, over and over I emphasize the word "decision." It means, literally, "to cut off." As a coaching staff, we "cut off" options and decide to go in this or that direction.

I have a well-worn joke that I use too often:

My doctor put me on a diet, but it wasn't enough food. Now I am on two diets.

When you follow any diet for about two years—and it simply doesn't matter what you decide to do—all diets bring about the same results. Most people don't follow a single diet for a whole day. A typical dieter begins the day with the Bagel Diet, slides to the Grazing Diet, adds in the Fast Food Diet and then finishes the day with the Drinking Man's Diet mixed with the Omnivore's Diet.

I would like to say, "I jest," but we all know this is more truth than hyperbole.

So, as a staff, we need to make decisions. We must stay true to that decision process. But, things happen.

Memorize that: *Things happen.*

Plans change. As a coach, I believe you actually need to plot and prepare for plan changes.

A local university, for example, has lost their starting quarterback for six of the last eight seasons. It makes sense that the staff would plot and plan what to do with the back-up quarterback.

Moreover, I can't think of a better way to say it than this:

"No battle plan survives contact with the enemy."
~ Helmuth von Moltke the Elder

This is why I don't like training in perfect conditions or training at the same time every day. I have lifted and thrown in competition at eight in the morning. I have deadlifted at 3:00 a.m. I have competed in rain, snow and fog so bad the officials couldn't see the discus after it left my hand.

I'm not sure that was safe.

I hate plan changes.

But, I am comfortable preparing for them.

The next key is game changers. These are tools, events or people who come along and completely "change the game."

Obviously.

Fosbury's high jump technique

Jaws and Star Wars—the summer blockbuster

Anabolic steroids

I hate that last one, anabolic steroids, but you can't ignore the impact on sports. Oddly, I have had more than a few experienced athletes tell me the real impact is amphetamines. The downside, I have been told, are little things like insomnia, lack of appetite and uncontrolled rage.

But, hey, more weight on the bar!

I have had several game changers in my career. Certainly, adding the Olympic lifts and the loaded carry family to my training changed me for the better. My annual discus camp adventure changed my thinking as both coach and athlete.

Assessing game changers is the easiest thing I do: When something has a massive impact on improvement almost overnight, we need to rethink and retool everything to adapt and adopt this new idea.

Barney Stinson from *How I Met Your Mother* is right:

"New is always better."

Unless it is not.

Constant assessment has to be tempered with appropriate measurements, appropriate adaptability and appropriate long-term vision. Again, in sports based on stopwatches and tape measures, assessment is easier than it is in rugby or American football.

Game changers lead us to our next core principle: constant upgrading.

Chapter 4
Constant Upgrading

As a coach...as a parent, as a neighbor, as a coworker, as a spouse...we need to always be vigilant about getting better.

Upgrading means more than just buying new equipment every year. I know of universities that annually buy millions of dollars of equipment, all magically branded on all sides for every photo opportunity, but still teach a jumping reverse curl instead of a power clean.

I upgrade constantly as a strength coach. The first—and we will come back to this again in the leadership discussion—is that I visit people and gyms. I've been inside the homes, gyms, garages and backyards of some the biggest and brightest names in the field. I know Bret Contreras is right about his glute research because I sat down next to the computer with him while the machine (insert technical name for something out of *Star Trek*) calibrated and measured...something.

I've had coffee in the morning with some of the best coaches on the planet before either of us showered or brushed our teeth. It's not romantic, but this is how I learn.

I upgrade first and foremost by "being there." I get the key information—the core ideas—without having to repeat the experiments and experiences.

Next, and Laree Draper will attest to this as I drag her along with me, I sit up front at workshops and clinics and LISTEN! In Hebrew, there is a great word, "shema," that means "listen," but think of it as Mom telling you "LISTEN!!!!" when you broke a family rule. I try to listen to speakers as if my mom was explaining my recent series of errors, sins and omissions.

My biggest secret for constant upgrading is this:

I often do nothing with the new information.

It's true. After sitting in the chair, doing the hands-on, reading the book and watching the video, I often realize, "We have this covered." Sometimes, I simply don't have the budget, both in time and resources, to go all in with some new idea we are doing in some form already.

And, there is always a chance I am wrong: I think we are already doing it, but the fault lies with me and my ego. This is where relearning comes in. I might not be a good learner, but I seem to be a very good rerelearner.

The next level of upgrading is equally simple: We might sprinkle in a few of the ideas here or there. There have been times when I didn't appreciate this sprinkling for a while.

I was doing sled pulls long before realizing it was massively improving my performance. The kettlebell swing took me a few years of deliberate swinging to appreciate. I still wonder why I didn't appreciate pullups from the beginning of my career. Preparing for my first kettlebell certification involved countless reps of KB clean and press mixed with pullups. I looked good, felt good and easily passed the cert. When someone asked what I learned, I said, "Pullups."

It's not like these are some kind of secret.

And, there are times when I almost want to toss out everything I did before and start all over. This would be true with the Olympic lifts, Tim Anderson's *Original Strength* and with loaded carries. In each case, I measurably performed better. This is where, once again, constant assessment and constant upgrading chase each other's tails; it's often hard to discern whether you are assessing or upgrading.

When something works better—note: "better" without measurements is a loaded word—you have to have the courage to tear down and rebuild everything as quickly as you can.

And, soon…you and I will be sitting in the front row trying to learn some new way of making it even better.

Chapter 5
Ignore Perfect

I often speak to college classes. I guest lecture both live and online. Online is actually fun. My dog Sirius Black likes to stick his head in front of the computer camera and make a cameo. Sadly, when I return the next session, the students seem to be focused on when Sirius is going shove his face toward the camera.

During the Q and A, I generally answer questions about things like neck position in this exercise or that one, mesocycles and supplements. Most of these questions won't really help the student early in a career. Then comes the next layer of questions. It usually starts with "If."

> *If you had to design a perfect gym...*
> *If you had to put together a perfect program...*
> *If you could only do one exercise...*

I understand this need.

In a sense, the student is simply asking:

"Please...just tell me what I need to know and what to do."

Oddly, I do the same thing. Whenever someone goes to a workshop or cert, I always ask the same question:

"Hey, what's the ONE thing I can use from the workshop?"

Years ago, I was sitting on my back deck with some elite military operators and I asked that question to one of the guys.

"Oh. You're an Alpha."

I'm sorry?

"Yeah, Alpha predator...great white shark, killer whale. One tool."

It took years for me to fully understand the length and breadth of this "one tool" insight. Let me take it to the absurd:

Tyrannosaurus rex may have been one of the greatest killing machines in our planet's history. But *T. rex* is terrible at pushups. *T. rex* might be your best option for land-locked carnage, but a horrible choice for the President's Physical Fitness Test.

The Alpha is perfect for one thing.

The problem with "perfect" is that there is a high cost in every other area of life and living. My friends in professional basketball are warned by the league that their great height might also impact their longevity.

Striving to lift more weight than anyone else is going to lead to joint issues...among other things.

My "perfect" training environment is a warm shed next to a field so we can O lift, do loaded carries and throw all in the same space. A bodybuilder might ask about the lack of a leg press machine at my perfect gym.

My perfect is not your perfect.

I was once asked at a conference the classic question:

"If you can do only one exercise, what would you do?"

Overhead squats?

The young man followed my answer with, "What if you don't know how to do overhead squats?"

I was stumped.

My perfect exercise was NOT perfect!

One lesson that resonates over my lifetime in athletics and academics is this: Pretty good is pretty good. Keep looking for "better." Keep upgrading.

Perfect can be a moving target.

The perfect vacation for a five-year-old involves rides on small trains, songs about a small world and a kiddie pool. For a 19-year-old college kid, it might involve sun, booze and late nights. Today, my perfect vacation includes long daily walks, swimming in cold water and afternoon naps.

Remember, even Mary Poppins was merely "practically perfect in every way."

Keep upgrading. Keep assessing. Ignore perfect.

Chapter 6
This Isn't Moral Theology

There are no "good" or "bad" exercises or training systems.

Let's review, once again, why I hate going to parties. Anyone involved in fitness, health, longevity or performance will probably have these same issues.

The problem?

Like *Soylent Green*...it's the people!

I'm often minding my own business at a party, trying to figure out if corn chips go with clam dip (of course they do!) when someone will come over and ask me...

"Hey, you're into, like, cannonballs..."

(Kettlebells)

"And lifting and stuff, so is it true..."

Here we go.

Let's make the list:

Squats hurt your knees.

> *(No, the way you do them hurts your knees.)*

Deadlifts hurt your back.

> *(No, the way you do them hurts your back.)*

Coffee is bad for you.
    (No.)
Wine is bad for you.
    (No.)
Veggies are good for you.

    (What do you mean by veggies? Corn chips are corn!)

And I can go on. My nutritionist friends tell me it's much worse for them as, since everybody eats, everybody is an expert on food.

It's this "good/bad" thing that drives me crazy. I constantly argue that exercises, exercise equipment and programs are tools. You simply need the right tool for the job. I sum this discussion of appropriate use of these tools like this:

Could we do X?
Done correctly, yes.
Should we do X?
It depends.

When it comes to food choices, we tend to fall into this "good/bad" trap too. Sweets are evil and veggies are good. If you get fat, well, you are sinful!

Oddly, even nonbelievers and some of my young atheist friends go right to the Seven Deadly Sins when it comes to discussing obesity:

Sloth
Gluttony
Greed
Wrath
Envy
Pride
Lust

When people decide to lose fat by insane fasting or strict low-calorie diets and rigorous exercise routines, I always wonder if in the back of their minds they think their "sinful behaviors" of gluttony and sloth need to be countered with torturous extremes.

Hesiod told us, "Moderation in all things." As a child, I was taught that virtue lived in the "mean of the extremes." That was great to memorize for a test, but living a life of moderation demands awareness and practice. It's easy to say, "Moderation in all things," but saying no to a seven-layer dip is challenging.

I'm sure a reasonable portion is fine. Oh, and please pass the corn chips and clam dip. Thank you.

Speaking of moderation, two of my favorite writers share absolutely extreme visions of moderation:

"Complete abstinence is easier than perfect moderation."
~ Saint Augustine

"Moderation is a fatal thing. Nothing succeeds like excess."
~ Oscar Wilde

I can't say it better than the author of *Ecclesiastes*.

Pete Seeger, the great folk singer, a favorite of my brother growing up, put this to music with the song *Turn! Turn! Turn!*:

> *To every thing there is a season,*
> *and a time to every purpose under the heaven:*
>
> *A time to be born, and a time to die;*
> *a time to plant, a time to reap that which is planted;*
>
> *A time to kill, and a time to heal;*
> *a time to break down, and a time to build up;*
>
> *A time to weep, and a time to laugh;*
> *a time to mourn, and a time to dance;*
>
> *A time to cast away stones,*
> *and a time to gather stones together;*

> *A time to embrace,*
> *and a time to refrain from embracing;*
>
> *A time to get, and a time to lose;*
> *a time to keep, and a time to cast away;*
>
> *A time to rend, and a time to sew;*
> *a time to keep silence, and a time to speak;*
>
> *A time to love, and a time to hate;*
> *a time of war, and a time of peace.*

Yes, there is evil in this world.

Yes, there is good.

No, we are not talking about good and evil when it comes to workouts and ways of eating.

But with the squat, be sure to sit down BETWEEN your legs.

There, that's good.

Chapter 7
Everything Works!

In *Never Let Go,* I gave two basic principles:

> *Everything works.*
>
> *Everything works…for about six weeks.*

As I review my athletic career and my time as a coach, this point seems to leap out of my memory and scream, "TRUTH!"

As usual, I had to learn this lesson the hard way.

Not long ago, I made a list of the 10 "mistakes" of my career. Let me list them:

1. *The cult of the bench press*—I fell for "Whadiya bench?" as the question of questions. Luckily, I got addicted to the bench press in 1971 and was "cured" by Dick Notmeyer in 1974. For the record, I probably benched more weight as a 162-pound high school senior than most people will ever lift. And…it didn't help that much!

2. *I joke about this all the time: "It worked so well, I stopped doing it."* My ability to ignore what works is now the cornerstone of my lectures. I think we all do it: What works is often so basic, fundamental and, frankly, boring, that we all fall in love with the bright new shiny promise and fancy promotion. It never works; focus on what works.

41

3. *Sadly, even with great mentors, I still often ignored the map.* Coach Maughan told me in 1977, "Lift three days a week; throw four days a week for the next eight years and you will be great." So, I lifted six days a week and threw twice a day trying to get there in four years.

Performance, like life, has speed limits.

4. *Of course, this last point leads to my biggest issue: overtraining.* I was working with a local guy well established in all the dark parts of performance. He noted that the biggest issue with American athletes is overtraining.

I asked, "Do I overtrain?"

"Dan, you are the poster child of overtraining."

Of course, recovering from overtraining—and the surgeries that go with it—takes more time and effort than appropriate training does.

5. *I ignored a lesson from Tommy Kono and all of the great Olympic lifters: balance serious O lifting work with periods of general training*...what we often call "bodybuilding."

As usual, I ignored advice about moderation and I would max out the day after an Olympic lifting meet to see if I could do more. It worked...until it didn't. Listen to those who have gone before you.

6. *Unless they are druggies.* This isn't a moral theology exam; I am simply pointing out the obvious. If someone took amphetamines before workouts, dope before meals (to get hungry) and used steroids, the training program is going to be different than if you use coffee as your go-to drug of choice. One friend told me, "At most, I improved 10 percent from the drugs." Ten percent is pretty good for simply popping a pill. If you are clean, listen to the clean.

7. *Instead of drugs, I fell for the tinctures set.* Sadly, I have thrown out my collection of failed magic pills as this would have been a lot of fun to walk down memory lane. Once you have paid for horny goat weed, it's difficult to not laugh out loud at yourself.

I fell for magic dust over and over again in my career. Not one thing outperformed good food and smart training.

8. *Magic dust, tinctures, potions and lotions were just the start.* I also fell for the bogus recovery stuff. True, meditation works for me; sleep tapes, saunas and hot tubs are all fabulous too. But, I also tried to heal a necrotic hip by looking sideways and wiggling my finger. Stick with the basics here.

9. *Nautilus training.* I completely bought into this stuff. I had a Nautilus gym membership and followed the rules exactly. And, in full candor, I made great progress for a few weeks. Then I stalled. My performance in the discus went down, down, down.

I still think this method of training has value, but the cost of each machine could buy a complete gym. And a car and a truck.

10. *CrossFit.* I loved—and still respect—the programming back in 2003 and 2004 when Lauren Jenai was doing the daily Workout of the Day (WOD).

I loved the idea of learning new things and "practicing" as a central tenant of training. Then, it went off into the paramilitary macho stuff that feeds some people's egos. "Regularly learn and play new sports," the last point of the famous "Fitness in 100 words" concept is good advice for everyone. Sadly, as with Nautilus, performance in my sports went down under these workouts.

By the way, even those early horrid supplements worked. The placebo effect is real and recent research indicates it works even when the person knows it is fake!

My little list of lessons underscores the value of variety and variation. Pavel Tsatousline famously explained variation as "same, but different." There might not be a better truth when it comes to long-term success in performance and life. In the area of nutrition, "same, but different" is great advice.

At the Olympic training center, the nutritionist told us to eat "protein and veggies" and "drink water." That sounds restrictive until you do the food math. It is estimated there are 20,000 to 200,000 different edible plants and animals. If we go on the low side—20,000—and you choose to eat just one animal and plant variety at every meal, you will have 400 million options to mix and match for the next few weeks.

I joke…but not much.

Everything works. But the things that work day in and day out over a career are going to be the fundamentals, the basics. These are the tools passed down from one generation to another, one coach to another coach and athlete to athlete.

Yes, there will be some variation. But not much.

Chapter 8
Achieving a Goal versus Achieving Success

…are not the same thing…sadly.

I have achieved many of my goals in life. I wanted to be a college athlete. I wanted to have advanced degrees. I wanted my career to be fairly independent.

I achieved all of those. I also wanted to be an Olympian. I wanted to be on the national team. I wanted to play football at the university and professional levels. I wanted to be Lori's boyfriend. I wanted to finish my doctorate.

Those are all "Nopes."

As I looked back at my successes in life, I began to realize that many of my high points had little to do with my goals. Ignoring real life, let's look at my top 10 moments in sports.

1. 1967—Winning hit in a softball game

Every lesson I know in life, sports and everything else comes from that day in 1967.

2. 1974—Westmoor football game

"They" were supposed to be the best team in our league's history. They were at minus seven yards of offense at the end of the first half...we were up 35–0. I memorized their scouting report and knew nearly every play. My last play was a sack for 15 yards, one of 17 tackles that night.

3. 1979—San Jose PCAA meet

Paul Rodondi told me to move my feet to the left a bit at the start of the discus throw and I threw my lifetime best with ease.

4. 1982—Softball League

From centerfield, I caught a short fly ball, tagged second on the fly and ran down the guy coming from first: an unassisted triple play.

5. 1996—Winning caber throw, Murray Highland Games

I had one attempt left at a nearly impossible caber. A dad of another competitor told his son, way too loud, "Well, you've won...no one will turn this." Jeff Armstrong told me later that he told the dad, "You just gave Dan the victory."

Turned it. Perfect toss.

6. 2001—Baton Rouge, the National Weightlifting Meet, last clean and jerk

If I make the lift, I'm National Champ. If I miss, I take fourth. Tiff walks over and, um, "reminds me" to make the lift. I did.

7. 2004—Ohio State Twilight Meet

After three weeks of discus camp, my legs were shot. Mike Pokowski comes up and tells me the local Ohio guys were making fun of me for being so old.

First throw: 55 meters and I showed them! Mike walks over: "I made that up."

8. 2005—Fast Action Football League

Time is over. They had just scored to go down by one and we have one "untimed" overtime two-point play.

The QB scrambles back and forth, back and forth. When he finally throws…BEHIND ME…my legs do the impossible as I leap up, punch the ball and back roll into victory.

And, no, I can't do that now.

9. 2008—Seattle, National Championships Discus

I entered the ring on my last throw behind by one inch. I smiled and threw 17 feet farther to win.

10. 2010—My daughter Lindsay's state championship shot put throw

Last throw…best throw. I only cried a bit.

Numbers one and four are intramural softball games. Ten is my daughter's victory; two and eight are football games (one was a county rec league), and three and seven are not even first place wins.

If you are striving for just achieving goals, I'm not always going to be able to help you. Your DNA, discipline and luck might be far more important than me saying "two sets of five."

But, success?

I live by Earl Nightingale's definition of success:

"Success is really nothing more than the progressive realization of a worthy ideal. This means that any person who knows what they are doing and where they are going is a success. Any person with a goal toward which they are working is a successful person."

Earl went on to say he could not think of anyone more successful than teachers aspiring to make a difference in their students' lives. Let me be so bold as to add coaches.

I have always wanted health, fitness, longevity and performance as part of my life. What you see on my list is six decades of competitions. But, the competitions and the trophies pale when compared to the friendships, the love and the fun.

Finally, I have to include a curse my father, Albert John, used to give, "I hope you get everything you want." It took me years to understand this was a curse.

It took the original *Star Trek* series to get my mind wrapped around what Dad said. In the classic episode, *Amok Time*, Spock's wife (T'Pring) figures out a way to get rid of Spock and keep her lover, Stonn.

Spock [after T'Pring explains dumping our hero]: *Logical. Flawlessly logical.*

T'Pring: *I am honored.*

Spock: *Stonn, she is yours. After a time, you may find that having is not so pleasing a thing after all as wanting. It is not logical, but it is often true.*

Chapter 9
After the Peak is the Cliff

This is one of life's lessons that's just hard to swallow. Every so often, a movie or television show will grasp this truth, but it is just not something people want to talk about too often. I sat through enough bad high school valedictorian speeches to know that "commencement" means "to begin," but the zoned-out students and parents worrying about the party rarely heed the implied warning.

All too often, brides focus on the wedding and miss the marriage.

If you ever hit a physical peak, be sure, as Delaine Ross told me, to take as many pictures as you can because you might not ever get there again. The next step after the Greater Mister Midvale Bodybuilding Championships is pizza and doughnuts.

The next step after a peak...is a cliff.

I walked home from the library in 1970 with a book on training. I got home, pulled out our old Ted Williams Sears barbell set and started training. I got strong. Then I got stronger.

I played football for Southwood Junior High and South City High. I wrestled. I played soccer and basketball. I was MVP in track and field at South City, Skyline College and Utah State University.

I had thrown the discus very, very far. For basically nine years, I just got better.

I wasn't ready for what was next.

I had my college degree. This degree, my father argued, would open the doors to the gold brick-lined path to success. Now, he was right. It just took longer than I imagined at the time.

Life caught up with me. It was time to start a career or something. I was 21 when I graduated and that's, in hindsight, a bit young to make a lot of the decisions I had to make. I could have used a year of travel. Instead, I decided to keep pushing ahead.

And, after working at a cheese factory from 10:00 p.m. to 6:30 a.m., then taking courses in my masters, then coaching and training...I crashed. Skipping sleep for days can do that to a person. It took me years to learn that you just can't keep going after it. You can't keep striving for the top. You can't keep rubbing your nose on the grindstone.

Something has to give.

Oh, I was rewarded well and l loved it. Championships, records, travel and free education are all wonderful. But, I missed a key truth and it took me years to understand it.

Mark Reifkind, with 42 years in the trenches as a coach, always reminds us, "The next step after a peak is always down; you can either step back or fall off."

I think all of us have felt it in some way. It's a life truism, like "buy low, sell high," that we all know...but sometimes we forget we know it.

My book *Now What?* (you'll find an excerpt in Appendix Six) essentially answers the question "what do you do after the peak?" I've seen champion athletes return to practice the following Monday; they know the season has ended, but, well, now what?

We see *Now What?* in all areas of life.

It could be the day after the baby comes home. It might be when you finally publish that book, story or poem.

My daughters used to joke about "fifth-year seniors" at their high school who would be at the games, dances and events a few months after graduating and, on paper, moving along.

It's a tough truth in life and I am convinced that Peggy Lee stated it best:

> *Is that all there is*
> *Is that all there is*
> *If that's all there is, my friends*
> *Then let's keep dancing*
> *Let's break out the booze and have a ball*
> *If that's all there is*

I've won championships and wondered why I went through the hassle. I know people who loved the wedding, but hate the marriage. Retirement often leads to isolation and loneliness.

It's not just in success either.

One of the toughest lessons I learned as a coach is the early edge. Years ago, I read that you should always join fledgling sports BEFORE they become popular so you can dominate the early wave. There is a great advantage to driving your child around, taking them to elite coaches, elite tournaments and elite training camps.

Your kid gets the edge.

Your child might end up the best 10-year-old discus thrower or tennis player in your region. Early specialization works. Your little darling might compete against kids who just found out last night that there was a competition. Perhaps this morning, someone showed them how to hold the discus or racket.

Eddie will crush them. Be sure to take a picture with this trophy because early specialization, like peaking, has a cliff.

The cliff is the reality that the other kids will start practicing, maturing, growing and taking this seriously too. Those early advantages quickly run away like the tide in Galway Bay.

I've seen it happen in high school sports: The young lads with the club experience do very well their first year. Then, overnight it seems, everybody catches up. It's a tough experience to watch as a coach and teammate. The superstar 13-year-old is soon relegated to the scout team.

It also is a truth about drills. As we often remind the athlete, "The drill is not the skill," it never seems to latch on in the brain. There is a value in doing the "whole-part, whole-part, whole-part-whole" method as a foundation of teaching and coaching. Show the whole movement or event, break it down into pieces, and return over and over to the whole movement.

All too often, the athlete assumes that the part—the drill—reflects the whole in kind of athletic logical proof: "If *this* improves, *that* must improve."

Sadly, that isn't always the truth. I have seen young throwers in all four of the disciplines (shot put, discus, hammer and javelin) fall in love with the standing throw—a drill—as they are dominate in this show of strength.

The standing throw is a drill. The standing throw is a nice way to warm up. And, that is it. I have worked with people who simply could not learn the full event and continued to just practice the drill. It's the drill, not the skill.

As a freshman in high school, I went to a big track meet literally up the stairs from my home at South City High. As we got ready for this meet, a massive boy from another high school, began warming up with us.

I asked him, "Are you a freshman?"

He responded, "I'm a big mother."

Yes. True. Literally. That's what he said.

I threw with my elementary spin technique and achieved a mark of 72 feet. He did a standing throw of 113 to command the competition.

Let's pop ahead to part two of this story, which I continue to love to tell all these years later.

As seniors, we went down to his school for a meet. By this time, puberty had kicked in…a bit…for me and I was better. That day, I threw well over 160 feet and he…

…did a standing throw of about 115 feet. I relished reminding him of his comments just a few years earlier in windy South City. Relished it.

Standing throws are a drill. We call this "transference." Honestly, transference is the hardest thing to understand in many parts of life. Constantly, we hear the term "correlation, not causation," but correlation is so pretty, so alluring, so confident.

Like Ulysses, we sometimes need to plug our ears with wax to block the Sirens and cover our eyes from the mermaids. Correlation, believing that *this* HAS to lead to *that,* is so seductive in coaching. It brings us to the whole issue of "looks like Tarzan." "He HAS to be good…he looks the part."

We do this in everything. Someone "looks" presidential. *Moneyball* had great insights into how some scouts think a player's girlfriend indicates his level of confidence. If she is attractive, he must have confidence. I cringed at that scene in the movie. We often assume the vehicle a person drives indicates wealth, income or financial acumen. I'm not sure any of it is true.

Actually, I'm pretty sure it's not.

In sports, people are always talking about peaking. I just don't believe in it. If it worked, by rule, every athlete would have at least a seasonal best at the Olympic trials. Now, you can argue weather or pressure, I will agree, but how do you not know to prepare for the weather or pressure?

It's because…it's really hard to peak. I tip my hat to Marty Gallagher who uses linear progression to build the greatest powerlifters in the history of the sport. Yet, people miss the fact that Marty poured everything into two 12-week peaks a year and spent the rest of the year getting his athletes to eat better, rest better and fix issues. In the sport of powerlifting, he proved it could work.

But, as we once discussed over dinner, you need to take time off after a 12-week peak. The next step is a cliff!

In addition, we find the same issue with "enough is enough."

I learned this the hard way so many times in my career. Once I was strong enough, I could never just let it go. Of course, "Never let go" is my signature line, mantra and life vision; letting it go is not going to work well.

I always strived for more volume, more load and more work. And, I always fell off the cliff.

I got an email from someone who listened to a podcast where the interviewer asked me about my injuries. I was completely candid, and later this podcast listener decided he should point out the obvious:

"Don't all of your injuries and surgeries make you wonder if you did things wrong?"

Oddly, when someone says something stupid, we respond with, "No kidding, Einstein." It's sarcasm, from the root to "tear flesh."

Yes. I did things wrong!

Don't do all the wrong things I did. Hmmm. That seems simple enough.

After graduating from college, I hit the cliff as an athlete. It wasn't until years later, I realized that in every other area of my life things were blooming and blossoming. Of course, being so driven as an athlete makes a person blind.

I was safe around mermaids.

Chapter 10
Self-discipline is a Finite Resource

The first chapter of *Never Let Go* is about free will. Since free will is such an important aspect of religious studies, I also include this chapter in the readings for my students. It's too long to make the point right here, but some students really seem to get a lot out of it, you can find this in Appendix One.

Some of my female students have written through the years that they were vindicated by this chapter. Trying to juggle kids, college, job, home and husband left them little energy to make desserts from scratch or train five hours a day. There is a certain wisdom in understanding that "I can do this" and "I'm sorry, I can't do everything."

One student wrote a scathing review of the material. The student disagreed with every point and every example. The student was convinced that all people need to do for six-pack abs, millions in the bank and a perfect life is to put their nose to the grindstone and work away.

Of course, the story doesn't finish here.

A few weeks later, one of this student's assignments looked "odd." I did a simple check and discovered that 100% of the assignment (an important one) had been cut and pasted from another student's work.

Thankfully, the name at the top had been changed. The student failed my course.

This is not triumphal on my part; I truly liked this student and the interaction disappointed me. But, it was not unexpected. It happens.

When I wrote the original article, I noted that free will—the ability to use self-discipline to will yourself to do something—is like a can of shaving gel. You use it, you use it...then PFFFFLT... empty.

For many mothers, from the moment those kids pop out of bed and start demanding, asking and sobbing for this and that, the can of free will begins to empty.

My wife has a great insight for raising kids: Pick your battles. We made chore lists and a menu to counter the kids' natural need for things like tacos, burgers and frosty cones that were littered on ancient savannahs of pre-historic humans. We eliminated many issues over appropriate media by not allowing television on school nights.

Those battles only had to be fought a few times. Picking those fights early allowed us to skip all kinds of other worries down the line. Frankly, I can't say our home life was an idyllic landscape of unicorns and rainbows, but we didn't have a lot of real issues.

I often miss this myself: I would wake up in the morning to protein-filled oatmeal and coffee. These had been prepped the evening before and the timers were set. This gave me time to go for a walk or hot tub...or just read.

The Sunday shopping provided everything for that evening's meal and I would often set the slow cooker with dinner just before leaving for work the next day. The meal was ready when I came home, so I had time to train. I would walk into my home gym and lift, drag out some equipment to do loaded carries and get some throws in my backyard.

While cleaning the dishes, we would make the next day's breakfast and perhaps even get ahead on the dinner too. Because our kids didn't watch TV on school nights, they tended to read Harry Potter or Calvin and Hobbes and go to sleep early.

Having these habits—these menus, shopping lists and chore lists—allowed me to focus on my training while working full-time.

I kept my can of shaving gel full. I keep it as full as I "can." (There's your pun.)

A common question that arises in many workshops is: "How can I get my clients to have more discipline?"

It's a great question. It's easy to answer and tough to do.

Coach Maughan could sum the path to discipline with two phrases:

"Make yourself a slave to good habits."

"Little and often over the long haul."

And, after 40 years of reflection, I realize that both of these are the same thing.

Chapter 11
Fundamentals Trump Everything Else

Hmmm. Basics work best?

I'm not much of a fan of basketball, but look at what these three greats all say about the sport:

"I wasn't real quick, and I wasn't real strong. Some guys will just take off and it's like, whoa. So, I beat them with my mind and my fundamentals."
~ **Larry Bird**

"When I was young, I had to learn the fundamentals of basketball. You can have all the physical ability in the world, but you still have to know the fundamentals."
~ **Michael Jordan**

"Can I jump over two or three guys like I used to? No. Am I as fast as I used to be? No, but I still have the fundamentals and smarts. That's what enables me to still be a dominant player. As a kid growing up, I never skipped steps. I always worked on fundamentals because I know athleticism is fleeting."
~ **Kobe Bryant**

Recently, LeBron James noted that his key to ongoing success is insuring that he sleeps nine hours a night. That's a fundamental truth.

Most people still struggle with this truth of life. Master reading, writing and arithmetic, and the rest of your education will be easier. Learning to slow down and drive defensively will save you thousands of hours in rehab. Drink water and eat veggies.

You KNOW this.

Do it.

The last point of my Ten Commandments is "Take a moment to appreciate those who went before you."

The instant I wrote this on my list of 10, I realized that without the stories, this list of the 10 Commandments of Coaching, although good, lacks context.

Let me share my story, my 40 years with a whistle and a lifetime of learning. Let me tell you about my teachers, coaches and mentors.

Part Two: Mentors
Appreciating Those Who Went Before

Chapter 12
Sister Maria Assumpta

Sister Maria Assumpta is one of the cornerstones of every book I have written. Her story involves a moment when I was in the second grade. (Let's insert my standard joke: Second grade was the best three years of my life.) Sister walked up to the chalkboard and drew a compass with these words on the points:

Work

Rest

Pray

Play

She was discussing balance in life. She warned, long before the word "workaholic" was coined, that some of us would work too hard. Others would choose to rest too much or engage in slothful behavior and never get out of Mom's basement.

And some—and we all know someone—would choose a path of pure play.

Being a nun, a term derived from the feminine of "monk" for those women who are in communities of chastity, obedience and poverty, she never mentioned praying too much. For those of you who don't pray or meditate, this can also be alone time or enjoying nature or art.

That would NOT include binge watching subscription TV.

This happened in the early 1960s. My age was single digits and I doubt I remember much else from that year. Oh, I imagine I learned sticking letters into words and words in sentences and the basics of a dozen fields and probably how to play games, but I can't honestly remember much. My brother Ray went to Vietnam that year, so that has to be part of my memory gap.

For whatever reason, her compass stuck with me. It's my foundational vision of life.

In the 1990s, I had a full-time job and I was training as a national-level thrower. I also was the father of two girls and my wife traveled for work every week. One Sunday morning reading the newspaper, Tiffini found me a full-time job (I'll give you more details later). Now I was to have *two* full-time jobs. I made her a deal:

"Yes, I will do this, BUT…I insist we buy a hot tub."

On my 40th birthday, I came home to a hot tub.

If you work harder, plan to rest harder.

Soon, Tiffini could be found every morning well before the rest of us woke up, sitting in the hot tub with a cup of coffee. I swear our daughters survived because, well, Mommy got some alone time.

I noticed that if I plan to increase all four points of the compass, I can handle almost anything in life. I actually improved as a discus thrower when I took on a new sport, Highland Games, because it was fun—it was play.

Drinking Scotch Whisk(e)y and eating ribs between rounds of throwing appealed to me at some level.

As I reviewed this life balance insight I got from Sister, I began to rethink why our intentional community workouts are so excellent.

When I moved back to California in 1990, a story I'll expand on later, Dan Martin asked me to work with him a bit. He found a location, Coyote Point, and a group of us met there weekly for a fun little session.

It became, and remains, the cornerstone of my approach to training.

When we train with an intentional community, we laugh, work, rest, learn, clean up, eat and explore. We are truly human. But, there are also times where I need to take my dog for a walk and just listen to nature.

We need both play and pray, work and rest; we need all four points of Sister's compass.

We have fun. Challenges are work and play.

I have dozens of them and some are very difficult, like squatting with your bodyweight on your back for 50 reps. I find it fun watching someone else do that one. You'll discover my thoughts about challenges in Appendix Five.

Sometimes, the simpler I try to make things in training, the more I tend to confuse people. People often miss the obvious. In the book *Think Like a Freak,* one of the great secrets of life turns out to be:

Don't ignore the obvious.

If you want to get strong, lift weights. Repeat. If you want to do this for decades, you need to find some fun in it, some other people to join along with you and, sometimes, the joy of being alone. That should be obvious.

Sister Maria Assumpta's compass idea has impacted every aspect of my personal and professional life. As I sneak up on 60 years with the barbell, remember that balance gives me this: I feel better, look better and perform better in my "real" life.

It's all about the balance.

Chapter 13
The Winning Hit and Dale Kursten

In one of my first published articles, circa 1996, I told the story of my first trophy. Here is the article:

On my gym wall, I have a small shelf. On it, there is a small trophy that bears the stamp "S.V. 67." For the record, it stands for "St. Veronica's, 1967," the first trophy I ever earned. I earned it one year before my wife was born.

Although I often joke about my funeral—for example having Frank Sinatra's One for My Baby, One more for the Road as a closing song—I am serious when I ask that somebody remember this trophy.

It is a lesson in, well, how the universe works.

I was the world's worst baseball player. My batting average was three zeroes. I hated sports, all the while my brothers were getting their pictures in the local sports section every week. As the right fielder, I was safe until I batted. Then, I would close my eyes, swing like mad three times and sit down.

And, as in all great stories, we were heading for the championship game.

I went to the local high school the night before the game and decided to learn to hit. Throw the ball up, close my eyes and swing. Ball up, close eyes and swing.

As I tried to learn to hit, one of the local high school heroes, Dale Kursten, saw me madly flailing away. He walked over and gave me a few lessons. Keep your eye on the ball, swing level and make contact. A few easy hits later, he said goodbye.

And, of course, it all came down to the last inning.

With two outs and a man on third, our captain turned and asked, "Who's up?"

Me.

"Oh, great. We are going to lose."

With that pep talk, I walked to the plate. Dale's words from the night before echoed, "Eye on the ball, swing level, make contact."

And, I did. The ball slid between the fielders and I made it to first base. The guy on third scored and we tied the game. Later, we would win. A few weeks later, I was given a trophy.

At my sister's 20-year high school reunion, she mentioned this story to Dale. It didn't register. Oh, he had heard about my athletic career, but was stunned to learn he had anything to do with it.

I see those minutes of his guidance as a turning point.

What is difficult is that, like Dale, we never really know when we will impact a person's life. It may be the greatest of the challenges of the Golden Rule: Do unto others.

In essence, we are called to live this message every moment of our waking lives.

As I look back on these events of 50 years ago, I still wonder if I have done enough to help others as much as Dale helped me.

From that day on—and it is hard to explain this to some people—I had my trophy. I was an athlete. I fell in love with competition and teamwork.

Sports became my first love.

My first love taught me about life.

Chapter 14
The Invisible Man on First is Out
Because of Pitcher's Hands

"Coach, I'm going to concentrate on basketball."

During almost every year coaching at Judge Memorial Catholic High School, a boy would quit all other sports to "concentrate on basketball." I had teacher friends who would pretend to stare at a ball after hearing this, "I'm concentrating on a basketball," and we would laugh. Often, the boy would be cut his senior year because the head coach had a theory that if a senior didn't start, he should be cut.

When I helped at Bingham High School, the track coach, Jeff Arboghast, a man who should be sainted, would lament that the football coach wouldn't allow his football players to do anything but year-round football. After the autumn of their final year, most of these boys would be looking for something to do since few were offered chances to continue playing at the collegiate level. Many would go out for track and field and fall in love with one of the disciplines and ask, "Why didn't I do this all through high school?"

I dunno.

I get questions all the time from parents about how to get little Billie or Bobby Sue to dominate the nine-year-old division in some tiny town. It's caused me hours of thought—a good thing—but usually I reply with a vague response. I won't take the money offered either. I don't like it.

I have been around long enough to see the long-term effects of the kids who were pushed, prodded and pulled by their parents. Rarely do we see success, but, yes, every parent will point to those one-off athletes who pulls off early specialization and succeeds. Often, that same athlete ends up in the celebrity tabloids with embarrassing stories as much as in the sports section.

I don't like early specialization for a lot of reasons; you can find research easily on why it is a bad idea. But there's a much bigger issue for me: It's literally a question of justice. Or, at least, learning about it.

This idea that we can take a child and guess the future always made me wonder. Certainly, if the kid is unusually tall or fast, we have some ideas, but for the rest of us mere mortals, it takes a while to figure out our gifts.

I thought I would be a great linebacker; I ended up playing corner. But…I was a much better discus thrower. Later, I discovered I was born to be a hammer thrower, but it was too late, or so I thought. Then, I discovered the Highland Games and my best event was the hammer(s).

Go figure.

I was lucky in my life. For whatever reasons, my mom and dad banned us from all kinds of organizations:

- Boy Scouts

- PAL (Police Athletic Leagues)

- Pop Warner Football

- Boys Club

My mom had a built-in mistrust of a lot of things not related to her church. I am sure it had its roots in her family's history of being from Northern Ireland around the time of Independence.

Don't get me wrong: She had a deep love for many of the police officers she "adopted" through the years. There were always a few doughnuts and a fresh pot of coffee ready for when they arrived.

It's funny to think about this now: I grew up with brothers fighting in Vietnam and armed police officers having coffee in my kitchen. My daughters grew up sharing a bathroom with Olympians, Special Forces guys and strength coaches from around the world.

It's only different by degrees.

Since we didn't play on organized teams with practices and schedules and tournaments, my family and friends played sports all the time.

We played.

For Christmas and birthdays, we would get new basketballs or footballs and play with them until the first layers of leather rubbed off. I always thought home court advantage was the idea that you had to know how to use the bladder popping through the ball to one's benefit.

We played.

It was a rare day when we weren't scurrying up and down Ramona and Wilms Avenues, running patterns between two parked cars (impossible to defend, and also impossible to advance the ball) or heading up to the high school to play ball (baseball).

Certainly, I would wear an occasional "SV" shirt for my church team (St. Veronica's School in South San Francisco), but it wasn't until my freshman year of high school that I actually put on a full uniform to play football for Southwood Junior High.

Yet, by playing countless games of street football, pick-up basketball and sandlot baseball, I learned things my classmates from organized teams never learned.

I learned the fine art of judgment. I learned fair play. I learned literally every position in every game.

We always played baseball in front of a wall or back stop, as we never had enough players to include a catcher. So, when you were batting, you also fielded the balls and strikes and threw them back to the pitcher.

It was important to name the field you were hitting to so the Invisible Man on first could beat the throw before you got out because of pitcher's hands. If you understood that, you probably played a lot of sports like I did.

There were no officials; instead, we had to address close plays by discussing things. Yes, it could get heated, but fair play always leads to more play. Occasionally, we would vote on things; sometimes we would use logic and sometimes we would use something one rarely sees today:

"Okay, you get this one. But, the next close call goes to us."

Sounds fair. Let's get back to the game.

My issues with early specialization will be discussed more shortly, but this might be the biggest problem I see with club sports and organized sports for kids:

The adults make the decisions. The adults make the rules. The adults coach, screen, recruit, plan, adjudicate, organize and reward. The chosen few kids (often the coach's) get the short-term benefits of trophies and awards. The rest of the children play with daisies and spit on bugs.

In our games, we had to umpire, referee, play catcher while batting, share gloves with the opponent and keep in mind dozens of things like score, strikes, balls, outs and where we put the Invisible Man.

If one of us cheated, it meant nothing. Well, we would all know the truth and you probably would "get yours," whatever that meant to us, somewhere down the line.

Of course, occasionally, one of us would do something so egregious that we took it to a higher authority:

Mom.

You didn't want to get Mom involved. You see, if you couldn't play nice, there were always chores and school work. We learned to play nice. We judged fairly. We made appropriate rules.

Talent, by the way, didn't matter. We needed bodies to fill the fields and courts and all of us had spent the years mastering the games. If new neighbors moved in, it was a joy to see the new faces, male or female, join the squads.

In our neighborhood, the only way to stay warm while the fog rolled in and froze us to the bones was to pick up a ball and run with it.

And, let's be honest (my father's favorite qualifier), in numbers we found safety.

It was a different time.

And...I just don't see this anymore. Years ago, a boy walking his dog was a common enough sight, but, at least in my experience, I don't see it very often these days. I don't see groups of kids playing neighborhood sports. Even in schoolyards, this seems to be vanishing.

Oddly, my concern isn't for the threat of obesity or the health and wellness of these children and teens: I worry they will never learn the fine art of negotiation after a pass interference call, the judgment skills of fair or foul balls and the subtle art of calling an offensive foul in basketball.

These are life skills that are difficult to learn in law school and debate class, but oddly simple in the playing field.

The three witches in *Macbeth* said it best about the kids in my neighborhood discussing judgment calls in foggy South San Francisco:

"Fair is foul, and foul is fair:
Hover through the fog and filthy air."

Shakespeare seems to have understood play(s). Fortunately, he never concentrated on basketball.

Chapter 15
The Orange Library: Three Books

My elementary school was a basketball powerhouse. Several of my classmates went on to play college basketball, including at schools like Cal, Hayward State and Sacramento State. Ron went to the Air Force Academy and Peter played football for St. Mary's.

We were blue collar kids and knew college was "the answer."

I wasn't good enough to play with my class team. But, I knew I would be fine in football and track and field. Our school insurance wouldn't allow us to play football at school, but when we did, I liked the contact and collisions.

I also liked the tactics of football. You play. You stop. You re-gather and go again. The adjustments in football happen by the second. I loved that you could hurt us with this play and then we would adjust and stop it dead. Yes, it's a physical game; I have the scars and surgeries to prove it.

It's chess with collisions.

Since my family wasn't really a football family, I went off to the local library to learn more about the game.

I always loved the library. I think I checked out every book on oceans, physical training and football. I always enjoyed finding a book on Native American woodcraft on one shelf and then finding a book on Italian brick oven cooking a few stacks away.

When I got to the library, I went to the sports section to find books on football. Then, I walked over to the health area and looked for books on building muscle. Finally, as I went to check out the books, the librarians offered their picks for the week.

Three of those books became the pillars of my training and thinking for the rest of my career.

1. *The Sword in the Stone*, T. H. White (the book the librarians recommended), which became the foundational book of my life. This sequence toward the end of the book is a great way to look at training:

> *The Wart walked up to the great sword for the third time.*
> *He put out his right hand softly and drew it out as gently*
> *as from a scabbard.*
> **~ T. H. White**

Young Arthur (Wart) is given his power through advice from his friends, including:

> *Power springs from the nape of the neck.*

> *Use those forearms held together by the chest.*

> *Find your tool.*

> *Never let go.*

> *Keep up a steady effort.*

> *Fold your powers together, with the spirit of your mind.*

This advice became the cornerstone of my coaching.

2. *Seven Days to Sunday*, Eliot Asinof, from *Wednesday on Ken Avery*:

> *"I worked on my body all the time. I learned from German gymnasts. I did Chinese pushups, kip-ups, flips. I walked on*

my hands, studied body balance. Body momentum trans-fer—that's where you can move around in the air without hitting the ground. I worked on the trampoline, did rope climbing, lots of tumbling. In my frosh year, I could do only 10 pushups, 35 situps and three chin-ups. A year later, I did 111 pushups, 500 situps and 25 chinups. I would work out while I watched TV. I would roll out of bed in the morning and do pushups and the U.S. Marine squat jumps.

"My mother gave me ballet lessons to build up my legs. I learned the second position, the plié. I wanted to build up my groin muscles, the calves, the thighs. I could dance pretty well at that. I wanted to be graceful as well as strong. She taught me a lot.

"In my junior year, I made linebacker. I was able to knock down big guys weighing two hundred pounds behind the line of scrimmage. I was quick. I got even quicker. In the spring, I ran the high hurdles, shot put, threw the discus, ran the half-mile.

Threw the discus.

It's funny to read that now and realize how much these three words impacted my life.

3. *Body Building and Self Defense*, Myles Callum

"This method (isometrics/tension) is based on a new the-ory of muscle growth [the book was published in 1962]. *German and American scientists and doctors have found that a muscle can grow at only a certain rate. And, accord-ing to this theory, it doesn't take as much work as we used to think. If you flex any muscle to its maximum power and contraction, and hold it there for six seconds, once a day, the scientists say, the muscle will grow in strength just as fast as it can grow* [in strength!!!].

"Whether or not this method of muscle tension can ever really replace weight-lifting is still a matter of controversy. Some scientists say it can; endless repeating of strenuous exercise, they say, 'does not make the strength of a muscle grow any faster.' Weight-lifting, however, may make the size of the muscle grow faster."

Decades after reading this, I am still unpacking these two paragraphs.

The summer after my eighth-grade graduation, I began training seriously for fall football. I didn't know it at the time, but I was already armed with great information.

And…I learned an important lesson: Books are the fastest way to learn the basics.

Yes, you need to dig in and do the work, but following the well-worn path walked by others saved me years of my own trail-blazing.

Chapter 16
Dave Freeman

I graduated from Catholic Elementary school in 1971. After eight years at St. Veronica's School, I transferred to Southwood Junior High to begin a new journey. It was an interesting transition. From Irish nuns to public school is big enough, but I was also going to play football. At 118 pounds of pure "too small," it was obvious to everyone: I needed to lift weights.

It was at this time that I was introduced to Southwood's lifting program. In a portable building, the school had outlaid about 15 of those cement-filled weightlifting sets everyone from my generation remembers as their first barbell.

Mr. Dave Freeman spent little time explaining the "rep-set" system of 8–6–4 because everybody—except me—knew what to do. That's part of the brilliance of the program. You learn it once and then you lift. It was a program that stuck to me ever since.

The program was very simple. First, groups of four boys were given a bar. The bars ranged from very light, maybe 25 pounds, up to nearly a hundred pounds.

Each cohort of boys would lift one at a time, put the bar down, and then the next boy would lift. The four would constantly switch from lifter to watcher—the bar never stopped moving. The three sets wouldn't take very long.

In fact, sometimes it was hard to catch our breath in time for our next set.

The reps were very simple:

First set: *8 repetitions*

Second set: *6 repetitions*

Third set: *4 repetitions*

The goal was also clear-cut: When you got all 18 reps, you moved to the next barbell when we returned to work out in two days. Some students would not progress quickly, but others soon found themselves with the heaviest barbell.

Like me.

The program involved four lifts:

- *Power clean*

- *Military press*

- *Front squat*

- *Bench press*

Each lift was done in the 8–6–4 rep format. The bar was cleaned (once) for the set of military presses and the bar was also cleaned (once) for the front squats. Each workout, the athlete cleaned the bar from the ground to the chest 22 times. If, as some people believe, the power clean is the king of the exercises, that's a lot of reps with the king!

To hurry up the training, there were times when Mr. Freeman recommended combining the power clean and military presses. One clean and one press, repeated for a total of eight reps. This was done with a lighter weight. One could also do the front squats after the clean and presses too. This, the combination of power clean, military press and front squat, remains the basic format of my "armor building" workouts all these years later.

Each day to warm up, we had to run two laps and an obstacle course. The two laps were about 600 meters. The obstacle course had a wall, various upper body challenges and some balance walking. All in all, this wasn't a bad program.

Three days a week:

>Power clean: *8–6–4 reps*
>Military press: *8–6–4 reps*
>Front squat: *8–6–4 reps*
>Bench press: *8–6–4 reps*

Mr. Freeman also kept the weightroom open before and after school. Throughout my career, I have always opened the weightroom after school to do my own training and help as I can with other faculty and students. Some of my best training insights have come from these sessions.

He and the rest of the PE staff also did something that still makes me think: *This is genius.* Three times a year, we were tested over three days with 10 or 12 events. We trained up for it for weeks. I remember most of the tests:

- *Pullups*
- *Pushups*
- *Situps*
- *Shuttle run*
- *40-yard dash*
- *600-yard run*
- *Six-minute run*

There were others, but you get the point. Each event was scored by the instructors and we accumulated points.

Some of my classmates had it dialed in; if you added one pullup, I was told, it was worth more than running "this much better" on the 600…and easier. We would work on our events during free periods and ask each other advice about the task.

The day after we finished, Mr. Freeman would hand out our awards: They were various-colored felt triangles. As I recall, the white was the entry point, and from there it moves to blue, red, green, black and, ultimately, to gold. Guys trained for months trying to earn a gold felt triangle.

Read that again: *a gold felt triangle.*

It was a piece of cheap gold-colored felt, cut into a triangle to be sewed, as or in my case, glued, on to our PE shorts.

You might miss my point: 13 and 14-year-old boys would take time away from adolescent idiocy and stupidity to train hard and smart to win a piece of felt. This was my first introduction to the value of standards and measurements. If you want someone to achieve, put up a barrier and tell them to "jump over this." Then, raise the barrier.

My brother Gary, who seems to have a rare ability to make everyone angry, often notes that the problem with modern education is that they put the high jump bar down to one foot. All the kids jump over the bar and receive a gold medal. The kids know it's a joke and throw the medals away.

In 1971 and 1972, Coach Freeman simply offered different colors of felt. Some of my classmates didn't care about these and, not surprisingly, many of them didn't set the world on fire. But, to the rest of us, that piece of felt was worth sweating and straining during our free time to achieve.

As I was setting up my gym for a morning workout, I thought: "Wouldn't it be great if we did this with adults." And, just as the thought formed, I was reminded of FitRanX. I am a huge fan of the system Nick Rians has put together. There are eight levels, three age groups, and male and female standards.

That's 48 levels, and in those levels, things break up a bit more by height and weight.

If you tell someone you are Level Five, a FitRanX person knows what you mean…and where you are going in the future.

Let me give you an example of the testing. This is for me, my Level Five test: I'm male, over 56 years of age, six feet tall, and weigh just under 225 pounds.

Strength Tests

Pullups: 5 (one-minute rest)

Dips: 10 (one-minute rest)

Double KB front squat with 24k 'bells: 10 (one-minute rest)

Double KB press with 14k 'bells: 10 (one-minute rest)

Single-leg deadlift with 14k 'bell: 10 per leg (one-minute rest)

Suspension knee tuck: 25 in one minute (one-minute rest, then right to the triset)

Triset One, three sets with 30 seconds rest between sets (six minutes of work)

High box jumps: 30 seconds

Double KB swing, clean, squat with 8k 'bells: 30 seconds

Clapping pushups: 5 in 30 seconds

Triset Two, three sets with 30 seconds rest between sets

KB alternating swings with 12k: 30 seconds

KB low windmill with 12k: 20 seconds per side

Double undulating ropes: 30 seconds

Nothing in the FitRanX system is hard by itself, but the accumulation of fatigue makes me laugh out loud as we suddenly find a 'bell that is "woefully too light for the Great Me" making us squirm in pain.

What to do after Level Five, you may ask?

Level Six!

And, like that gold felt patch I got from Coach Freeman, I will spend extra time on my weekly movements to bring the whole system up to the appropriate level.

Mr. Freeman also coached football, basketball and track. He was always fair and answered every question I ever had. He was a coach's coach.

As I remember him, I realize how much I try to model myself after him.

Chapter 17
Bob Jacobs
and High School Biology Class

I have been in school since 1962. I continue to take adult education courses, online classes and sit up front at workshops. I love learning and connecting the dots from one field of study to another.

Sadly, my family and friends don't have my same enthusiasm for Celtic trivia, strategic developments and WWI poetry. But I share it with them anyway.

I've had marvelous teachers. I've had Irish nuns, WWII vets and poet laureates teach and lead me through practically every subject one can study. One teacher, Bob Jacobs, changed my approach to learning.

I have tried to find Mr. Jacobs since I went off to college. My brother Richard, who worked with him, couldn't tell me where he went...save something like "south." That's not exactly GPS.

Mr. Jacobs taught high school biology. I also took some electives from him, including ecology. There was something remarkable about the way he taught materials and I adopted it... when I finally understood the method.

This was the early 1970s and Mr. Jacobs had long hair and a beard. He would rally students to clean up the bay from litter (San Francisco Bay) or the local beaches. Litter and oil spills marred one of the most beautiful areas on earth. Fixing this was as simple as showing up and carrying out junk.

Oddly, after I moved away from the Bay Area, the state began a vigorous campaign against litter and other polluters. I left in 1977 to go to Utah State and returned full-time to California in 2010 when Tiffini was transferred to the City, a story that comes later. The difference in the air quality was stunning. The lack of litter and roadside junk was also inspiring. In other words, it works. I hope, somewhere, Mr. Jacobs is happy.

He warned us one class, "I don't know how, but the environmental damage is going to have an effect on your adult lives." As I watch Irish farmers deal with drought and read about massive firestorms destroying much of the western United States, I can only see, sadly, his vision for us in the future.

Mr. Jacobs had a hook as a teacher: Rather than read from a book or assign busy work, he lectured on every unit. But he lectured on the most fascinating areas of the sections. When we studied single-celled animals, he taught us about amebic dysentery. Tape worms and pin worms were the next series of lectures, and he spent a good week teaching us about shark and shark attacks.

We were on the edge of our seats.

When it was time for testing, we read what we had to read to expand our knowledge about the other two kinds of fish scales that were not the shark variety. I can probably retell the whole shark lectures to this day.

I can still see his drawings of shark anatomy and his walking around the room highlighting what to look for in a shark attack. This is also where I first learned about feeding frenzies. (Insert stupid pun about a high school cafeteria.)

He hooked us with great stories and fascinating aspects of biology. For a blue-collar school, we were treated like fellow travelers in science. He lifted us up.

In my career, I try to utilize the same technique. As a classroom teacher, I strive to find the unique and the interesting. I focus hard on finding what Joseph Campbell would call "the hero's journey."

I look for odds and ends that make a subject come alive. Often, it is simple things like explaining the word "POSH (posh)" or "son of a gun." (POSH means "Port Out-Starboard Home, the expensive seats on a trip to India. "Son of a gun" is a child conceived on a ship.) I explain at nearly every workshop that "fit" comes from the Old Nordic word "to knit."

Mr. Jacobs taught us (me) to hook the audience, to entertain with stories and let the learning happen naturally. His humor inspired me to find my own rules for teaching history.

Let me share this with you, my *10 Commandments of Teaching or Learning History:*

- Never be so sure something that "everybody knows" is correct.

- Everybody in history…dies.

- War, as horrible as it is, speeds technological change.

- You can be guaranteed that anything that has "always been done this way" has not been.

- Obviously, if it could be done again and everybody knew what was going to happen, it would be done different. However, none of that will ever happen.

- We will never know the whole story.

- "There is nothing sad—except history."
  ~ T. H. White, *The Sword in the Stone*

- "Nothing is more unfair than to judge men of the past by the ideas of the present." ~ Denys Winstanley

- The "twin towers" of the historical method are chronology and geography.

- "If they did it to Him, they will do it to us. It is something that we can expect." ~ Saint John XXIII

That last one is what I tell young teachers after their first bad parent-teacher experience.

I have used Mr. Jacobs' methods as a teacher for 40 years. Not once has teaching ever felt like work.

It's like fishing: I'm trying to hook the listener.

Chapter 18
Ray DeJong
and South San Francisco Football

Coach Ray DeJong was an institution at South City High. He played football for Cal and played in two Rose Bowls. He had nine league titles (I played on his 1974 championship team) and won over 150 games. He, like many of my coaches, also fought in WWII.

I was coached by a generation of people who understood sacrifice. They had a radically different view of "hard." I played football when water wasn't allowed at practice...somehow, it would make us soft. We hit often—full contact and collisions—and we spent a lot of time getting up and down off the ground in an exercise called either "up-downs" or "grass drills."

After I graduated from high school, they allowed water at practice. I can't help, at some level, to think, "These kids with all their advantages—when I was their age, I walked to school uphill...both ways."

As a small side note, I have yet to meet a person who doesn't think young people have it much easier than they did. Somehow, everyone I know pulled themselves up with their own bootstraps or whatever cliché we toss out when we think our youth was spent on a deserted island fighting off wolf packs and shark attacks every night and day.

I seem to think that way too.

At first, I wasn't going to include Coach DeJong in these mentor memories. As a child, my goal was to play under the lights at South City High and run out on the field to one of the greatest fight songs of all time. But Coach DeJong wasn't much for coddling or small talk, and I don't have a lot of stories. He was good to me and often asked my opinion about opposing players because I wrestled or competed against them in track.

But, I thought his impact was just that: He led us out into the lights of Rue Randall Clifford Stadium and let me legally hit people.

It wasn't until his memorial service that I realized his impact on me and my thinking. Coach was criticized by fans and former players for "taking too many hits to the head," not changing things very often or being old fashioned. Of course, we were one of the great California football powerhouses and very few All-State kids from other parts of the nation could have played much for SSF. We had former players in the NFL come back and teach us how to step up our game. Many of my teammates went on to play for Pac 12 schools (Pac 8 at the time).

Jerry Littrell in a preview of the County Championships noted:

"They (SSF) plod along doing a few things well—very well. And, if they should perchance get a lead on another team, they can force them to play their game and become doubly effective.

"That very simply is the South San Francisco High football team philosophy. When they play their game, the Warriors execute well and can kill a team with finesse."
~ San Mateo Times, November 27, 1974

At the memorial for Coach DeJong, Tiffini went through the various memorabilia on display. What caught my eye was a small piece of cardstock that had this on it:

Towards Tight End

> *R-47 Dive L-23 Dive*
>
> *R-47 Dive Pitch L-23 Dive Pitch*
>
> *R-47 Dive Option L-23 Dive Option*
>
> *R-34 Delay L-36 Delay*
>
> *L-36 Blast R-34 Blast*
>
> *L-42 Slant R-28 Slant*
>
> *R-37 Wedge L-33 Wedge*
>
> *R-37 W-Motion L-33 W-Motion*
>
> *R-37 Wedge-Fly L-33 Wedge-Fly*
>
> *R-44 Trap L-26 Trap*
>
> *R-49 Quick L-21 Quick*
>
> *R-28 Power L-42 Power*
>
> *R-39 Sweep L-31 Sweep*

Towards Split End

> *L-47 Dive Option/Pitch R-23 Dive Option/Pitch*
>
> *L-37 Wedge R-33 Wedge*
>
> *L-44 Trap R-26 Trap*
>
> *L-39 Sweep R-31 Sweep*
>
> *R-42 Slant L-28 Slant*

I'm pretty sure this was the "hot sheet," the offensive plays for a game—November 28, 1974. This was my last high school game, on Thanksgiving, against San Mateo for the county championship.

The San Mateo Times headline said San Mateo's problem was "Same Old SSF." The fans and Littrell were right: DeJong found a formula and stuck with it.

And, yet, what hit me as I stood there with Tiffini is not only could I write out the entire playbook from 1974, but I was pretty sure I could line up and run the offensive plays. I think I can show you what all 11 people did on every play.

But here's the thing: I was a defensive player.

Coach DeJong's system was so simple that I could easily explain where all 11 people line up, what to do and when to do it…45 years after wearing the blue and white of SSFHS. And I rarely practiced on offense.

Systems stick.

Here is an example of his brilliance: If a play had an odd number, we snapped the ball on one. If it was an even number, we snapped it on two. With just one word, in the 1974 season, we all knew where to line up on offense.

On defense, each of us had three jobs. If we all did those, we basically took away the first 33 things the opposition could try to do against us. It usually worked.

Coach DeJong was a "systems" coach. If the first step doesn't work, we simply move to the next thing. We generally never panicked; we just kept trusting the system. If we all worked together, it worked.

And, I know: It is the cliché of clichés. But, that doesn't mean it doesn't work. When we lost our last game, Coach DeJong took all the blame. When we got off the bus, he put us in a room—we still had our cleats and uniforms on—and apologized: "We lost because of me." He then thanked us for a great season and told us to enjoy Thanksgiving.

This is a lesson that resounds with me more each year:

When we win, the team played well.

When we lose, it is my fault.

There are many famous coaches who do not ever learn this lesson.

As I look back, the great lesson of playing American football—and coaching the sport—is the organization. As an offensive coordinator, I had 25 seconds to get 11 boys to line up legally, move on the same command and proceed with their jobs. As the play progressed, we adapted to the play of the opponent. Coach DeJong did this with:

Right, 23 Dive

I read and discuss at length the concept of cues in coaching; play calling in football is the ultimate in cueing. Our job as coaches and trainers is to continue to search for more elegant and nuanced cues that say so much with so little.

That's the art of coaching—saying so much with so little.

Chapter 19
Dick Notmeyer and the PBBC

It is not possible to overstate Dick's influence on my life. The physical changes of Dick's training system and nutritional vision certainly impacted me: I showed up to his gym on day one weighing 162 pounds. Four months later, I weighed 202. I went from being a good high school athlete to a Division One MVP under his care. We will come back to this, but there were far more important changes.

On the emotional side of things, Dick guided me through the waters of my dad's second conviction for drunk driving. It was a tough time in our home. Dad lost his license and I had to drive him places; he also had to do some jail time. Having said that, this would have been the first time in probably five or six years when Dad didn't come home drunk. I used to get nervous about 5:10 every night. If Dad wasn't pulling in then, later he would show up sloshy and pretend it was just a long day. Losing his license kept him from the bars and gambling halls.

My dad was simply a guy who couldn't hold his booze. Any amount of alcohol would get him google-eyed and slurry. He embarrassed us at church events, weddings and gatherings. After Mom died, he began nightly binges again. Between his chain smoking and drinking, I am surprised he lived 11 years after Mom died.

I loved Big Al. I still do. I have always been comfortable with seeing beyond people's problems and appreciating their gifts. Certainly, this is something I learned from dealing with Dad's issues. I think it is something we are beginning to lose in society today; perhaps it's the ease in which we share and spread information with literally the touch of a button.

Good people can do dumb things. Memorize this. It will apply to you too, by the way.

As my senior year in high school came to an end, the teachers went on strike. I still support it, but it was the most important time of my final high school track season. I was throwing well, but the pressures of my home life and the pressures of getting a scholarship really began to tighten me up. Then, basically, school closed. The district brought in scabs and I was still expected to go to school. To get there, I had to go past the picket lines where my brother Richard held a sign.

My season ended with me throwing the best toss of my life out of bounds at the Sectionals.

It was a foul.

It didn't count.

Boom. Done.

Oddly, I had very little coaching that year. For whatever reason(s), my throws coach seemed to go out of his way to ignore me or tell me of my shortcomings. It was probably a good thing, as self-discipline is the cornerstone to track and field success. As I gathered my gear, he came up to me and asked:

"Why did you throw it out of bounds?"

Seriously. He asked that.

And then high school was over for me as a student and an athlete. I was going to go to San Francisco State. There was no interest in me as a thrower at any other school, so I picked where my brothers had gone to school.

Later, I discovered the coach had done nothing to encourage colleges to find me; a couple years later, Coach Maughan told me he would have given me a full ride out of high school with my grades and discus marks.

I didn't go to SFSU.

Things were about to change for the better.

Fortunately, our head coach, Pete Giachetti, came by to tell me the coach at Skyline College wanted to talk with me. Coach Bob Lualhati showed up at school while I was training with the college discus—the high school discus is 1.6 kilos; the Olympic or college discus is two kilos. He told me my workout throws were better than the Skyline College school record and glowingly told me about the opportunities found in choosing the junior college route.

Although we had already sent money in registration fees to SFSU, my mom was fine with changing my decision. It was, and remains, one of the best decisions of my life.

When I got to Skyline, Coach Lualhati wanted me to start Olympic lifting. Skyline had recently hired Kees Tuinzing to run an advanced physiology lab. We also had one of the first par courses—the outdoor circuit training loops that remain some of the smartest general training units for most people. Skyline was miles ahead in the areas of physical education: water tanks for fat loss measurement, systems for testing carbon dioxide and oxygen, and tons of innovative equipment.

Kees taught me the basics of the O lifts. I quickly learned the power versions of the Olympic lifts, which is where you pull the weight high and catch it with minimal knee bend. I had to learn the squat variations because, as always, that's what I learned from magazines.

One day, Kees told me to go to San Francisco and check out the Sports Palace. Not long after that, I pulled my Honda 200 up next to the gym and walked in. After asking about the O lifts, the guy at the front told me to "Come back tomorrow for a local lifting meet."

I got there much too early and sat around in a folding chair. As the meet began, I felt like I should have competed.

At the first break, Jim Schmitz, later Olympic Team Coach, announced his thanks to "Dick and Joy Notmeyer" for helping with scoring and refereeing. I had read the names in *Strength and Health*. I looked for them and I saw Joy wave to the crowd.

Soon I needed a bathroom break. As I walked in, I bumped into Dick. I told him I needed to learn the O lifts and he invited me to his gym on 790 Moana Way in Pacifica.

"Come to my gym Monday...about 2:45. When you get there open the garage door and come in. It's the Pacifica Barbell Club (PBBC) and we will make you a member."

"One thing, you have to pay your dues."

Got it. What's that?

"25 cents a week. Oh...and you have to swear to not use your newfound gains for evil."

The PBBC was the back room behind his garage. I was expecting something more elaborate, but like when Luke Skywalker meets Yoda, size does not matter.

I found a training home.

Dick's sense of humor has been a fountain of joy in my life: Dick can tell a story. No matter what happened, Dick had a story for me. Need to lose weight? Dick would go into a story about a guy who never missed a workout and turned his life around. Gain weight? Protein and front squats were the secret to turning this guy's life around. I hope I became one of his stories.

Dick's walls were covered with pictures and "clubs." You could enter the situp club, bench press club or, the big one, the gym records. My name dominates the 198 and 242 weight classes—and, yes, that's a big deal to me.

From that Monday until the day I die, Dick's influence on me was and is profound.

The first workout wasn't anything special as the O lifters were taking it easy after Saturday's meet. But soon I would be snatching, cleaning, jerking and squatting rep after rep, set after set, five days a week for two or three hours a session.

All for a quarter.

The program was simple:

Monday
Snatch
Clean and jerk

Tuesday
Front squat
Jerks off the rack

Wednesday
Snatch
Clean and jerk

Thursday
Off

Friday
Snatch
Clean and jerk

Saturday
Front squat
Jerks off the rack

Sunday
Off

And, 99% of the time, that was what I did. My hands hurt at night and I was sore everywhere…all the time.

My body quickly responded. I soon could only wear t-shirts because my traps and shoulders were blowing up by the day. I wore sweats because few pants in the 1970s were structured for big quads. Disco was king and pants were tight, but I like to keep my pants from ripping at the seams when I sit down.

A few months after joining, my brother Gary, who had just gotten married, was visiting our home. I walked in the door and he looked up and said:

"Holy shit!"

I had been physically transformed.

I found a place where I could get world class coaching and a million laughs. Dick had stories about 25-pound cats, surfing, fast cars and growing up in San Francisco. Literally, almost daily, I produced new personal records and there seemed no limit on my progress.

In my first three weightlifting meets, I made 17 of 18 attempts with PRs in every lift and total. Within a year, I would always be the strongest discus thrower at track meets. Oddly, I didn't win many O lifting meets because Northern California at the time hosted multiple future Olympians and future Olympic medalists in my age and weight class. Looking back, I was really good. But I was a good-sized fish in a big pond.

Dick summed up the O lifts with three key principles:

Leg strength

Pulling strength

Tranquil mind

It's that third one—tranquil mind—that helped me the most. He taught me not to be anxious. I needed to learn to relax and he figured out how to do it: make me laugh. I still use the "smile" technique to ease myself in all situations. I would certainly lose again in life and competition, but I would never again choke under pressure.

Dick also believed in hard work. "Greatness comes to those that dare to sweat, dare to strain and dare the pain," he taught us.

I did all three. Trust me: There is nothing like sitting down on a bench and watching a pool of sweat from your chin grow so large that someone asks you to wipe it up because, and I quote, "that looks like a wading pool."

Of course, my coaching career would be a blank canvas without my favorite Dick Notmeyer quote:

"He who lifts the heaviest weights...gets the strongest!"

With Dick, the name of our favorite magazine, *Strength and Health*, was also the key to life. If it wasn't healthy or if it didn't lead to heavier weights, Dick warned me not to do it. Smoking was especially sinful in Dick's view. White flour and sugar were almost as bad. Even though anabolic steroids worked, Dick told me, they are NOT good for your health.

"Anyway," he told me, "they get you to where you would be in about two years of proper training."

Wow!

"But when you stop taking them all the gains go away."

He then pointed to his arm and made the "pffffffffffft" sound of air going out of a balloon, "With proper training, it stays."

He was right. Actually, he was even more right than we knew: Most of my friends who used PEDs are either dead or extremely limited in movement. It's a rare week when I don't hear about a friend or former rival who has died.

It was strength AND health.

My second year, Eric Seubert, a South City grad and Skyline teammate, joined me in training. It helped to have someone talk to about the various injuries, aches and pains we enjoyed daily. We were terrors in the cafeteria, eating everything not kept away from us.

On our free days…wait, we didn't have any free days.

Eric threw the shot for SC, so we were at track meets all over California. On those rare days off, we went to the beach to hang out or just eat pizza at The Village Host in San Bruno.

Looking back, these were all good times. We occasionally went to parties with high school friends, especially one friend who would always host a party when a new Led Zeppelin album came out. He would take the album out of the wrapper like a blessed artifact and insist on quiet as he played the new record.

Eric's older brother had a party one time and I was invited. One of the guys at the party started making fun of Eric for lifting. He was using the usual language of the time, "You queers all rub oil over each other."

Finally, the guy asked, "What good is lifting?"

This is such a good memory.

Eric said, "This!"

He took the guy by his arm pits and push jerked him high up the wall and held him there.

For a long time. I mean…a really long time.

Finally, Eric's brother walked over and said, "You made your point, let him down."

Whenever I need a little pick-me-up about the bullies of our world, I think back to that guy's legs kicking and swaying as Eric pushed his head and shoulders into the wall.

For Dick and Joy's 50th wedding anniversary, I put together a booklet about our training and a glossary of terms from the gym. Many parts of the glossary are funny stories about black widow spiders, jumping out windows and standing far too close to someone in a public urinal.

The other thing I tried to share was the unique training methods we used due to lack of equipment or money. Sometimes we did things that were probably more wrong than right, but much of the exercise was the fun of doing them…PBBC style.

The most complex exercise ever invented is Dick Notmeyer's behind-the-neck presses. We will discuss this in a step-by-step manner, although it still won't make sense:

1. Place the bar at the end of the bench. Part of the fun of this exercise is loading extra plates. You see, with the bar straddling the bench, adding weight to one side makes the other side flip up. Great fun for the whole family when the bar swings up and careens into a lifting buddy.

2. Sitting on the bench, grip the bar in the snatch grip.

3. Stand up with the bar. Lean back to pull the shoulders back.

4. Dip the bar to the knees, snatch the bar overhead and sit on the bench—ideally, all in one movement.

5. Begin pressing the bar behind the neck. Get that goofy, hyper-smile grimace you can look at in the mirror.

6. On the last rep, let the bar come down and then stand up.

7. Gingerly, replace the bar on the bench.

8. Add weight on one side, allowing the bar to flip up and hit a training partner. Laugh. Have Dick once again explain that you need to keep your hands on the bar when adding weight.

9. Repeat until everyone has been hit by the flipping bar.

Dick became a legend in my circle of friends and family. I remember people commenting, "This guy's 47? He looks 27!" Forty years later, Dick still lifts and walks and insures he gets enough protein every day.

He remains my role model for strength and health.

Chapter 20
Robert Lualhati and Skyline College

I think we all have certain Golden Ages in our lives. I look back at the 1990s when I had two little girls pounding up the stairs on Saturday mornings to get breakfast so they could watch cartoons as a bright golden haze in my memory. My senior year in college was another: Everything just got better every day. Certainly, my trips to Ireland have been perfect, the Emerald Age of my life.

But, day in and day out, my junior college years might have been the best years of my first two decades. I had my Honda 200 motorcycle and drove to school, then over to the PBBC. I would come home to a happy house as Dad no longer drank alcohol. My nieces and nephew would visit and I would torture them as all uncles do naturally. My neighborhood friends were willing Merry Men for every adventure.

We crammed people into trunks of cars to watch drive-in movies and shot off to the beach to play at a moment's notice. I liked Skyline academically and my professors were very good. My counselor was right: At Skyline, the professors only job was to instruct and "they will know your name after the first week."

It was a magical time. With my physical size increasing, I was getting a fair amount of attention. Some of my high school friends would ask questions about what was happening to my body. Famously, Rita Harrington started poking my trapezius muscles at a party. Finally, with great tenderness, she leaned in and asked, "What the f--k are those?"

Skyline's track team was very good. We would have defeated most Division One teams in a dual meet. The dual meet is disappearing; it is a track and field meet with just two teams competing. Sadly, this is killing track and field. Fans understand "we beat them," but struggle understanding the sheer madness of Invitational and big track meets.

Most of my team went on to compete at the next level.

Coach Lualhati loved track and field. He worked tirelessly for the program. I'm not sure any other team had the little extras Coach would do for us. For example, at the end of our season, he would give each of us a booklet with every mark, every record and the full yearly bio of each member of our team. I still have mine.

But, you had to earn that Skyline uniform.

It's no longer there, but at the time, the school had a dirt hill in the back. It was 200 meters and the last 30 meters were more of stairwell. To earn the uniform, you needed to do 10 of these. The first one was awful and it got worse from there.

I earned my uniform with John King. John was a massive guy with a gentle soul. I had been at St. Veronica's with him, but he went to another nearby high school. My junior year, on a kickoff, he blindsided me and made me a highlight tape. He hit me across the chin with his helmet and my feet went vertical. At least, that is what I saw on film...I don't remember much.

By the day of the 200-meter hill test, John had gone off to a famous college football program and returned home. He didn't fit in with college football, but he was a great teammate.

I think I could have done it alone, but John made it easier. He was dying up every single one of these torturous runs, but he was nothing other than positive walking back down. I think back to his math:

"One-fifth finished."

"Thirty percent there."

"Halfway."

"Only two more after this one."

We both got our uniforms.

My social life was limited due to all the travel, but it was a great time for me. I didn't have girlfriends or really "party" like others my age, but I enjoyed life. There were some lonely times, but all in all, it was a wonderful time.

Skyline was very good with media. We got lots of press for our team and it was nice to wake up in the morning and have Dad show me my picture in the paper.

By my sophomore year, the school had developed an amazing athletic department. We won the state in soccer, basketball and track and field that year. That's pretty impressive.

Our track team was amazing. The one drawback is that we were going to as many as three track meets a week. I had to train after competitions just to get my volume in. Our sprinters and hurdlers were slowly coming apart as the season progressed.

At one point, I pulled a muscle in my back. We had been in mini-vans up to three times a week traveling as many as 20 hours roundtrip. Adding this to the throwing and lifting daily and my back spasmed. It would knot up for hours at a time and the only relief was sitting in the fetal position.

I had a massive black and blue mark at the bottom of the injury where the blood pooled. I struggled to sleep or get up and down off the couch. Every time it got a little better, I would hop in the van for a trip to Southern California and injure it again.

Slowly, the injury improved.

This actually worked out well for me: It made me slow down, ease up and learn to relax. I took some time off. I finally recovered.

The season ended well. I won the Small College State Championship in Porterville. Their thrower was picked to win the discus with his hometown advantage. I didn't beat him by much, but I still have the plaque on the wall in my gym.

I ended my time at Skyline graduating with highest honors, the school record, was MVP and co-captain of the state championship team, and held my individual win.

It was time to step up to the next level.

Chapter 21
Ralph Maughan: The Greatest Aggie

After my 9th grade year, my brother Richard and his wife Diane drove me down to Track and Field News. I wanted books on the discus throw. Fortunately, I picked up the *Track and Field Omnibook* by Kenneth Doherty. I am convinced that the first edition remains the best of the series as his insights into the holistic methods of coaching have never been explained better.

The discus throw section did not disappoint. Certainly, the drawings of the discus, done in Doherty's style he called "movies on paper," didn't give a completely clear picture, but the information was fabulous. I was eager to read L. Jay Silvester's training programs and see the clarity of given by his coach, Ralph Maughan.

The next time I went to the library, I looked up Utah State University and found that Ralph B. Maughan was still the head coach. Of course. He would be head coach of Aggie track and field from 1951–1988. I decided that day that I wanted to throw the discus for Utah State University and Ralph Maughan.

It always stayed in the back of my head. At the time, I was a skinny freshman who had to tie a knot in his sweat pants to keep them up.

But I had a dream. I had a goal.

Coach Maughan didn't know about me yet. He was busy living an amazing life. Let me just mention a few things:

- He received a Purple Heart and a Bronze Star at the Battle of the Bulge.

- He was drafted and played for the Detroit Lions.

- He was national hammer champion and made the Olympic team.

- His hobby was engineering and advanced mathematics.

- He raised two wonderful children and several generations of college men.

Of course, dreams and goals don't always follow a straight path. I needed to throw a lot, learn the Olympic lifts from Dick Notmeyer and give up a normal teenage life. Six years after reading that book, my dad, who had turned his life around in just a few months, called up to me, "Danny, telephone call."

I picked up the phone.

"My name is Ralph Maughan. I am the head coach at Utah State University. I would like to offer you a full-ride scholarship."

Dreams can come true, even in real life. It wasn't going to be perfect, but this was such an important decision in my life. There was one issue: USU is in Logan. So, we cracked out the atlas and started searching for Logan in the state of Utah. We started at the bottom and…well, it took a long time to find Logan at the top right of the map.

It wasn't like San Francisco. It was small. It was far away from anything. I didn't know it then, but that would be perfect for me.

Coach's methods were the basic "basics" and I didn't respect them enough at the time. Within days of reporting to school, Coach gave me two phrases that remain the foundational pillars of my life:

"Make yourself a slave to good habits."
"Little and often over the long haul."

As I have said many times, it's easy to tell a Division One athlete about the importance of habits. It is very difficult for that same athlete to understand what "the long haul" truly means. I use the terms "shark habits" and "pirate maps" now, but during our first face-to-face meeting, I had been given the framework for success.

Coach asked me about my journey to USU. I told him the *Omnibook* story and he laughed. I guess the workouts weren't exactly the truth, but let's leave that alone. He then told me about a great USU thrower, Glenn Passey. Sadly, Glenn died as I was writing this section.

Glenn was the Utah State school record holder in the discus. Ultimately, I would just miss breaking that record by three inches, but I weighed 231 and Glenn weighed 178. That's not a misprint. He was the size of an engineering major.

But, Glenn trained "differently." Growing up on a farm, he had a tremendous grip from years of farmer walks. His work capacity was enormous. He was also famous for picking and tossing 40-pound hay bales over and over in the barn. I can't imagine a better foundation for a thrower: His farm work prepared him perfectly for elite throwing.

He told me once, "We didn't lift like you guys."

At the time, I dismissed this point and I still regret it.

"I was told you had to press (Olympic clean and press) and snatch your bodyweight. And, clean and jerk maybe 20 pounds or so more.

"Each fall, I would take a few workouts to get up to those levels, and then stop lifting. I would come back every so often and test myself. If I got weaker, I would train until I got those standards again. Then...stop."

It is genius. If you are up to the standard in the weightroom and not throwing far enough, it's not the lifting that's the issue: You have problems in the discus ring.

In my world of strength training, all too often we have the "more is better" approach in the weightroom. Passey, preparing for multiple tours in Vietnam as a helicopter pilot and later coach at the United State Air Force Academy, didn't have a lot of extra time to spend.

I didn't understand this for decades.

Coach Maughan believed in just a few lifts: the quarter squat, the push jerk and the power curl. He thought hill sprints and stadium steps twice a week were far more important than the weightroom. If you think about Coach's ideas, you can see that we were mimicking Glenn's farm work.

My greatest regret was overtraining in weightlifting during my time at USU. Coach was right: I was now an elite thrower, not a lifter who throws. Three days a week in the weightroom was enough. I didn't need to prep for O lifting meets. I should be sprinting hills. I didn't. I kept trying to do the PBBC program on top of discus and hammer throwing and academic work.

I was wrong.

Utah State revolutionized discus throwers. Most throwers do the USU techniques without knowing it. Coach and his throwers utilized the wide leg at the start and quick feet across the ring. It took me a while to learn it. When I did—basically my senior year—I added 15 feet in a week. That's pretty good.

Coach had a good sense of humor. He had a plaque on his desk: *Be reasonable, do it my way.* He could simply say a few words to cut to the point.

Every thrower had a story about Coach. Once a guy complained that everything Coach Maughan said was negative. He insisted that Coach Maughan say only positive things.

So, the thrower got in the ring and threw.

Coach paused.

And paused.

Finally, "You are holding the discus right."

I have my own little story: I was throwing 180 feet over and over and Coach just kept telling me to do this or that. Basically, everything I did was flawed. Finally, I said:

Coach, these are pretty good throws.

Coach took out a handkerchief and wiped his eyes.

"Well, after watching my guys throw 230 feet out of this same ring, this is just hard to watch."

I shut up and went back to work. And, I got better. Coach always appreciated that I earned good grades and one time added, "If your brains were in your feet, you would throw farther."

My senior year, I went all-in with his advice and I had an amazing year. I had, according to Coach, "the best year any thrower has ever had at Utah State." I was his High Point Man (MVP) and went to the Nationals. I also had a 4.0 GPA and life was good. At the end of the year, Coach asked me to come back in the fall and be the strength coach for the track team because so many of the guys were beginning to train like bodybuilders rather than track and field athletes.

I'm not positive, but back in 1979, I might have been one of the first strength coaches ever. Of course, I just focused on what Dick and Coach Maughan had taught me; I kept it simple with full body movements and squatting. And, yes, I made sure the athletes ran hills and stairs.

Those who followed this well-worn path did very well.

Oddly, one of the most important moments of my life with Coach Maughan happened in the winter of my senior year. Because I threw the indoor weight—the indoor hammer throw—I often went to track meets alone with Coach because the event was held hours before the official meet started. Our driver was Randy Wilson, Coach Maughan's son-in-law.

One trip, Randy was asking questions about World War II. At first it was obvious that Coach didn't want to talk. Then, and I have seen this look from WWII and Vietnam War vets, he looked out the window and started to talk.

He mentioned the sound machine guns made and how he could tell American or German weapons just by the speed of the rat-tat-tat. He talked about the frostbite and the first dead German soldier he saw by the side of the road. He went deep into his memory during that long drive.

That night, Randy took me aside and said that Coach NEVER talked about the war. Coach kept quiet about it; this had been a first for him.

The stories made me realize what I was doing might not be so important. Discus throwing and sitting in a classroom was pretty easy stuff for a 21-year-old boy. Being shelled and shot at by Nazis in the winter of 1944 changed Coach Maughan; he loved life, his kids, his grandkids and all of us.

Survival clarifies purpose.

I'll tell you more as we go along, but I went on to get my bachelors and masters while coaching for USU. I then moved down to Salt Lake City to teach at Judge Memorial Catholic High School. I continued to travel to Logan to visit Coach Maughan long after he retired in 1988. His retirement track meet—his family set up a surprise alumni track meet and banquet—capped his career as an Aggie.

That was the day I met many of my heroes. I discovered Glenn Passey's insights into the discus, the importance of the overhead squat and how simple it is to be great in throwing... and in life.

It was also the weekend after Tiffini and I got married, so it was a chance to spend some special time with my wife in my life's journey. My teammates were unanimous in their praise of my new bride and we had lots of fun.

Years after he retired, he spoke to the Utah State Track and Field Association. His clarity in coaching was still so fresh: He summarized all of coaching and life with some very simple ideas. He explained his "two-day lag rule" to stunned young coaches. Coach had discovered that athletes can train hard the day before competition and lose almost nothing. But, TWO days before competition had to be easy.

Historically, Thursday practices at USU—meets were generally on Saturday—were ghost towns; nobody went very hard nor stayed very long. These, of course, are hard-earned and hard-learned lessons. Before that, most of his audience literally ran their athletes into the ground.

He also said you could probably summarize most of track and field with a few phrases: "Attack with the knee" and "Continuous acceleration."

I have helped jumpers, vaulters, hurdlers and throwers just by teaching an aggressive knee drive. Of course, acceleration is the key to so much of athletics; Coach was vehement about the importance of the phrase and the concept. He also finished the day by reminding the coaches that we should only recruit two things, "speed and smarts," as those are two qualities we can't really change. I still laugh at that.

Sadly, not long after that, I started noticing some changes. Parkinson's disease began to catch up to him and his vision, always an issue from the War, got worse. He figured out a way to read my articles by using a projector and a screen to read them. I'm not sure I have ever been more honored.

He died on July 3, 2006, the same date as my parent's anniversary, and the importance of this day in my life wasn't lost on me. He has been called "The Greatest Aggie." Utah State's mascot is the Aggie, and I can't argue with this designation.

If I ever used a touch of sarcasm in my training or asked out loud why we are wasting so much time at practice when we could be doing other things in life, you are hearing my inner Coach Ralph Maughan.

He was the original life coach. He saw sports as a way to make life better.

Chapter 22
Cheese Factory and Master Degrees
A Multi-year "Now What?"

I had a big issue after I graduated from Utah State: Now what? That makes a great title of a book and a reality check for many of us. I had been "perfect" so far: elementary school, junior high school, high school, junior college and now the university degrees.

I had five diplomas in eight years. My father had always been convinced that a college degree set one on the royal road to riches. You know, he was right! It just took longer than I thought.

It was at this time I was getting ready to marry my first wife. I linked my throwing success to our relationship—a classic logic issue—and we got engaged. To support us, I often worked up to three jobs. Now, in her defense, she also worked as a waitress at a little place in Logan that still survives, but an issue was starting to show: her spending habits. We soon found ourselves with stacks of bounced checks and cancelled credit cards and it was difficult to dig out of that heap.

I started working the night shift at a local cheese plant scrubbing cookers. Work started at 10 at night and the shift finished at 6:30 a.m. It was wet, messy work. I almost lost my sight one night when a machine spit out chemicals, but my friend "Steely Dan" picked me up and carried me to the eye wash station. It took hours to dilute the caustic chemical enough that it felt safe to let me go home.

I would sleep a few hours, then head up to USU to coach in the weightroom. I wasn't sleeping much and had little energy for anything. I tried to train, but the days were killing me. Fortunately, Ross Peterson, one of the members of USU's fine history department, told me about an opportunity to get my masters in history while earning a nice stipend.

History was a good fit for me. I like the use of chronology and geography and loved the lectures. I found a place to both work and learn. Later, I picked up another job working for the Utah History Fair and that taught me many lessons of traveling and organization.

Not long after I married, my mom's cancer returned and soon she died. My professors were wonderful and helped me in every way possible. I was amazed at the kindness of Norm Jones and Carol O'Connor.

Eleven years later when my dad died, I would be supported by the Judge Memorial Catholic High School community. It's inspiring to remember the help and comfort so freely given.

Working on the degree and coaching in the afternoons started to ease my life. I did a smart thing: I sat in on the freshman survey courses—and taught occasionally. I knew a lot about United States history as well as ancient and western civilizations. But, I needed to have my knowledge *linked together.*

This insight has served me well throughout my life: It's really important to find your niche, that area you really know. But you must also be sure to embrace the big picture.

My friends were surprised one year when they saw me coaching hurdlers. But hurdling, as Coach Maughan taught us in our track class, is closely related to the jumps, the sprints and the throws. Concepts like "attack with the knee" work as well in the hurdles as they do in the high jump as they do in the javelin.

Connecting the Links later became the title of a booklet I made for my religious studies students. Religion literally means "to link back," and seeing the links, seeing the connections, is a key to both coaching, teaching and learning.

This was foundational material for my career. I was learning the key to coaching and teaching: linking things together. When we talk about a drill—whether you hate or love drills—the drill must link into what we are trying to get the athlete to learn and do.

In my career, I have done lots of things that didn't carry over to the field of play:

Monkey rolls

Jumping jacks, burpees and most conditioning nonsense

Nutcracker or Oklahoma drills

Most blocking sled drills

Actually, much of American football practice

Jogging

Voodoo recovery ideas

Most stretching work in team sports

Of course, I can also include the sheer waste of time and energy we produce at most training sessions. I will always regret having 92 people standing around watching a coach teach a quarterback to take the snap from the center. No one was doing anything except for those three.

I test myself on this often: Whenever we come up with something brighter, bigger and better, I step back to see if it helps with the big picture.

If it does, I become the idea's biggest fan and missionary.
If it doesn't, I try to dustbin it as fast as I can.
The big picture:

It's the key to long-term success in every field.

Chapter 23
Tim Carr

As I look back over my career in teaching and coaching, there are dozens of people who come to mind who helped me over the various walls and obstacles that crater through school corridors. Teaching is a tough profession. Job one is literally to take attendance. Taking attendance is to simply insure that the little ones are safe and sound. Learning is not the focus. Being in the room is primary; the lawyers are clear about this.

Often, to become a teacher, it helps to know people.

I'm a believer, first and foremost, of the magic quality of social capital. It's that marvelous thing you get from friends and family that gets you backstage passes, the locals' admission price (free) and the after-parties of life. I never intentionally mine my social capital, but I can see, in hindsight, the value of it. I can also see how it has opened doors.

Tim Carr was the Dean of Discipline at Judge Memorial Catholic High School. He was a pillar, an icon, of this school. My brother Ray and Tim had become friends in graduate school. This, of course, opened a door for me when a job opened up at Judge.

Tim, as I discovered later, was the only administrator keen to hire me.

A former Judge student had graduated from college and she also applied. I had a masters in history; she had a bachelors in history.

I could coach football, wrestling, chess and track; she would not be able to do after-school activities as she was actively trying to get into graduate school. I know all of this because we later became very good friends…and remain so to this day.

Judge was a funny place at the time: If you went to JMCHS, you were considered the best choice for faculty, even if it meant you would be teaching the brothers and sisters of your high school best friends. Of course, that is fine and I am sure many places deal with this same issue.

Tim went to bat for me over and over. What ultimately secured me the position is that the other applicant withdrew her name. Begrudgingly—and I mean that—I was offered the position. I accepted.

From 1982 until 1996, I thrived there.

But, I thrived for a good reason. The day before school started, I came back to campus after an orientation—the women leading the orientation said "We don't need to reinvent the wheel" a dozen times at least—and Tim called me into the office.

Basically, Tim was just checking in. There were so many things I didn't know. But I didn't know what I didn't know and I was very comfortable with beginning the next day.

Tim then leaned back, lit his pipe and told me a few things that remain the foundation of my teaching and coaching right up to the moment I type this sentence.

"You know, Dan, you are going to have some kids with some pretty lousy lives. Their parents are flakes; these kids have been lied to and promised things their whole lives that never came true. They get shuttled from Mom to Dad and back again. Adults, in these kids' experience, are flakes.

"Sitting next to them is a kid whose dad is a lawyer and whose mom is a doctor. They fly to Europe on a whim and the kid has had every advantage.

For this kid, you can sit in your chair and ask, "What do you feel like learning today?" You can wing it. You can play records in class and have free time. This kid will still get into college, grad school…and will do just fine.

"But, those other kids, they need an adult in their lives. They need you to be organized, balanced and sane. You need to have a routine, a schedule and consequences…good and bad. You need to point the way."

It was, and remains, the most important thing I have ever heard about the gift of teaching. I'm not there to entertain, I am there to teach. To lead. To educate.

Sure, we can have fun, but always as part of the structure of the class and course. Stories that expand a lesson, puns that reinforce the terms and jokes that open a window into the material are welcome. It's okay to have fun, but it must be part of the journey.

Sister Maria was right about work, rest, pray and play years before I met with Tim.

Tim nodded a bit, then added one more point:

"The students need three pillars here: academic, activities and social. If kids get all As, but don't have an appropriate social life, they won't last long in college. If it's just sports, life won't be easy after high school. The successful students…in life…are those with the best balance. It's like a stool: You won't be comfortable on a one-legged stool."

This became one of those truths I bumped into time and again. The students with good grades, active afternoons and friends "worth the name" seemed to always be doing great years after graduation.

The one-dimensional kids would suffer from Bruce Springsteen's *Glory Days* syndrome or get kicked out of college for terrible grades by trying to fit four years of partying into the first quarter of college life.

Then, he said, "Good luck…see you tomorrow."

And, for the next 13 years, I never missed a day.

I was convinced that my athletic career might be finished and I would become a high school coach. But, my path back to competition had already been paved.

Chapter 24
Dave Turner

The fall of 1980 was a transitional period for me. As I look back, it is a whirl of good and bad. I had been married a few months and the financial issues were starting to bend things. My mother was strangely quiet about her cancer treatments, and I began full-time work on my masters in history.

I continued to help the throwers at Utah State while being the strength coach. Some of the athletes followed my advice and ideas, but many chose to skip lifting or just train like bodybuilders. Their path did not lead to superlative performance. I had learned a lot in this year after graduating from college: I was working in the cheese factory and juggled coaching, a few classes and full-time work.

Then I got a piece of news: The first Utah State Weightlifting Championship would be held in Salt Lake City a few months down the line. I started training again and contacted Dick Notmeyer, who agreed to review my workouts. I started sending him weekly letters with my training and he would reply with ideas and insights.

As you might guess, the turnaround of the letters often meant I had already either improved or gone south by the time Dick's return letter arrived.

My training was good. Then, I got a call at 3:00 a.m.

"Mom just died."

On October 2, 1980, my mother, Aileen Barbara McCloskey John, died after a rather quick battle with breast cancer.

Travel. Funeral. Sadness.

Things start to swirl a bit in my memory, but I know I decided to train hard for this weightlifting meet. I sent in the registration and prepared myself.

Two weeks before the meet, the captain of our powerlifting team found out his 100-kilo lifter wouldn't compete at a big local meet. I said "yes" and I still don't know why. I weighed in at 9 a.m. on Saturday morning and I still hadn't deadlifted at 2:30 a.m. Sunday.

I've told the story a million times, but how it went was this: When the last person missed a deadlift, I asked the official, "What's the next jump?" He said "628," so I went to the platform and made the lift and we all went home.

This did little to help me prep for the Olympic lifting meet to follow, but it makes for a good story.

Two weeks later, perhaps 20 people descended on some place in the west side of Salt Lake City for the state weightlifting meet. It was at this time that I met the organizer, Dave Turner.

Dave deserves to be in halls of fame, but I doubt he will get in. Singlehandedly, he built Utah Olympic lifting. He ran meets, judged, lifted, organized and coached O lifters for decades. He was a middle school math teacher who developed a team called the "Hercules Barbell Club."

I'm still a proud member.

I won Best Lifter that day in 1980 and began a four-decade relationship with the Hercules Barbell Club.

Dave coached his team three days a week in a working closet just off of his school's auditorium. The walls were filled with motivational pictures and the simple programs Dave uses to teach the lifts.

I always warn my interns and friends when they go to train with Dave: It's going to be a hard hour.

Wait, an hour? Yes, we start at 3:00 and go until 4:00.

Exactly.

Dave begins with a short meeting reminding the team about upcoming events and the usual details of performance sports: Fill out the form, send the check, show up.

Dave then has the team go through a full body flexibility warmup that is a series of classic movements done one after another.

We all grab broomsticks and we do overhead squats, followed by front squats, and then a cardio-like few minutes of snatches and clean and jerks with the broomsticks.

Dave reinforces the terms used in lifting: "Get set," "Push the floor," "Jump," "Dip" and "Down."

Once, and Parker J. Burns was with me doing this so we have third-party verification, we went for 20 minutes. It was exhausting.

Then, we do Dave's daily program:

- *Snatch:* Eight sets of doubles—a "double" is two perfect repetitions

- *Clean and jerk:* Eight sets of singles—a "single" is a perfect repetition

- *Front squat:* Five sets of five repetitions

- *Press:* Five sets of three repetitions

If your form is perfect, you add weight the next workout, if not, you stay at the current weight. I know, I know, it looks easy on paper. Try it...then, tell me it's easy.

As I review this after 40 years of experience, I realize Dave is teaching his lifters how to lift during the warmups!

I stole this idea for my discus throwers: Our throwers warm up with the basic movements…over and over and over again… of Stretch–1–2–3. They hear the terms, do the movements and warm up their bodies and their techniques at the same time.

One thing I struggle to explain is how the Hercules program includes variation. Dave's workout is always the same…with one variation. The athletes all do the same program, but they start at different lifts.

A typical variation:

> *Clean and jerk:* Eight sets of singles
> *Front squat:* Five sets of five
> *Press:* Five sets of three
> *Snatch:* Eight sets of doubles

One day an athlete might start at the clean and jerk and finish with the snatch. The next workout, the front squat is first; the next…press, and the next week begins with the snatches and finishes with the presses. A little variety is nice—that's all a beginner needs.

The genius of Dave's system is two-fold; first, the athletes are preparing from the moment they enter the gym to lift on the platform at a meet. All their training is focused on the two meet lifts: the snatch and the clean and jerk. The front squats and the presses are the strength moves.

Then, at 3:58, we clean up the weights, put our hands together and shout the motto of the Olympic Games:

"Citius, Altius, Fortius!"—*Latin for "Faster, Higher, Stronger"*

Dave has coached me in my 20s, 30s, 40s, 50s and 60s—no, I don't lift like I did in my 30s, but I still lift. I appreciate his friendship, his coaching and his genius.

Dave reinforced a truth: If you are going to perform, you MUST practice like you perform. Dave's template of getting everything done in one hour became my model for coaching track and field and, later, all my coaching opportunities whenever possible.

If you are going to get everything finished in an hour, you have to know what you want to do…

And do it.

Dave also has an advanced program for peaking at larger meets. This is the 10-week template:

	Day One		Day Two		Day Three
Week	**Press**	**Front Squat**	**Pull**	**Front Squat**	**Total**
One	60/3/5	72/2/5	80/2/5	72/3/5	80
Two	64/3/5	72/2/5	84/2/3	72/4/5	68
Three	68/3/5	72/2/5	88/2/2	72/5/6	84
Four	72/3/5	72/2/5	92/1/2	76/5/5	72
Five	76/2/4	72/2/5	96/1/2	80/4/4	88
Six	80/2/3	72/2/5	100/1/1	84/3/3	76
Seven	84/2/2	72/2/5	104/1/1	88/2/2	92
Eight	88/1/1	72/2/5	108/1/1	104/1/1/	80
Nine	Total 76		Total 80		84
Ten	Total 76		Rest		Meet 100+

The first number is the percent.
The second is the reps and the third is the number of sets.
Day Three will be explained on the next page.

Day One

Press: push jerks or jerks

Front squats

Day Two

Pull: snatch-grip high pulls and clean-grip high pulls

Front squats

Day Three and the Last Two Weeks

Total: Practice as if this an Olympic lifting meet. I found that doing a long workout helped. Full warmup. Snatch up to your opener, then make three perfect lifts. Repeat for clean and jerk.

The numbers: The first number is the percent; second is the reps and the third is the number of sets.

I recommend the full warmup and stick work too.

Dave gave me a program in 2010 that culminated all of his years of experience. He told me, "I had you in mind for this program."

Hercules Rack Routine

Day One

Snatch: 80% for three singles

Low front squat isometric: 100% for a six-second hold in the rack

High snatch pull isometric: 100% for a six-second hold in the rack

Push press: 60% for three sets of two

Day Two

Clean and jerk: 80% for three singles

Mid clean pull isometric: Two x 100% for a six-second hold in the rack

High front squat: Two x 100% for a six-second hold in the rack

Lockout: 100% for a six-second hold in the rack

Day Three

Total with at least 80%. Meet conditions

On Week Eight: *Test or compete*

Monday: Total with 76%
Rest all week

Meet: *Go for records*

Again, do the full daily warmup and broomstick work.

So, not long after burying my mother, I lifted in the first Utah State Weightlifting Championships. I was awarded Best Lifter and have competed in the championships numerous times since then. I've lifted with Dave Turner in gyms, correctional facilities, fire stations and garages. I competed alongside him, his sons and his grandsons representing Hercules BBC.

Dave kept me competing until I had the spark to step it back up again.

I honor our friendship.

Chapter 25
The Scandinavians and Tiffini

I've been keeping a journal since 1972. Sometimes reading the entries breaks my heart as I am doing way too much crap and ignoring the basics. Then, I see some absolutely genius training programs and, of course, I quit doing them because…I am an idiot. My first journal still makes me smile:

March 25, 1972

> *1. Incline bench press, 65 pounds, 8/8/4*
>
> *2. Bench press, 65 pounds, 8/6/4*
>
> *3. Squats, 65 pounds, 10/10/10*
>
> *4. Toe raises (regular, toes in), 65 pounds, 20/20/20*
>
> *5. Pullovers (full range), 10 pounds, 8/6/4*
>
> *6. Incline flys, 20 pounds, 8/6/4*
>
> *Tried to do press (65 pounds), experienced pain in left elbow. (Applied fast heating minute rub)*

Later, I added a note on the top:

> *3-3-78: First meet way back at 72 feet. Second meet versus Alta Loma 89' 10" for first place and a win over Harno.*

I always make a little joke when I share this workout: "Hey… and I was drug free!

The first journal served me until December 13, 1974, and I had to find a new one. That first track season, I got all the weights from my neighbors and ended up benching on my back porch, 132½ pounds for 8/6/4. Why that weight? That's all I had.

My next journal has "US History II" on the cover; my brother Phil bought it for a class and never used it. I tore out the first pages of his notebook and used it from February 22, 1975, until June 2, 1977. I was to go from 118 pounds in bodyweight to 231 pounds through those journals, win four straight conference championships and pay for all my education throwing the discus.

As I review them, I see I don't usually make notes like I did that day on 3-3-78. I sometimes shudder at the decisions my younger self makes, but the lessons learned usually made me better in the long run.

There are times I want to reach back and give a helping hand. When I returned from the Middle East, I was concerned about my "dire" finances:

> *October 15, 1985*
>
> *Situation*
>
> > *1. About $600 owed on skis and plane tickets*
> >
> > *2. Probably $600 on taxes. Fed.*
> >
> > *3. Maybe $200–300 on state (taxes)*

I was heading out in a few months to visit my sister and dad in Vermont and I was worried about these massive debts I had incurred. I was a poorly paid teacher and coach and $1,500 in debt scared me to death.

I would love to loan me a bit of money now that I can afford things better.

So, in 1985 and 1986, I struggled with some financial issues and I was dealing with a few physical issues from my time in Egypt. I probably would never have returned to competing, but

I opened the morning paper one day and the headlines on the sports page talked about the Utah Summer Games and the amazing efforts of an athlete in the discus.

The throw wasn't very good. My first thought was, "I can do that without training."

A switch flicked in my head.

I started lifting and throwing again. My bodyweight had fallen to 185 with the illness and I had forgotten how sore things get when you lift weights.

A year later, I won the discus at the Utah Summer Games and beat the old record by a long way. Reviewing my journal from this period made me realize it was probably the most important period of my career.

Cue Ravel's *Bolero.*

It had been almost a decade since I competed for Utah State. Still, I was welcome at track meets throughout the states of Utah, Colorado and Idaho. I couldn't afford to travel very fancy, but my two-toned Volkswagen was up for the challenge. The two tones were rust and lime green; the bumper was held on with a weightlifting belt and the back seat had caught on fire when I put too many books on the seat.

So, early Saturday mornings, I would pop out of bed, deal with the rain, sleet and snow of Utah spring and go throw the discus. At a meet in Ogden, I threw well and Coach Maughan came down from the stands to congratulate me.

"Things have changed."

Coach was right. Out at the circle, the athletes were screaming, yelling and stomping around between throws. These guys were much larger and louder than my generation. Things had changed. Most of the guys were ripped, yet were able to maintain bodyweights sneaking up on 300 pounds.

Some of you might guess part of the reason for the change. We will just move along.

I met one of the throwers from down south, James Bischoff, and we started to talk. James had been training with some throwers, all from Scandinavia, and he outlined some of what he was doing with them, which I'll explain shortly. On May 9, 1987, I wrote this in my journal:

1. *Warm up with sprints*

2. *Plyometrics three times a week*

3. *Three sets of eight with the straight-leg deadlift; twice a week for flexibility*

4. *Deep squats: a set of five, a set of three and the big last set with seven reps*

5. *Dumbbell everything you can think of twice a week*

6. *High pulls twice a week*

7. *Throw twice a day*

For the next few years, I would be lifting and training with full-time athletes while I tried to work a full-time teaching load and coaching. It wasn't a formula that would work, but I was to learn so much.

These guys read everything on lifting and throwing…and thought of little else. We talked at length about the central nervous system and how to test its "freshness." I was told about the pencil tap test where each morning one woke up and grabbed a piece of paper. Then, in 10 seconds, make as many marks as possible (dots are best). Then, count them and compare to the normal results.

If you slow down 10 percent, it's a day to take off. This little test gives a glimmer of sight into CNS fatigue.

Later, Mike Rosenberg came up with a way to do this on a computer using the space bar as the tap test. You can still find these in app stores, but Mike should always get credit.

My new friends were excellent technicians. They had the discipline to keep hammering away on a problem until they pushed through it. With James's help, we were able to make a weekly template of training that served me well for a little while.

Monday

Morning Session

Warmup

Sprints, 4 x 30; 5 x 20

Evening Session

Warmup

Altitude jumps, 4 x 3

Depth jumps, 6

Vertical jumps, 3 x 4

Straight-leg deadlifts, 3 x 8

Max situps

Squats, 5-3-7

Tuesday

Evening Session

Warmup

Pushup jumps, 4 x 3

Max dips, 2 sets

Military press, 2 sets

Curls

Shrugs

Light snatches

Wednesday

Evening Session

Warmup

Standing long jump, 4 x 5

One-legged hops, 2 x 2 x 6

Form sprints

Thursday

Off

Friday

Morning Session

Warmup

Sprints, 3 x 40; 2 x 30; 4 x 10

Evening Session

Warmup

Altitude jumps, 4 x 3

Depth jumps, 6

Split-stance jumps, 3 x 6

Two-legged hops, 3 x 6

Straight-leg deadlift, 3 x 8

Max situps

Squats, 5–3–7

Saturday

Evening Session

Warmup

Pushup jumps, 4 x 3

Dips

Military press

Curls

Shrugs

Clean-grip snatch

Quickly, of course, I started falling apart.

My back started cramping and my legs felt awful a lot of the time. I kept pushing as best as I could, but I couldn't keep up this kind of training.

It's okay; the lessons I learned during this period were well worth it.

At this time, I was asked to speak to a group, a mix of young athletes and parents, about being elite. My experiences with these guys helped me through the talk, *What makes an athlete elite?*

> *1. The athlete no longer is on a steep learning curve. The athlete, in other words, is no longer improving in quantum leaps from year to year or season to season. Lifts, for example, no longer double over two years. Improvement is slow.*
>
> *2. The athlete has a year-round approach to one sport.*
>
> *3. The athlete uses some form of intense training camp or focused training of some kind each year.*
>
> *4. The athlete uses high levels of strength training before the competitive periods. Save for lifters, as strength levels go down, performance should improve.*
>
> *5. The athlete has made a personal choice to be elite.*

Expanding on the first point:

> *The athlete no longer is on a steep learning curve. The athlete, in other words, is no longer improving in quantum leaps from year to year or season to season. Lifts, for example, no longer double over two years. Improvement is slow.*

Yuri Sedych, still the world record holder in the hammer (and it has been a long, long time since he set it), told me a very simple definition of "elite" a few years ago at dinner:

"If you improve every year, you are elite."

The athlete no longer improves by leaps and bounds, but at the same time is still improving.

Expanding on the second point:

> *The athlete has a year-round approach to one sport.*

I often caution people to follow Andrew Carnegie's advice:

"Put all your eggs in one basket…and carefully watch that basket!"

True, there is a time and place for all of this. It is fine to take a month, six weeks or two months away from your focus and try other things. But the bulk of your time, energy and focus have to be on that one basket of eggs.

Expanding on the third point:

> *The athlete uses some form of intense training camp or focused training of some kind each year.*

Get out of the comfy confines of the local spa and go see what the best are doing. Go to a clinic. Take a certification course. Find out what is really going on.

Get your hands dirty and relearn (or simply learn) the basics. If there isn't a formal camp to go to, book a hotel room near a gym or place you need to train and go there and immerse yourself in the place.

Expanding on the fourth point:

> *The athlete uses high levels of strength training before the competitive periods. Save for lifters, as strength levels go down, performance should improve.*

I learned this years ago from John Powell, the great discus thrower. The explanation was so simple I nearly cried: The body, especially the nervous system, can only be asked to do so many things at once.

I continually encourage people to get strong earlier in the year, then focus on the other qualities for the sport.

Expanding on the fifth point:

The athlete has made a personal choice to be elite.

I have written time and again about goal setting. Many people wash over the articles with a blank face and ignore the importance. It comes down to this: If you want to be great—the best—you need to make the choice to do it.

You might have the genetics to do it, but natural talent only gets you so far.

You might have a mom or dad pushing you to do it, but, in my experience with some of my athletes, that can be a millstone around your neck.

And, you make this choice by setting goals. If you want to get extremely low numbers on your bodyfat tests, you are going to have push away and push aside temptations in the form of sweets and fatty goo nearly every day, if not nearly every hour.

You have to have courage in reserve to achieve great goals.

But YOU have to have it. No one can do it for you.

That summer, 1987, found me training harder than I had ever trained before as an athlete. Sadly, my performance as a discus thrower began to drop. It was clear I was not heading in the right direction.

But I was going in the right direction in my life. I just needed to say "yes."

In August, football season came around and I had to stop serious training. I was going back to my monkish life.

That is, until one of my assistant coaches asked me a favor.

"Hey, Dan. Will you go to a party with me?"

No.

"It's a graduation party for my brother. He graduated from the U and his girlfriend is setting me up with some girl."

No.

"I'll drive and bring beer."

Hmmm. He had me there.

Yes.

I'm glad I said "yes."

On August 21, 1987, I went to a college party. I was 29 and 51 weeks old, hanging around with college kids. This wasn't what I had been hoping for on the eve of my 30th birthday.

There I met the woman he was being set up with that night. Her name was Tiffini. In a few months, we would be engaged and on May 14, 1988, we would marry.

I'm the worst wingman ever.

Tiffini was 19. She understood my sports and my passions. She has always supported my career and career choices. She could see when I was overtraining and knew how to talk me down off the ceiling after bad days.

That football season would have its ups and downs. We were undefeated, then lost every game. It was just that kind of year.

In hindsight, my favorite part of that 1987 football season were the Wednesday nights: I tutored economics while I ate hamburgers.

Chapter 26
Lessons in Performance are Lessons in Life

As I said, in 1985 I got very ill when I studied in the Middle East. Obviously, I had a great time, but I picked up something bad at Medinet Habu when I had to decide, in 120-degree weather and no shade, whether to go without water or drink what was available.

As we read in *Dune,* I had to make a water choice.

It didn't go well. In two weeks, I lost 40 pounds; I rarely made it through a meal without sprinting to a toilet. I still struggle with a few small issues—according to my Tiffini, I have the bladder of a baby.

The memories are golden. The nighttime boat trip on the Nile, the full moon rising over the Suez, and a dinner discussion with an Israeli general certainly are memories that will forever glow within me. I swam in the Dead Sea, the Sea of Galilee, the Jordan River, the Nile River, the Mediterranean Sea and the Red Sea. These experiences made me a better teacher, a better lecturer.

But, I paid a price with my health.

It was a great time, but came at a cost. Oddly, this is exactly the kind of cost-to-benefit ratio that paid off in my coaching career.

Getting out of bed every morning weighing 40 pounds less is a mixed blessing. Certainly, my joints felt better, but I felt "just plain lousy" (and if you recognize that old TV commercial, you are, like me, showing your age).

I was living in a basement, sleeping in a fold-out bed that was a crappy couch and a much worse sleeping platform. This was just before I met Tiffini and, as I often joke, I know she didn't marry me for my money!

Usually, when my wallet is thin, I like to say, "Well, at least I have my health."

I didn't. I was poor, lonely and sick. But I had my dreams. I had my goals.

Besides feeling lousy 24 hours a day, I also found out that my department head decided I needed to teach economics to the seniors that fall semester. It was late August and school started the next week.

Fortunately, I had a good friend, Galey Colosimo, who was also teaching econ; he could keep me a few days ahead of the students.

I think I was a natural economics teacher: "cost to benefit" sums most of coaching and training; "opportunity costs" explain why so many people quit early and "asymmetrical risks" remain the foundation of how I spend money to not only have fun, but also to protect and insure my family's lives and wealth.

Soon, of course, it became obvious that what I taught in economics was exactly what I learned in sports.

And, the lessons in sports reflected what I learned about life.

As I learned from Bob Jacobs, "life" was the perfect hook.

I refer to this now as the Four Fs:

> *Fitness*
>
> *Finance*
>
> *Food*
>
> *Friends*

British statistician George Box famously wrote: "All models are wrong, but some are useful." I completely acknowledge that comparing this to that—apples to oranges—is always fraught with problems, but it seems useful.

Coach Maughan's simple point, "Little and often over the long haul," seems the cornerstone of the Four Fs.

I can't repeat enough the four "truths" I have found in almost all fields:

> *Little and often over the long haul*
>
> *Focus on quality*
>
> *Foundations first*
>
> *Master the basics*

Years ago, I read about another way to approach these "truths," the Four Laws of Ecology, discovered by Dr. Barry Commoner, a cellular biologist and college professor.

The Four Laws of Ecology are:

> *Everything is connected to everything else.*
>
> *Everything must go somewhere.*
>
> *Nature knows best.*
>
> *There is no such thing as a free lunch.*

He goes on:

> *"Exploitation of nature will inevitably involve the conversion of resources from useful to useless forms. In nature,*

both sides of the equation must balance, for every gain there is a cost, and all debts are eventually paid."

Commoner's Laws are true in all areas of the Four Fs. Number Four, "There is no such thing as a free lunch," is a foundational truth of most of life, living and the universe.

Debts are eventually paid. It's a rare week when one of my performance-enhancing-drug friends dies far too early or other friends get crushed by bad credit card debt. As Rocky Balboa said: "You gotta pay the piper."

As an economics instructor, I was gaining a toolkit to explain the coaching methods that would help my athletes succeed. Much of what I teach in workshops are thinly veiled economics lectures.

I quickly realized that as wonderful as microeconomics and macroeconomics may be, we all need to know supply and demand and GDP—but we had a massive gap in PERSONAL economics. My students could argue domestic trade policy, but they couldn't balance a checkbook.

In full candor, most still struggle. So, I came up with some simple ideas for my students.

First, the baby steps:

1. Copy both sides of everything in your wallet; put it in an envelope and put it someplace you can access it if you lose your wallet. If you travel, make another set (including your passport) and give it to someone you can trust to help on the road. It's probably a good idea to have a master password document and have that available too.

2. Schedule an annual physical, dental appointment and eye exam. No matter how much you make in income or enjoy in various forms of savings, not having your health will drain everything.

This is a good idea for everyone in your family too.

3. Begin an emergency fund. Even if you are in debt, having $1,500 easily accessible will allow you to weather the minor issues in life. I've had the hot water heater go out on Christmas Eve—things happen. A little cushion provides a better night's sleep.

4. In addition, grab a jar or envelope and start stuffing any spare change or cash into your "fortune fund." Every day would be wonderful, but do what you can. And, every time you add a little, remind yourself of that distant goal.

Honestly, if you can do these easy steps at an early enough age, you won't have as much to worry about later in life in the area of finance.

The next step is to determine "Where are you?" It's also the first thing ever said by God to humans in *The Bible*, so maybe this is more important than we think.

Take an inventory of everything you have: all the stuff, cars, places and money you can tally. Then, total all you owe in loans and credit and whatever else you might owe to someone or something else.

The first time I did this in 1987, I was barely above water. Knowing where my money was going was the first step to getting my feet on dry land again.

Tracking your cash flow is the first step to being debt free and to achieving your financial goals.

And, yes, skipping that daily fancy coffee habit at the chain franchise might be the little bit of extra money that brings all your financial dreams home.

You might notice something as you do this annual "Where are you?" a few years in a row. You might see that you are spending money on things, but not yourself and your family. I had it explained to me like this:

"Stop spending money on your assets."

If you own a wonderful car that demands excessive care and maintenance, you are spending money on things. Which, of course, is fine…

Unless you would like to spend money on you and yours. I have a friend who once asked me how I can afford to vacation yearly in Ireland. He owns a SUV that probably drinks more gas going to the grocery store than I use in my economy car in a month.

I told him, "I don't spend my money on assets."

That sailed right over his head.

Your assets might be crippling your goals and dreams. Think about those things you have that eat away at your happiness.

Then, look at debt.

We all know the rope that debt puts around the neck of personal progress. Becoming debt-free is a lot like losing bodyfat: There are millions of "secrets" about how to do it, but it will come down to some sacrifices and consistent efforts.

After achieving no debt, the next steps will keep most of us happy and sane:

1. *Remain debt-free.*

2. *Buy quality goods and services.*

3. *Choose wisely when it comes to matters of the heart.*

4. *Invest deeply in your and your spouse's(!) education and career advancement.*

Let's keep this in perspective: Your finances support all the other aspects of life, at least where I live.

It is no secret that rich people today have better access to health care, education and the various forms of power.

But, there is something that can be achieved by everyone: happiness, bliss.

Joseph Campbell's interviews with Bill Moyers really helped me wrap my head out his phrase "Follow your bliss." Later, Campbell insisted he should have said, "Follow your blisters."

Whenever I strode forth doing things I love to do and that make me happy, the universe conspires to keep me on that journey. I have had my share of nine-to-five jobs and I appreciated the money, friendships and opportunities. But, when I do things I truly love—things that make me happy—I never seem to actually "work."

Follow your bliss. Be sure you find a way to enjoy 24 hours a day…every day. Life is too short not to love what you do.

Remembering Sister Assumpta's compass, when we start discussing finances, we seem to resort simply to "Work." I grew up and I live in a capitalistic system. I've seen Adam Smith and Karl Marx both right and wrong as I have journeyed through life.

I have an excellent liberal education—the education of a free person. For me, any and all new technology is a new tool: nothing more, nothing less. I have been trained to adapt, add, subtract and flow with new ideas and new ways of doing things.

So, "work," yes, is part of finances.

But, it is just *part* of finances.

Chapter 27
Adapting Economics Lectures to Life

Sometimes, people miss the big picture here. Certainly, I honor and respect work, labor and the rewards of a job. I am a believer in the absolute dignity of work, but I also believe there are two kinds of jobs.

The nine-to-five job pays the bills, picks up insurance and provides for the basics of life. What a wonderful thing it is to have a nine-to-five job that fulfills your soul, feeds your passions and makes you leap out of bed in the morning. I've had that happen a few years in my teaching career when the students were bright and eager to learn the subjects that made my heart rise.

And, yep...there are times when I hated every second of a school day. We used to discuss being hamsters; the moment the classroom door closed, our teaching staff would start spinning our wheels.

If you are lucky, you find a career that allows you to work with passion. You make a difference. You love what you do.

For me, I soon discovered I was lucky: Not only did I love my nine-to-five job most of the time, I was also able to make a little more money by doing the things I loved.

I loved coaching American football and the throws in track and field. I made very little for it, but I kept copious notes and typed (before computers, we had these things called "typewriters" that didn't have great memories...none actually) and re-typed my ideas, teaching progressions and vision of performance.

When the internet came around, I typed those concepts into my first website. The free materials soon started a life of their own and exploded across the web.

Years later, I was asked to speak for an hour at Charles Staley's Boot Camp and discovered I could make a living from my writings. I go into detail about fitness writing in Appendix Two.

For the next 10 years, I juggled full-time teaching, coaching and "professoring" (online instructor in religious studies) while managing a growing career in giving lifting workshops and writing for a variety of strength and fitness magazines.

In 2009, *Never Let Go* was published. Tiffini took me aside.

"Your books and workshops are doing well. Is it time to do this full-time?"

At that moment, my passion—writing about and coaching lifting—became my full-time job/career/life.

It was wise for me to take a moment to not only look at the bountiful gift I had in doing full-time that which I love, but also to assess this new opportunity.

I could do this all day, every day.

And, that was wrong. It was short-sighted and I realized I would probably soon hate what I love to do. I had to make sure I kept my compass intact:

> *Work.*
> *Rest.*
> *Play.*
> *Pray.*

Most of us forget play, rest and pray. I always make sure to take care of all four points of the compass.

Economics taught me the fine art of getting to the point, the "do this" of life. Okay, here is the Four Fs "Do This" list:

Food: eat protein, essential fats, water, veggies

Finance: be debt free, build an emergency fund, purchase quality goods and services

Fitness: get 8–9 hours sleep every night, daily walking, do the fundamental human movements

Friends: in relationships, focus on those "worth the name"

That last line comes from Jerome K. Jerome, one of the most quotable humans of all time:

"Let your boat of life be light, packed with only what you need—a homely home and simple pleasures, one or two friends, worth the name, someone to love and someone to love you, a cat, a dog, and a pipe or two, enough to eat and enough to wear, and a little more than enough to drink; for thirst is a dangerous thing."

Boats make wonderful quotes for authors looking to make a point. Two of my favorites:

"The boat is safer anchored at the port;
but that's not the aim of boats."
~ Paulo Coelho

"Only the guy who isn't rowing has time to rock the boat."
~ Jean-Paul Sartre

Calling forth my inner Sister Maria Assumpta, my favorite prayer is also a boat poem:

Thy sea, O God, so great,
My boat so small.
~ Winfred Ernest Garrison

The experience of teaching econ prepared me for fatherhood too. When my daughter Kelly graduated from the eighth

157

grade, I wrote *From Dad to Grad* for her. This section, "On Investing," will remain true for a long time.

Sir John Templeton said it better than I can. When asked about investing money, he gave two words of practical advice: "Do it."

Now, having said that, there will be questions that will arise: first, why am I telling an eighth grader to invest? Well, any money you invest early in your life will have that wonderful gift called "time" to earn more and more and more for you...without you doing a thing. The second reason is simple: You must always look long term in life.

Invest in stocks, unless you really know something about another field. Use mutual funds for stock investing...I don't mind full-time people keeping an eye on my money. I simply don't have the time or skill to invest full-time. If you know real estate, buy land. But, remember how hard it is to unload land, gold, jewels or antiques when the market drops.

Never invest in things that eat. Never invest in stuff you don't understand. Never invest in someone or something who calls you on the telephone. Never invest in something or someone who promises "easy money."

Easy money is the road to no money. Don't fall for it.

The best investment would be "you." Get all the education and skills and degrees and diplomas you can get early as you can get them. The next big investment would be your spouse...yes, it is an investment. Don't make a bad investment by choosing a bad spouse.

The biggest investment you may ever make is having children. But, that is another discussion for another time.

Always, always, always think long term. Things go up and down; life goes up and down, stocks go up and down.

When investing in stocks, bonds or life, invest...but keep a safety net too.

Chapter 28
Champagne Wednesday

A few years later, I was asked to teach another course for our department. We had hired a new person with a narrow teaching focus. I moved from econ into other areas.

The new econ teacher wasn't very good and was failing most of the class. I was asked by the senior football players to help them as a tutor. We agreed to meet every Wednesday at a hamburger place after practice. They bought my meal and I taught econ on napkins with a burger in hand.

Pretty soon, I asked if I could bring Tiffini. They agreed it would be fine and offered to buy her dinner. This became Wednesday Night Date Night. Later, Tiffini would change the name of this weekly celebration to Champagne Wednesday.

That was a LOT of benefit for a very low cost.

It was on one of these dates when Tiffini and I had our *Field of Dreams* moment, as we like to joke. Here is the scene from the movie:

> **Ray Kinsella:** *So what do you want?*
>
> **Terence Mann:** *I want them to stop looking to me for answers, begging me to speak again, write again, be a leader. I want them to start thinking for themselves. I want my privacy.*

> **Ray Kinsella:** *No, I mean, what do you WANT?*
> **Terence Mann:** *Oh. Dog and a beer.*

Tiffini asked me, "What do you want?"

I started speaking quickly. I described the home of my dreams, the dogs, the gym, the kids, the library, the decks, the sauna and the writing area. I discussed annual trips to Europe and making donations to organizations that need help.

She nodded and said again: What do you want?

Oh. Dog and a beer.

Be careful of what you want as you might get it.

On a date in a hamburger place surrounded by varsity football players, I described…in EXACT detail…my life decades later.

Chapter 29
Discus Camp
John Powell and Bill Witt

Jumping back for a second to set this up, my high school sophomore year, 1972–73, doesn't generate many memories for me. I remember distinctly walking up a flight of steps on my first day of high school and thinking, "This is my first day of high school. I need to remember this."

That's all I remember.

After football season, Claude Gregory and I began going to the all-comer meets at the College of San Mateo. We were in the same grade, but Claude could drive. I wouldn't be able to for a while. Moreover, Claude was a pole vaulter and he needed the jumps.

So, we hopped in his classic Chevy and went down every Saturday...as best we could.

One Saturday, the discus competition was a bit stiff: John Powell and Tim Vollmer, fresh from the Olympics, were there to throw the discus. I am proud to say I hung on for third place that day.

There were only three of us.

Afterward, I asked them for help on the discus. John explained both the concept of the Backwards Seven and the idea of Two Circles. They told me a bunch of other stuff, but I hadn't yet realized the importance of writing things down, so I forgot all of it.

John has an ability to find a simpler way of explaining things with fewer words, less talk and less stress. "Figure it out" is something John tells athletes when things break down.

"Figure it out."

Using the brain does marvels for performance.

John went on to win Olympic medals and break the world record in the discus. I followed his career closely, but I would only see him throw occasionally at meets. I certainly read anything I could find about him, but, generally, we just went different directions.

Then, in 1993, with two kids in the home, I needed some help.

My athletic career was spiraling.

After I recovered from that parasite illness and an odd back injury in 1985, I had slowly returned to competition and improved every year. In 1991 and 1992, I was Olympic lifting at the national level with a best in the snatch of 314 pounds (142.5 kilos) and a 385 (175) clean and jerk. As I look back, I notice, AGAIN, that I was trying to be elite in too many things. 1993 was a poor throwing year.

About that time, in *Track and Field News,* I found an ad for a discus camp…in Ohio. I called the number and John Powell answered the phone. We talked for a long time and I reviewed my story about throwing with them in 1973.

Tiffini, God bless her, was all in for me to go. We had two kids, ages one and three, and not much money. Tiff was excited for me and told me to go. I bought the ticket, sent a check to John and looked ahead to this adventure.

On the first day of camp, I met Bill Witt. He was blur of organization, yellow pads and note cards. Later, I would learn that Bill ran the camp and he had to deal with all the stuff John forgot to deal with. Little things like checks, cash and credit card information would often end up in the wrong place.

Bill, I soon began to realize, was the center of this whole operation.

Bill is a high school math teacher in Pennsylvania. He is famous for taking his calculus students white water rafting and demanding excellence in academics. He always focuses on everyone else's needs first and he might be the most caring man I have ever met.

He was also a college discus thrower. In the mid-1980s, he began coaching and needed help. He contacted John Powell and they agreed to a visit in California. Bill stayed a while and, soon, John Powell and his friend, Brian Oldfield, would join Bill for a discus camp at Dennison University in Ohio.

This camp was hard for me. I was in my early 30s, but the humidity and four throwing sessions a day began to add up. Thursday night, Bill came over and invited me to his room for some beer and pizza with the coaching staff. It turns out that Bill had told John I needed to be a coach at this camp.

From that day on, Discus Camp became an event in our family, like Thanksgiving or Christmas: We all looked forward to our annual visit. My daughters "grew up" at camp, joining the group in all the fun. They went swimming, rode golf carts and ate cafeteria meals along with high school, college and open throwers.

It was a joy. But for me, meeting and getting to know Bill changed my life.

Bill and I are opposites in some ways, but we tend to bond at everything important in life. I think I taught him some important life lessons.

SEPs: "Somebody Else's Problem," from *The Hitchhiker's Guide to the Galaxy.* He used to worry about countless things and I did my best to show him that many things are, almost always, SEP.

Laughing at friends: Preparing our Highland Game BBQ one year, Bill accidently got the lighter fluid on his kilt. If you have never seen a man on fire sprinting around trying to rip off his kilt…well, you are missing something amazing.

Understanding spouses: Bill once told me, "I bet you calm right down when your wife is around." Tiffini arrives. The next day, Bill walks up to me, "I can't believe it…you are WORSE with her around!"

As I look at this, I realize I didn't teach him much. But Bill, he changed my life.

Certainly, spending time problem-solving with Bill, a born mathematician, really helps one see gaps in logic. He can quickly see through bogus training nonsense…unlike me. I fall in love with the new, pretty and shiny stuff.

Bill is also adept with tools and handicrafts. When we get an "idea," Bill prototypes it with duct tape and PVC pipe. Oddly, these ideas turned out to be the best teaching tools I have ever used as a coach. This would include x-sticks, slosh pipes and the caber trainer…a 40-foot piece of light PVC with a weight on the top, held vertically to teach the body stiffness.

Bill has the ability to come back to an older idea and refine and redefine it, making it better and fresher. Bill had this idea of taking every drill tool and technique for each event and typing them on one page. Then, he laminated the page.

This way, he keeps a kind of living checklist we could look at and realize, "Oh, we have been skipping this."

I use this simple idea for most of my coaching. It's a rare time when we don't have something on the wall of the gym or in my coaching notes stating: "Don't forget!"

It's amazing how often I forget the best ideas.

Bill Witt has been very good to me. His patience was remarkable in teaching me the importance of "settling" in the throws—that instant when all the forces build up and the athlete must wait to hit it. A decade after he first explained it to me, I finally got it.

Bill spent hours with me working on the javelin, allowing me to set the national record in the weight pentathlon; my javelin numbers were holding me back.

He also gave me some great advice at Kelly's wedding taking me aside not long before I walked my daughter down the aisle.

"Take a moment to enjoy the day."

Huh?

"Take a moment to enjoy the day."

Between bartender issues, tipping here and there, reminding people to do their jobs and glad-handing everyone, I took Bill's sainted advice several times that day.

Bill always lends a hand. Always. I have watched him pick things up, carry stuff for others, assist people upstairs, pull over and encourage and basically act the way we all know we should act. Instead of a good deed every day, he seems to do a good deed every five minutes.

As a coach, Bill has this amazing insight about drills. "It's a drill, not the skill" is the standard cliché of coaching.

Bill does something we don't often see: If a drill doesn't lead to throwing farther, instead of simply dropping the drill, he studies it a bit more. Bill will often find the issue with a drill and fix it with a broomstick or a cone or a band and magically the drill will be better.

Ideally, the athlete will now throw farther.

Jessamyn West's quote is a powerful reminder of the value of drilling:

"If you train people properly, they won't be able to tell a drill from the real thing. If anything, the real thing will be easier."

Bill makes drills "the real thing." Bill's life is "the real thing." And being his friend makes my life easier.

John Powell's impact on my career was obvious almost immediately. I changed my basic methods of teaching the discus. We did many more technical drills. I arranged training like circuit training in the weightroom. We embraced repetitions.

John's camp changed me and my family's lives. I still get the urge every June to hop on a plane and settle into nothing but discus for a couple weeks.

I miss it.

Chapter 30
Retirement
Winding Down and Family Time

In the early 1990s, I coached at the Upper Limit Gym, inter-acted daily with the NBA players and lifted and threw at national levels. I also taught full-time and still coached several sports. When the Upper Limit closed, I had to train at home again.

All I had was a barbell, two 35-pound plates and two 25-pound plates.

Oddly, that collection of weights that added up to 165 pounds would be the beginning of some of the best work in my career. I didn't have enough weight or equipment to train like I read in books and magazines. With two preschoolers and full-time work, I didn't have time to waste. That little barbell in the corner of the basement made me think.

Let me repeat that: *The barbell made me think.*

It would take a few years to "master" this, but my first discovery was rest periods. Now, in my defense, throwers and Olympic lifters basically rest as much as needed. In high school, I had one discus and I would throw it and it would slide. I would walk out, pick it up, toss it back a bit, and repeat this for hours at a time. Later, I would throw balls into a wall and get hundreds of throws in an hour. In a sense, rest periods were new to me.

I used a *101 Dalmatians* clock my girls abandoned for a Spice Girls clock to count the rest periods. When the second-hand hit the 12, I would go. Since the loads were light, I found that high reps and short rest periods were changing me.

I soon came up with what I called "the Transformation Program." It was a three-day-a-week program that would become a standard of my 1990s training template.

Day One

>   *Military press*
>   *Power curl*

Day Two

>   *Front squat*
>   *Overhead squat*

Day Three

>   *Whip snatch*
>   *Clean-grip snatch*

Each exercise was done with three sets of eight reps with just one minute of rest. I always included ab work too. It wasn't much, but I began to notice I felt very good.

For the chronically overtrained, not overtraining feels wrong. But it's right.

Since my options with a loaded barbell were 95, 115 or 165, I would play around with different loads and see how they impacted me. Every week, I would flip the order of exercises and soon found that if, for example, I front squatted first, it would be the warmup for the serious overhead squat. Next week, I would reverse that and overhead to warm up the front squat.

Later, I would read Clarence Bass's explanation of the Tabata protocol. I experimented with lots of ideas of doing the "20 seconds on, 10 seconds off," eventually to discover that only the front squat works with this idea.

It later became an internet phenomenon and I apologize to anyone who ever had to do some of the idiotic digressions of this fine idea.

My attempt with 115 pounds in the Tabata military press remains one of the stupidest things I have ever done.

That is a high standard of dumb.

It was during this time that I was beginning to make my annual trip to Ohio for discus camp. We used groups to train technique and I soon learned the value of circuit training for both individual and team sports. No one stands around. All coaching is done in small bites so the corrections relate to one thing. We all work hard and the time goes by quickly.

It was also at this time that Paul Northway entered my life. Paul's mom Susan was a music teacher with me at Judge. Paul wanted to learn to lift weights to get bigger for football.

He was in the fifth grade.

So, he got some equipment and a little bit of training from me and I didn't see him for a while. A few years later, his mom called and asked if I would help him with the discus.

I had retired from coaching after that season. I used to do that a lot, retire. Then, someone would need something and, before I knew it, I was busier than ever.

I didn't want to do this anymore, so I said to Paul: "I'll show you the basics. Then, you need to read this 75-page handout on the discus. Then...I want you to throw 1,000 times before I help you again."

I'm embarrassed to write that.

I spent a few hours showing him the basics of the discus. I said goodbye and thought I was done with him. Three days later, I got a call:

"I did the 1,000 throws…now what?"

It was then that I realized I might have my next champion. Paul originally just wanted to beat a classmate in the discus (he did), but later he became one of the best discus throwers in the history of high school track and field. His throw, 214′9," remains the National Catholic High School record.

With Paul, we experimented and "pioneered" some amazing training ideas. Most of our workouts were one hour, including weightlifting. Our school was very academic and I have always put schoolwork first. I have many former athletes who are professors, lawyers, doctors and other professionals; none of my athletes have ever made a real living tossing the shot or discus.

Paul helped design the One Lift a Day workout that allowed us to lift heavy but not expose ourselves to overtraining. Paul's mind understood both symphony and jazz—both his parents are musicians. He showed great discipline, but could still think around a problem.

Don't bring problems, bring solutions. Paul found solutions.

Paul knew the power lifts and Olympic lifts well, so we could focus on building load and volume. He was never the largest thrower, but always clearly the most powerful. His sophomore year, he threw farther than I did as a senior and ultimately threw 44 feet farther than me. It's strange to write that as I was considered good!

At the time, I had a white pickup truck and I would load my weights, all 165 pounds, and drive to throwing areas so we could lift between sets of throws.

This is when I began to understand the other roles that weightlifting provides an athlete. We were doing mobility and flexibility with the barbell (overhead and front squats), strength and power work, but also transferring the snap from throwing to lifting and lifting to throwing.

It was an amazing learning experience.

The most commented article I have ever written concerned the One Lift a Day program. Literally, here you go:

Each day, pick a lift. Do it. Go home.

I've answered hundreds of questions on the OLAD. Let me give you the details again:

Each day, pick a lift. Do it. Go home.

For us, it worked because we always stressed the basics and so the athletes lifted with excellent technique. Moreover, these were highly academic students, so they knew this was hard work, but the workouts didn't eat up hours of their valuable time.

This is one example of how we did this workout:

One Lift a Day

All lifts are seven sets of five. Ideally, wave the weights.

Monday

Power snatch, followed by quick whip snatches with a very light weight for eight or so

Tuesday

Squat, followed by max vertical jumps for eight reps

Wednesday

Straight-leg deadlifts—easy, to recover

Thursday

Off

Friday

Power clean or jerk

Week two was six sets of three.

Week three was the test week: warmup set of five, a triple and then strive for a maximum double.

Week four was easy bodybuilding.

We established a simple system based on the power lifts and the Olympic lifts that worked for a long time. It's the same basic model Dave Freeman gave me in 1971 and Dick Notmeyer refined for me in 1975.

I'm pretty sure it's going to be a model that works in the future too.

Chapter 31
Finished as a Coach

After Paul graduated in 1996, I took a job as an administrator and I was sure I was finished as a coach. Of course, "finished as a coach" never happened.

With my new position, it took me probably a year to lock down all the issues concerning the job. I still coached at discus camp and I enjoyed local Highland Games. One day, my IT guy hooked my computer up to this thing called the "internet."

I had no interest in it, nor did I see its value. I wasn't the brightest bulb.

But...I lucked out. My first visits on the net were to Clarence Bass's site. Here I read that Terry Todd was still talking about spring in the step and Bass had introduced Tabata to the world of fitness. I emailed Robb Wolf and learned about the Paleo diet and I got into conversations with Tamir Katz. Tamir urgently requested that I start a website and share my information.

I had to teach myself HTML code. I had to figure out picture sizing, GIFs and linking. Soon, my site was exploding with hits and follow-up questions by email. I still hadn't figured out how spam worked and had interesting conversations with Nigerian princes, lost missionaries and people concerned about my performance...not on the athletic field.

The early forums, like Old School, were amazing places. Occasionally I would find things in my home mailbox, like old York weightlifting books—someone would send them hoping I could use them. We discussed training and really had a wonderful community. Sadly, the trolls and awful people showed up and ruined all of this, but I had already made friends online.

At weightlifting meets, Highland Games and track meets, guys would walk over and introduce themselves and then say, "I'm BigGUNZ89" on the forum. Some people, like Mike Rosenberg, became family. It is still odd to explain to a wife:

"Honey, it's okay; we met on the internet."

Around this time, Tiffini found a(another) job for me in the Sunday papers. She used to love reading the want ads and comment on what I could or should be doing. Columbia College was looking for a religious studies instructor and it was a solid fit. For the next few years, two nights a week I would teach for three hours...after a full day of work at my day job. This class would open one big door for me: Columbia was looking to go "online" in education.

When I applied, I was told I had the most online experience. Having an email address and a basic website put me in rare air back then.

At our first meeting, we were told that perhaps once a year, 20 students would want to take our online classes. (You needed to say "online" at this time like you were opening a door to a magic room.)

Quickly, I was told that actually there would be five sessions a year. Not long after, I got a follow-up email that I would teach multiple classes. Today, it's not odd to offer 20 sections of this class per session. Online education has become far more popular than anyone imagined in 1998.

This was the time that when I got the job, I told Tiffini I would be happy to work this much, BUT I wanted a hot tub. Sister Maria Assumpta's advice was right: If I was going to work this hard, I needed to rest harder too. I used the hot tub to read, unwind and stretch. The hot tub became—especially in Utah's cold winters—a central feature in our daily life. If you just have to get away for a minute, hop in a tub in a snowstorm.

The late 1990s and early 2000s also brought back the Atkins Diet. Tiff had a doctor tell her that "no question" high protein diets were the best for fat loss.

I didn't believe it, but Tiff's progress soon got me to drop carbs too. We both leaned up and our blood profiles got better. For us, we moved from Atkins to Meat, Leaves and Berries, a shorthand for eating lots of veggies and fruit, along with poultry, meat and fish. We thrived.

Now, around this time, Tiffini, because of her success at the Loch Aidle Games, wanted to start throwing in the Highland Games. She did well and she had excellent footwork in the events.

But, she needed more explosion and asked me to train her.

This can sometimes work, husband coaching wife. Oddly, it worked for us and I am still amazed.

We had been meeting in our home gym for a while. Someone donated the Nautilus curl and triceps extension machine, so we would work arms up to three times a week. I also kept pressing and squatting one other day a week, but that was it for a while. Now, we needed to move to O lifting.

We were doing better financially—that had been an issue for a bit—and I bought small lifting plates so Tiff didn't have to go so heavy; I got Tiff her own bumpers and…off we go.

Soon, we were competing for the Hercules Barbell Club. We decided to go to the Masters Nationals in Baton Rouge, but Tiff didn't want to lift. She would focus on the state meet the week after the nationals.

To keep things short, I got my opener in the snatch and then missed the next two. I weighed just a bit over the 105-kilo limit, so was giving away a lot of bodyweight to my competitors.

I was in trouble.

Surprisingly, I did a smart thing: I stuck to my plan. I did the warmups and first and second attempts just like I listed them weeks before on the paperwork. On the third attempt, I had to make a decision.

I took a weight that would win the event; actually, I would tie my competition but win on lighter bodyweight. The problem was this: If I missed, I would take fourth place. I was nervous as this was a big lift for me no matter what my age, but a LOT for my late 40s.

Lincoln Brigham helped me stay focused. Then, Tiffini walked over.

"You know we can't afford to be at this meet, right?"

Yeah, I guess.

"This is a lot of money for us."

You are right.

"So, make THE F---ING LIFT!!!!!"

I sprang up on the platform, cleaned it with some struggle, held the jerk for three white lights and won the National Championship.

But, that's not the story I want to tell.

The next week, we competed for Hercules at the state meet. Tiff would end up going five for six and winning easily. Since I had snatched poorly at the Nationals, I pushed it that weekend.

The weight got goofy on a state record attempt and it twisted hard. When I had to dump it, I hit the ground and the barbell fell into my open hand while my elbow hit the wooden floor. Caught between the forces, my left wrist shattered.

Now, just for the record: My only competitor bombed (missed all three snatches), so I could be state champ if…if…if…

…I clean and jerked.

By the time I decided to take anything, the bar was set to 50 kilos (110 pounds) and with basically one arm, I made the lift and then went to the doctor.

It would take two surgeries to fix that wrist. I can still feel cold weather approaching, but at least it works well.

That day, my doctor told me something:

"I don't see how you will ever lift again."

Barney Stinson is one of the characters from *How I Met Your Mother*. Often, I thought he carried the whole show. One of my favorite things he did was announce:

Challenge accepted!!!

Often, of course, there wasn't an actual challenge, but Barney decided to take on this quest anyway.

My doctor looked at me said:

"I don't see how you will ever lift again."

I didn't have a Barney Stinson moment. I would like to say my lips quivered a bit, then I leaped up and said, "As God is my witness, I will overcome this and all who say nay!"

Actually, I just looked down and said quietly, "Shit."

I had been able to keep up at work by adding more traveling and meetings, but I suffered trying to type. In hindsight, the thing that may have saved me was those annual discus camp adventures in Ohio.

Mike Rosenberg asked if he could drive down to camp and bring some toys. Mike and I been talking via email and in forums for years by this time. He lives in Indiana, near Notre Dame and he, as we say in success, always shows up.

I warned the athletes about Mike and his tools—or "toys," as Mike calls these. We had been discussing the value of loaded carries on the forums for a while. I understood the sleds, both the dragging and blocking varieties, and their value. I just couldn't get my head around some of the other movements. By the time the Rosenberg weekend ended, I would toss out much of my weight training knowledge and replace it with carries.

Mike brought an interesting grip device with four different sizes for me to rebuild my grip strength. He had me do deadlifts with thick bars—extremely large grips making it difficult to grasp. He brought me a personal set of farmer bars too. Quickly, I was marching all over the field. With the narrow-gripped normal farmer bars, I could walk a long time before my left hand gave out.

Soon, I would farmer bar, dragging a sled. Then I would add weight to a backpack, then grab the farmer bars and pull the sled. In one weekend, I put together the framework of the next step of my career.

When I got home, I discovered an interesting thing: My farmer bars, as great as they were, were too light. But, with the left wrist still rehabbing, I needed to come up with a way to train hard and not get held back by just one joint.

So, I found an old bag, loaded it with 80 pounds of whatever I could find and started carrying it, "bear hug" style. These became bear hug carries. On the cover of *Never Let Go,* I am pulling a sled through snow and carrying a large bag. This, plus occasionally wearing an additional weighted pack, became the center of my hard training days.

It would take years to unpack why this worked, but it did.

When I first started to lift, isometric training as a technique was tailing off. It actually works well for specific issues, but it is certainly not the magic promised by some.

But many threw the baby out with the bath water (I love that phrase) when it came to isometrics: Teaching tension throughout the system is the key to strength. Teaching the body to instantly relax and then snap back into tension is the key to superlative performance. Loaded carries were teaching me to move with tension.

Later, I would describe things like goblet squats, overhead squats and farmer walks as "moving planks" and that phrase resonated with many people struggling to explain the role of carries in training athletes. The athlete learns to fill the body with internal pressure to counter the load, like a bicycle inner tube giving the wheel volume and, from there, speed.

It took a while to come up with a name for that "inner tube" strength. I called it "anaconda strength," and everyone seems to understand the term right away.

But then an odd thing started to happen. With my throwing hand uninjured and my left wrist "good enough," I started doing Highland Games almost every weekend. I was breaking records on almost every throw and people were asking what I was doing.

It was difficult to explain that I was simply picking stuff up and walking with it. There were no sets, reps or a system. It wasn't a pill, lotion or diet.

It had been the biggest gap in my training history. As much as they are now accepted as basics, fundamental training—my training—as always, was "odd."

Not long after the surgery, and the doctor's bad news, I sat down at my computer and decided to start a newsletter. I came up with *Get Up!* because the title inspired me to get going again.

After the first issue, Mike Rosenberg called and told me I needed something.

What's that?

"You need a mission statement."

Great. What's that?

Mike and I talked for an hour deciding on what I truly believe as a strength coach. We came up with this, July 2002:

1. The body is one piece.

2. There are three kinds of strength training:

- *Putting weight overhead*
- *Picking it off the ground*
- *Carrying it for time or distance.*

3. All training is complementary.

"The body is one piece" is a quote from John Jerome's book, *Staying Supple*. I find this foundational: There is no arm day, leg day, pancreas day or lung day. If you get sick, you probably shouldn't max squat. This ties into how I also see health, longevity, fitness and performance.

I still think that a workout of military press, deadlift and farmer walks (taken seriously) might be the "best" training one can do. When we wrote "Carrying it for time or distance," in 2002, I got telephone calls and emails asking me to explain what I meant by it. To this day, the most common answer I give about carries is, "Do them!"

The third point still boggles some people's minds: If you do tons of sprints in a game or practice, you don't need to do much in the weightroom. As we joked a few years ago, there seems to be two kinds of conditioning: conditioning and over-conditioning. We have to understand that if we work on this quality "here," we don't need to come back and do more "there."

Usually.

I began to travel down to Las Vegas to throw more with John Powell around this time. I flew out to San Diego for track meets and drove all over to compete in the discus. I was throwing the best of my life…at age 47.

I was invited to throw at the Modesto Relays, one of the traditionally important California track meets. My brother Gary drove me to the meet and my brother Richard joined us. In addition, my old high school track coach, Pete Giachetti, was there too. I also had a fan base of every person who remembered The Beatles.

It was miserably hot, so the four of us sat in a locker room to reminisce about the old days. I warmed up as I always did with easy, soft throws. My competitors took lots of throws and were throwing hard every time in the warmups.

Al Oerter, the four-time Olympic discus champ, once warned: "Long warmups are poison."

When the competition started, I got off one of the best throws of my life. The college-aged throwers competing against me all threw either fouls or poor throws. At the end of the trials, one of the throws coaches (a guy from a very famous throwing school in the LA area) took his guys behind a barrier. Later, I was told by a friend who could hear this that the coach was very angry and said:

"That m-----f----- is old enough to be your f------ dad and he is kicking your ass."

There was more, of course, and the crowd was loving it. I didn't win that day, but I threw really far. For any age.

This was a wonderful time. I competed in the ultraweight pentathlon which includes "tossing" a 300-pound weight. I broke the national record in the weight pentathlon (shot, disc, hammer, javelin and weight throw), did well in the Highland Games and competed in all kinds of track meets.

The *Get Up!* newsletter continued to grow with new authors and new insights. It was a heady time for me—this era showed me the value of the internet. I feel for those of you who missed this period: You could ask a question on a forum and the best and the brightest in the field would reply.

Then, of course, came the anonymous, the trolls and the losers. These drove the experts away and we are still seeing the divisive results of this idiocy.

Alas.

But, all of this came from the wonderful "illumination through injury."

Stu McGill has a book called *The Gift of Injury.* This is a hard concept for many people to understand, but the bumps and bruises along the way are essential for making the voyage to a goal. I use the word "voyage" on purpose, as the original root of the word meant "the provisions you packed for a trip." As you travel on this journey from "here" to "there" toward your goal, you are going to pack and unpack a lot of things.

What had been missing from my backpack was loaded carries. So, I added weight to my backpack, hooked on a sled and marched toward the best years of my career.

One day, it all changed: I got a call from my daughter, Kelly.

Chapter 32
Coaching One's Own Children

I was sitting in my office in downtown Salt Lake City. I was way ahead on everything and was reaping the benefits of check-lists, automation and delegation. I had plenty of time each day to take care of my online classes, my growing company and my actual job. I spent the weekends competing and my afternoons training.

Then the phone rang.

"The Office of Religious Education, Dan John speaking."

"DAD!"

It was my daughter Kelly.

Parents know a few things. One is that phone calls to the work number are not always good.

It turned out that her school needed new strength and track and field coaches. She was enjoying track as a freshman, but, in full candor, she was never coached. She wanted me to apply. I had been already offered the job and turned it down.

Twice.

Over a few weeks, my "no" became a "yes." I was changing careers from mendicant throws coach and your friendly neighborhood strength coach to full-time coaching again.

I knew with this change lots of things would vanish:

Hours of free-time to pursue my interests

Quiet (teaching in high school is not quiet)

Time pursuing MY athletic career

Saturdays and evenings to myself

True, I would win the Pleasanton Highland Games twice (2007 and 2008), as well as the National Masters Discus Throw during this time, but my weekly competitions and traveling were about to end.

One other thing: I was going to coach my own daughters.

I wasn't ready for that.

Before I began writing this section about coaching my daughters, which went from 2003 until 2014, I asked them a question: *What did you learn from me?* We were at dinner and I'm glad I had other people there to help me write down the explosion of answers.

"What did you learn?"

- Failure is essential…and okay.

- Master the basics.

- Last throw, best throw

- It's not where you start, it's where you finish.

- Squat lower.

- On vacation, don't get too hungry too tired or too hot.

- Water, coffee and wine

- Tension control for both deadlifts and not killing your kids

Obviously, "water, coffee and wine" is my standard joke about hydrating and "squat lower" will probably be on my tombstone. This meme showed up a few years ago and it still makes me laugh:

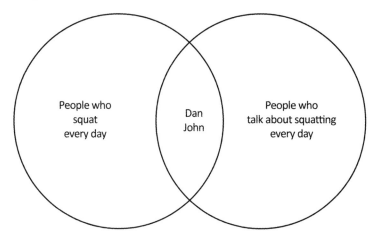

I have explained to my girls—and anyone else willing to listen—that the key to survival on family trips is one of the keys to overcoming addiction. Never let yourself get:

Too **H**ungry

Too **A**ngry

Too **L**onely

Too **T**ired

HALT!

I whisk my family into theme park restaurants at odd hours, insist on afternoon naps and strive to teach people to be comfortable NOT seeing every single historical site in a country in one day.

Kelly taught me to understand tension better when she did her first 275-pound deadlift and began sobbing after dropping the weight. She has said that deadlifting is one of the great preparation exercises for parenting.

Tension and arousal control are important when your kids are playing tag-team trying to make you lose your mind.

I was happy to see the first thing on the list: Failure is essential…and okay. I was always happy when my daughters took on something and it went a bit wrong. Each of them had moments growing up when they didn't get voted in to something or simply failed.

Hey! It happens! It's okay. As Frank Sinatra taught us:

> *Now nothing's impossible, I've found for when my chin is on the ground,*
>
> *I pick myself up, dust myself off and start all over again.*
>
> *Don't lose your confidence if you slip, be grateful for a pleasant trip,*
>
> *And pick yourself up, dust off, start over again.*

When Kelly graduated from the eighth grade, I wrote her that little booklet I mentioned earlier, *From Dad to Grad*. In hindsight, the following might be the best work I have done.

On Successful Failure and Failing Success

Most people are going to miss the point here, so let me start off by reminding myself that most people miss the point of anything related to success. I shouldn't worry too much about most people missing the point.

The point?

Well, you will have to bear with me a little bit, but the basic idea is this: Sometimes, NOT getting a goal or a dream spurs people into making a greater impact on the world than if they had fulfilled that goal or dream. And, the reverse is true too: Getting that dream can just flatten a person for years to come.

I have known a lot of college English majors who spend four years writing their own work in creative writing and poetry classes

186

and never write another essay as long as they live. They may spend hours red-penning semi-colons and the words "transitive verb" at the top of a student's paper, but never again write a composition. They attained the degree...and stopped writing.

Many athletes sweat and fight for four years of high school to get a scholarship to college, then quit after the first weeks of college practice because "it doesn't mean anything" to them.

In a sense, success can dilute the lessons of life. No, I am not telling you to fail; it is just that success seems to prod people into rethinking their attempts, their journey, their path.

Joseph Campbell commented on this several times when asked how the most renowned person in comparative religion never got his doctorate. No, Joseph Campbell chose not to do it and often encouraged his students to not go on either. He also warned them of getting buttonholed in a job that stopped them from exploring all the directions life presented them. He noted that people who earned their terminal degree and were next appointed to their dream job often "flattened" out. Much like Earl Nightingale warned us: "A rut is a grave with the ends kicked out."

Every four years, the world turns its attention for a few weeks on the Olympic sports. I am not exaggerating when I tell you that one of the worst kept secrets of Olympic sports is how many of the athletes quit...in fact, they can barely stomach thinking about their sport after the Olympics. Even gold medalists abandon the pool, track, field and court. After all the sacrifice and pain, "Here is your medal—thank you very much...next!" just doesn't seem to fulfill the athlete as much as the dreams of victory while training.

Those who fail to make their goals turn to coaching, writing or other forms to continue expressing their goals in other mediums. Or, they take those lessons learned and parlay them into a successful life...but, they don't just drop them and walk away.

Now, I'm not encouraging failure or the initiating of a "culture of failure." I coached football at Judge Memorial Catholic High

School for a long time and I realized a very unsettling thing: When we began losing games, my athletes were getting more out of losing than the winners did from winning.

When you win a game—as I had the good fortune to win many playing for South San Francisco High School—the team goes into the locker room and before you untie your shoes, the coach is talking about next week. The total amount of celebration in a winning locker room...for true winners...is often not very much!

But, the losers, the losers have hugs, tears, kisses, long speeches...usually from the prettiest girls. While the victors are thinking of yet another week on the grindstone, the losers are being cuddled and caressed back with a smile.

Okay, I exaggerated, but not a lot.

Don't let success flatten you nor let failure let you join the Loser's Club. Learn from failure, enjoy it if you can, but plug along into another expedition toward the top.

When you win, be gracious.

When you get your goals, dream of other goals.

At this time, I had been coaching 30 years. I understood tactics, strategy, preparation, peaking and technical work. I understood training arousal and tension.

And, I still didn't know much. I needed another phone call to wake me up.

I had been comfortable coaching in the weightroom at Juan Diego Catholic High School. Lots of things had changed in education in the decade I had been an administrator. Email arguments were a daily thing. Someone would "share" a joke with everyone and then people would get offended and share, with all of us, their outrage about the joke.

Endlessly.

Attendance at class was now computerized and a real pain for me since we didn't have working computers in the weightroom.

Students carried phones and learned to cut and paste material off the internet and claim it as their own. Books were being phased out in some areas. I spent hours loading up information online for my athletes as this, it seemed, was the only way to record schedules and results.

But, weights and sprints and throws were still learned and mastered through repetitions and time. Mastery continued to elude the quick fix. The internet generation seemed to struggle with this truth. I could help them there.

I was getting used to all the new surroundings when my coach's office phone rang.

"DAD!!!"

This time, it was my daughter Lindsay. As I said before, phone calls from the kids to the office is rarely good. She was, oddly, crying.

Lindsay doesn't cry.

"THEREISTOOMANYKIDSTRYINGOUTFORVOLLEYBALL ANDTHEYDON'THAVEENOUGHCOACHESANDSOIWON'TBE ABLETOPLAYANDALLIWANTODOISPLAYVOLLEYBALLWITH-MYTEAMANDMYFRIENDSAREALLCRYING…"

That's pretty close to what I heard. Just read it really loud while crying to get the feeling right. What I translated was this:

Saint Francis Xavier School needs another coach.

And…that coach would be me.

To sum my knowledge of volleyball at the time, let's write out all I knew:

    1. A ball was involved.

    2. There is no number two.

But, hey, I got the job. The first thing I did was sit down with several of our varsity volleyball players and ask a question:

What are the three keys to winning in volleyball?

The discussion changed my career and my coaching. Very quickly, they came up with three keys to winning:

1. Get the serve OVER and IN!
2. Protect the middle.
3. Play as a team.

In hindsight, I clearly remember the discussion on point one: The girls all started using their hands, then telling stories about this simple point. "OVER and IN!" Their emphasis was on making the other team make the mistakes.

"Forget the sidelines and backline, just protect the middle and don't let the ball fall in the middle."

Then I drove out to Saint Francis Xavier and met my team. I was honored to meet the proud "SFX II" team. There were a few issues:

Yes, I had my daughter Lindsay on the team. Good. I also had a girl who had a heart transplant the year before and was on serious medications. I had the two shortest boys in the eighth grade. I had a few other girls who had never played sports. Ever.

I only focused on what I could control, and what I could control were those three keys…now, the Three Rules:

1. Get the serve OVER and IN!
2. Protect the middle.
3. Play as a team.

When serving, I only counted the "overs and ins" and emphasized those stats. I tried to teach the kids to be a six-point spider web that expanded and contracted to protect the middle. We did individual skills, but much of the time was spent just working together.

During a game, if a ball fell in the middle, I would call a timeout and ask what rule we had broken. Clyde always said, "Number three." Actually, it was two, but…it was a good answer.

I quickly discovered we were called "Team Number Two." Since I have the brain of a nine-year-old, I told the team we need to chant "We're Number Two" after every timeout, break or cheer.

We're Number Two.

Now, yes, "Number Two" means something else in every school in America and the opposing team and coaches always had quizzical expressions on their faces as they returned to the court.

"Stay focused on the rules. Don't worry about all that other stuff. We can beat anyone if we play as a team."

It worked.

I am still amazed to say it worked. Because of my size and coaching job, people thought I knew what I was doing. I still don't completely understand the hand signals of the referees, especially the one where they seem to send kittens to the sky with both hands.

So, when I questioned a call, I had to ask in a certain way.

"Did you get that right? I'm just asking…okay, fine."

That usually gave us the benefit of the doubt down the line. We needed it.

The season wrapped up with a massive tournament with dozens of teams. I had to go off for a workshop, but I called my stand-in coach before and after every game. The coach (Tiffini) stuck to the game plan. She added some of her own insights and skills and the team responded very well.

At the workshop I was giving, as the day went on the attendees began to fall in love with the story. I was working with the military that weekend, and many of them were buying into a hodgepodge group of kids in Salt Lake City.

During breaks, I was huddled by men with multiple military deployments waiting on results. After every win, we shared high fives and hugs.

We didn't win the whole thing. That would be too good of a story. We lost to one of the wealthy school teams with every athlete on a club volleyball squad. We did bring home the first trophy ever in volleyball for SFX…third place. No one on our team went on to play volleyball professionally or at the university level.

But who cares? It was a wonderful time and the kids still share stories of beating far superior teams by sticking together and protecting the middle. And…it changed my life as a coach with some amazing lessons.

The lessons?

1. Ask around. Someone has done whatever you are trying to do. Ask.

2. I love the idea of "three things," as it always seems to work.

3. Focus on what you say you are going to focus on.

4. Poke a little fun at the problems. It helps to say "Hey, here's what I'm worried about," poke it a bit, laugh at it, hold it in your hand and watch it shrink away in shame.

5. Winning is not always about records and taking first place.

Lindsay went on to become the state champion and school record holder in the shot put. When she stood on top of the victory stand, the girl in second place—a full step down—was taller than Lindsay. I have to think, even today, that her victory was won in the lessons learned by playing with Number Two.

Chapter 33
Tim Anderson and Chip Morton

In 2010, I was asked—well "told" is more accurate—that I needed to take a certain course to continue my path in the kettlebell world. It was four days of videos and hands-on work and, in total candor, I have used very little of the material in the years that followed.

This happens sometimes: I teach a kettlebell course with certain lifts—most notably the bent press—that few clients, athletes or trainers will ever use. The bent press seems to have this odd ability to find old injuries and make them new again!

But, the lessons learned by doing the drills and practicing the moves seem to cascade down to other training needs.

The build-up to the bent press, the drills and movements I later organized into a 40-minute full-body warmup has great value to everyone. It became the foundation of our Thursday Tonic workout from the old meaning of tonic. "Tone," "tonic" and "tune" all come from the same root and I often tell people that sometimes, like a violin or a car, we need a tune-up.

Getting back to one of the great lessons of my career, there are no good or bad exercises. Sometimes something great, like the deadlift or squat, might be the worst thing we can do for the athlete or client.

And, of course, sometimes something silly or stupid fits the program perfectly.

The highlight of that particular four-day course for me was being teamed up with Tim Anderson. Tim had been working on this concept he called "Original Strength." It's a training system based on how infants learn to move, crawl and walk. Some of the movements are so simple, you would laugh it off at first. The six-point rock, basically doing air squats on your hands and knees— your feet make the sixth points—brought me back to quality movement quickly after a total hip replacement...so much so, the therapist asked me to demonstrate and then added the movement to patients when appropriate.

I don't think I would know what to do if Tim wasn't smiling. I always tell people, "He smiles so much because he knows something!" And, that is a truth.

Not long ago, I invited Tim to stay with me as I hosted a kettlebell course. I was hoping Tim would share his Original Strength work with the group. Well, "hoping" is a bit of stretch; I knew he would.

Tim decided to take this, a three-day Russian Kettlebell Certification, without touching weights in his prep. He crawled, he carried loads and he dragged things to prepare. But...no weights. No KBs. He decided to never panic or get close to panicking while training. If his tongue came off the roof of his mouth, he eased up.

Tim crushed the cert without "training."

That "tongue on the roof of the mouth" trick is so simple, but so effective. If you start to run the engine too high, your tongue comes off the top of your mouth. Certainly, there are times to push it, but Tim has taught me that backing off allows us to keep going forward.

I have learned that lesson many times and I always seem to forget it overnight.

Original Strength

Our most popular training day at the gym is Thursday. Since being a Utah State Aggie and Coach Maughan's tradition of "Ghost Town" workouts on Thursdays, it's always our "tonic" day. One of our regulars, Kevin Mass, loves the focus we have on this day of elegance and beauty.

I want us to move with grace…like artists, not bulldozers crushing a road. We quiet down. We move through our Original Strength movements. I hear lots of "ohhhhhhhs" as we go through Tim's materials. Here is a typical example:

Prone	*Neck nods*
Ear clears	*Find your shoes*
Elbow rolls	*Pumps*
Six point	*Rocks*
Nods	*Find your shoes*
Big hip circles	*Figure 8s*
Rolling	*Lower body rolls*
Upper body rolls	*Egg rolls*
Eight point	*Twist circles*
Tall kneeling	*Egyptians*
Standing with sticks	*Dislocates*
Figure 8s	*Wide-stance windmill*
Windmill sticks	*Kneeling windmill (KW)*

Pump: half kneeling to KW

KW, elbow to ground

KW, "hand off" windmill

Often the load is simply a broomstick or PVC pipe. Don't worry about the names of the exercises; we just use them to communicate and work as a group.

Tim has begun working with another good friend, Chip Morton, the renowned football strength coach. Wisdom springs from Chip and it is a joy to read their combined work. The influence of their material continues to impact me as I realize that basic mobility work demands to be fully integrated between every set of lifts.

That was clear to me early, but Tim and Chip have also made it obvious that we need to put these Original Strength movements in our track and field practices and probably every other sport session too.

I met Chip years ago at our discus camp in Ohio. He was coaching the Cincinnati Bengals and asked if he could visit during camp. Well, yes, of course, sure. We began a strong friendship and we try to bump into each other as often as we can to share work and insights. Chip thrives with athletes, especially those with "trouble."

"You just let them know you love them," he told me once.

He explained the issues with trust when it comes to well-paid professional athletes. Somebody, from fans to family, always wants something of the newly rich athlete and a good coach has to adapt to this feeling. Actually, it is a truth: Professional athletes are constantly being badgered by fans, friends and family.

Tim and Chip are truly two of the most grounded people I know. Yes, they know a lot about lifting and training, but it's what they know about life that most interests me.

I look forward to Tim and Chip's new thoughts and insights.

Chapter 34
Intentional Community

Back in December 2009, my first book, *Never Let Go,* was selling well and I was getting asked to speak at conferences, clinics and workshops all over the world. It was a strange time. I worked all day as a strength coach, but I was also teaching honors theology. I continued to teach at Columbia College, then every afternoon I would coach track and field.

Then, on the weekends, I would hop on a plane and teach at a clinic. Monday would roll around and…

What was keeping me together was the fact that it was my daughter's senior year. Lindsay had enjoyed a good career as a thrower and I was looking forward to helping her and her friends finish off well.

Tiff came home one night and said, "Listen, I have to get my name out there. So, I applied for a job in San Francisco…I won't get it…but I have to start moving ahead."

Great. Of course. I support you 100%.

She got the job.

They expected her to report in April. We were able to get that moved forward…to the day after Lindsay graduated from high school, the same week Kelly graduated from junior college.

197

So, as I worked two jobs and coached my daughter, I also had to start packing up a house with six bedrooms and three baths and lots of storage to get ready to move to the Bay Area. The pressure was high, but it all worked out: Lindsay won the state, Tiff got the job and I had the opportunity of a lifetime.

As I prepared the move, Dan Martin, a retired firefighter and frequent poster on the IronOnline Q and A forum, asked if we could get together occasionally and get a workout in. All I had left from my world class home gym was a single 28-kilo kettlebell, so I welcomed the idea.

Dan went online and found a place with easy access from the highways and close to my new place in Burlingame. It was at Coyote Point Park…and, as I hinted about earlier, a tradition was born.

While the moving company carried furniture into our apartment, I drove down to the park. Dan brought sandwiches and a mix of online friends gathered to train. This became a weekly tradition and the Coyote Point Kettlebell Club was born.

We each brought what we had. Some had equipment; some had youth and enthusiasm. Dan had sandwiches and I brought my coaching experience. We always began with everyone introducing themselves and a quick word about "what I need to work on." From those answers, I put together our session.

Often, the response was simply, "I just want to be here."

That answer unlocked the whole puzzle of training for me: Sometimes, people "just want to be here." They want to work out. They want to train.

But they want community.

It became obvious over time that these were becoming the best training sessions of my life. No one paid. There was no attendance taken nor expected. The people could do as much or as little as they wished.

We became a community.

Later, we figured out something that remains perhaps the greatest insight of my coaching career:

Intentional Community

This is term used in residential housing involving a like-minded group of people, often with a religious or "alternative" thinking bond, who come together to live. With the Coyote Point KB Club, we were a like-minded group of people who wanted to train, train outside, train hard and train together.

We met weekly for two years until some family issues brought us back to Utah—we started having grandchildren and wanted to know them. My grandmother died in 1925; my mother died in 1980 and I wanted my grandkids to know me. The moment we moved back, I spread the word that I would be hosting a weekly training group at my house. It swiftly moved from one day a week to three and then to five.

There are three things that make me love an intentional community. First, it does wonders with one's personal discernment and decision making. Whenever I decide to change something or add something new, someone kicks in with:

"Hey, I thought last week you said you were doing a 90-day program of…"

Well…yeah. Maybe I should finish what I started. The reason the kettlebell program called the "Rite of Passage" works so well with my group is that we have a collective will power that pushes us all to do it.

Briefly, the Rite of Passage is a three-day-a-week program of KB clean and press mixed with pullups that builds from three sets of 1–2–3 with each move to five sets of 1–2–3–4–5. We also toss in high-rep KB snatches or swings at the end of each session.

The second advantage of intentional community is that it allows for swift course corrections. I'm a huge believer in course corrections. My book *Intervention* is subtitled with the term "Course Corrections for the Coach and Athlete."

We hear this kind of thing a lot:

> "Maybe just add a little…"
> "Back off on that…"
> "You are getting that here, so you don't need to do…"

None of these are sweeping statements like "Throw this all away. This is worthless." It's a gentle nudge back onto the path.

Finally, and this can't be appreciated enough, an intentional community provides you with people looking at your "big picture." Depending on how things are going, you might hear:

> "You look a little rougher, stiffer…."
> "You look better…"

It's nice to hear this either way. I've been training on and off with Mike Brown for eight years. He has seen me through some highs and lows. When he sees me "right" again, I trust his insights. If he wonders out loud about some idiotic thing I am doing or the fact that I move like rusty iron, I appreciate his insights.

No, I might not like to hear some of this, but it is the most honest feedback of my career.

If there is something that makes great coaching, it's honest feedback.

Chapter 35
Connaught Rugby

As I was putting the finishing touches on this book, I was wondering what I would be learning next. These past two years, I have been sharing what I have learned and relearned as a coach and athlete, but I knew something "new" was bound to pop across my desk.

My wife and I take an annual trip to Ireland. We set aside money and time for a chance to walk for hours every day and swim in Galway Bay on the Emerald Isle.

We have become big fans of the Tribesmen, Connaught Rugby. And, through the various currents that push and pull us in the world of coaching, the strength coach, Johnny O'Connor, and I had a chance to meet and talk. He invited me to a Tuesday practice.

It's an honor to be around any elite program, but I was impressed with the standards of excellence here. I was allowed into the team meetings and Peter Wilkins, defence coach (Irish spelling) began to speak. Besides being funny, his summary of the approach for the upcoming weekend stunned me.

I don't know a lot about rugby. Oh, I enjoy the game, but the nuances leave me a bit lost. It didn't matter: I understood everything in the plan.

That's good coaching: The system is so clean and clear that a newbie can pick it up immediately.

But, then he explained one of his "big rocks" for the upcoming game: bounce.

Bounce.

It is the most elegant expression I have heard for the idea of getting back up and into the game.

Bounce. It's a combination of tumbling, grass drills, get-back-ups, Turkish getups and resilience.

The moment he said it, I adopted it.

As I told him later, I would use my standard method of stealing good ideas.

> *At my next workshop, I will say, "As Peter Wilkins always says, "Bounce."*
>
> *At the following workshop, "As Peter Wilkins always says, "Bounce."*
>
> *After that: "As I always say…"*

And, so it continues. As I begin my journey toward 50 years in coaching, something wonderful and marvelous will always be just around the corner.

Cervantes was, and always will be, right: "It's the road, not the inn."

Part Three: What I Think Now

Chapter 36
40 Years of Coaching and Reflection

"Not a bunch of programs and numbers."

That was the promise I made to myself as I began working on this book. As I look back over my career as athlete and coach, I realize that rarely are the real lessons "three sets of five."

Or, five sets of two.

I did a lot of smart things over these past 50 years. I have trophies and medals from six different decades in nine different sports (and more if you count things like flag football). I have done some things "right."

1. I showed up.

I show up. I continue to show up.

Workshops, certs, competitions…I show up. I still make it point to annually attend a multiple-day certification, sit up front, volunteer for everything and strive to improve.

I've been lifting weights essentially nonstop since 1965. That's a lot of showing up.

2. In 1974, I read an article by Dave Davis that stated that throwers mixed the power lifts and the Olympic lifts.

It was good advice then…and I have yet to see better.

3. I cook.

I enjoy BBQ and slow cooking. I try new recipes. I enjoy the journey of soup making.

I explore foods from other cultures and I sometimes make mistakes in the kitchen. Some of the mistakes have been good. Others…well, I have a big garbage can.

The lessons in the kitchen teach the same lessons of sports. It starts with quality ingredients, appropriate preparation and appropriate timing.

4. I have always had my own gym AND at the same time, access to another place.

In 1971, I saved literally every quarter and dime to buy myself my first incline bench. I have bought, sold and traded everything from massive Nautilus arm machines the size of small cars to a collection of 29 kettlebells to every kind of load you can imagine. My gym is open 24/7, but I also can use another facility for any reason that might pop up.

5. I competed.

I have stepped on the platform, the field, the track and the road for all kinds of events.

Competing teaches, with absolute clarity, one insight: It worked…or it didn't. "It," of course, is this thing we call training. "It" is the preparation. Competition judges preparation.

6. I have always emphasized community in my training.

Yes, I have spent countless hours—this is not a cliché but truth—alone in fields throwing or carrying things. But what makes me keep coming back to the gym and field is that people will be there. Jack Shroeder, the man who took me under his wing as a writer and made me better, used to always say, "People like stories and stories about people."

I love the stories.

7. I don't mind tossing things to the side.

People often ask me at clinics about "this."

"This" is an exercise, movement, idea or something I don't mention much anymore. "Ah…oh yeah, that! Yeah…I don't do it anymore because…"

And, that is the secret: In the constant search for a wee bit better, it's okay to get rid of things along the way.

8. I have always realized we can do better.

Maybe it is less of this and more of that, but the search for better is always on my mind. Loaded carries were forced because of a wrist injury, but they were a career-changing exercise for me…and my people.

9. I keep journals.

I have a record of every workout since 1971. I have lost one or two, but overall, I can tell you my training on the day you born. I would love to be able to brag about all kinds of things in my career, but the truth is in the journals. Sometimes, I look back and wonder, "Wow, I did that?"

And, sometimes I look back and think, "Wow, how dumb was that?"

10. I never, ever made athletics, sports, coaching or training the absolute center of my universe.

I always strived to maintain good grades as a student, progress with continuing education in the fields of history and religious studies, and read outside of the fields of training, nutrition and sports. Oddly, I think my best insights about sports actually came from studies in other disciplines.

The great insight from coaching happened when I realized that everything I learn(ed) on the field of play was true in the classroom. And everywhere else.

Chapter 37
The Big Picture
and the Five Lessons of 40 Years

The word "coach" means exactly that: A coach is a vehicle that carries people from here to there. After devastating losses or personal tragedies, sometimes the coach carries the athlete more literally than figuratively. Other times, when things are rolling, being a coach is just keeping the wheels moving.

A coach is someone who gets you from here to there.

In my workshops, I generally describe the idea of "A–B" with "A" being where you are today. This is where we might test and assess you and plug some numbers into equations. In track and field, you ARE your mark (distance, height or time) and not much else matters.

"B" is the goal. Now, many people have such ridiculous goals that I label these "A–Z" and try to break the next few weeks into more bite-sized chunks. Young athletes might dream of professional sports but not connect the dots that include showing up to practice. Or sleeping. Or eating good food.

Actually, most people have A/Not-A goals: Their goals are so vague and vapid, they are just pulling things out of the air.

"Not A" goals are when people say things like, "I should lose some weight." "I should exercise more." Every smoker I have talked to KNOWS they should stop smoking, but...

This is a tough thing about coaching. In a sense, everyone KNOWS what to do with just about everything:

Retire well? Save money now.

Healthy teeth? Floss and brush. See a dentist at least twice a year.

Lose weight? Caloric restriction and some kind of exercise.

Most people know what to do. Doing it, well, doing it is the key to success.

Helping people "do it" is coaching. At times, my job might simply be to applaud wildly at your success and other times I will literally "coach" you; I will carry you from here to there.

As I have reviewed my lessons from the past 40 years, I see basically eight areas that can help anyone with anything.

Maybe.

The first three are the "big picture." These three principles are commonly thrown around, especially in the business world, but coaches have to overcome obstacles that profit-making companies don't fully appreciate.

The terms can almost be clichés when we read the quickie business books: Leadership, big picture and adaption are common topics in the business section at the bookstore. Coaches have less time and fewer resources to prepare for victory. "Victory" might be overstating it; we could be talking about preparing for survival in some cases.

The next five I call "the five lessons of 40 years." These focus on my attempt to clarify the fundamental issues that deal with fitness, health, longevity and performance. Everyone does goal setting—I did it recently with a trainer—but getting goal setting to really "catch" is a much more developed process.

These five lessons are a few steps beyond what I might teach in a short clinic or lecture. I could sum them as:

- Goal setting

- Standards

- Nutrition

- Reasonable training

- Synergy—combining the elements

That is an excellent list. But, we need more tools and a deeper appreciation of the shifting winds in performance sports… and the challenge of fat loss, the dreams of a long life filled with quality living, and keeping illness from the door.

Here is the next section:

The Big Picture of Coaching

- Coaching is leadership

- Fractals and programming

- Deprivation increases capacity

The Five Lessons of 40 Years

- Getting people to become actors

- Measurements

- Do it or diet

- Snapacity

- Connecting the dots

Chapter 38
The Big Picture

"You can't see the picture when you are inside the frame."
~ Les Brown

I love the phrase "the big picture."

In college, my friend Crazy Jerry encouraged me to take philosophy courses with Professor Johnson. Jerry wanted me to learn the work of Ludwig Wittgenstein and I needed more credits to graduate. Unexpectedly, Wittgenstein's insights really prepared me for my life in coaching.

The first insight was that people can use words to mean anything they want.

Jerry and I would often dive deep into the waters of philosophy at social gatherings. (You can see why we didn't date much.) When we went too far, Jerry would stop the conversation with an interesting insight:

"You have a Toyota in your nose."

I didn't actually have a Japanese car in my nostrils. He was making a key point that really helped me as a coach and trainer: We humans have this ability to push air up from our lungs, play with our vocal chords and lips and form sounds that become words. Sadly, this is goal setting for most people.

So, Mrs. Henderson, what are your goals for this year?

Um, lose weight? Um, get in shape? Um, eat better? Um…

As we read in *Hamlet:* "Words, words, words." When most people set goals, they have little ownership for what comes out of their mouths.

My follow-up question, "What do YOU mean by that," has really helped me get people to actually own their statements.

Sometimes.

But it was the other great lesson from Dr. Johnson's Wittgenstein class that changed just about everything for me: the Family Resemblance Theory. Let me explain this.

My brother Gary has jet-black hair, dark eyes and is about my height, but weighs 70 pounds less. In fact, if you saw the two of us together, you would not think we were related. For those readers who don't know, I'm blond, blue-eyed and built a bit thick.

But, it is funny. Gary looks like my sister Corinne so much that people often thought they were twins. And Corinne looks like my brother Ray. Hang on, there are six of us. Ray and my oldest brother, Richard, look like they came out of the same stamp. My brother Rich could pass for my brother Phil's dad. And, although I may hate to admit it, I look like Phil. So, you see…Gary, who looks like Corinne, who looks like Ray, who looks like Rich, who looks like Phil.

When you go to your spouse's family party and look around, you might see the same thing.

When you see all six of us together, you will see how much Gary and I look alike. But, look, you have to see all six of us together. You have to view the whole picture.

Although Professor Johnson didn't use my family in his commentary, the moment he mentioned this, the light bulb went off in my head. It's the "big picture."

Let me give you another example.

Years ago, someone told me he expected fireworks when Mike Boyle and I were speaking together.

Why?

Well, it turns out that Mike does single-leg work and I don't really emphasize it much. Literally, this person expected Mike and I to get into the corners, wait for the bell and duke it out.

Mike and I agree on, I think, everything. When you step back and look at what his athletes need and what my athletes need...they need basically the same thing. Sure, hockey players need more of "this" and discus throwers need more of "that," but it doesn't mean we disagree.

When you step back and look at the big picture, good coaches tend to follow the same basic patterns, the same basic foundations and the same basic truths. If you tease out one or two things, you might find some differences—some variations—but overall, most coaches resemble most coaches.

These are the three things that are underappreciated in understanding good coaching:

- Coaching is leadership

- Fractals and programming

- Deprivation increases capacity

Let's look at these.

Chapter 39
Coaching is Leadership

We see leadership (and the lack of) in every area of life. One of my favorite conversations with young coaches, and a recent one with Lonnie Wade comes to mind, is about learning and teaching leadership.

When I had my life turned around from my experience in the Middle East and that small bug I carried around my stomach for a few years, I went to the local library and began listening to motivational audiotapes and reading success books. Earl Nightingale's classic *Lead the Field* changed my life. I have notes on all 12 tapes. One interesting thing is that my notes have up to five different colors of pen as I listened and re-listened to these tapes over and over and made new notes with each new insight.

Whenever I need to make a major decision, I pull out tape 12: *The Man on the White Horse*. I realize I can be part of the solution or part of the problem.

As a teacher and assistant coach, I have had many opportunities to see good leadership. Oddly, I have learned as much from poor leadership as I have from the Ralph Maughans and Ray Dejongs in my life.

As a teacher, I dealt with a series of less-than-stellar people acting as principals. I don't think this is unusual. Next to C.

Northcote Parkinson's Parkinson's Law, the next most universal truth I know is the Peter Principle:

"The Peter Principle is an observation that the tendency in most organizational hierarchies, such as that of a corporation, is for every employee to rise in the hierarchy through promotion until they reach the levels of their respective incompetence."
~ Laurence J. Peter

Beloved and insightful classroom teachers often become terrible administrators. In coaching, a brilliant coordinator will often flounder as head coach. Great athletes rarely make great coaches. Those who are gifted with genius or genius genetics often don't understand the fumbles, foibles and failures of the rest of us.

Universally, in my experience two things are true with poor leadership:

- Reactive...not proactive
- Amoeba responsibilities

The first is true in every aspect of life and leading.

One year as we approached finals week, the school ran out of paper. At the time, paper was king: There were no computers. We also had broken reproduction machines, no dittoes (now there's something from the past) and lacked all the other basic supplies. My friend Jim Markosian went down to the principal's office to address this issue.

The principal said Jim was insubordinate and threatened to fire him.

That's reactive.

A proactive approach would be to realize that outside of the first week of school, finals week will probably need the most volume of paper in the faculty room.

Proactive is what I recommend for so many things in life.

Shark habits and pirate maps deal with the myriad of "do this" daily stuff that can clog creativity. Checklists are master studies of getting the details right; like my friend Aonghus O'Flaherty discovered, trying to find a salad spinner in County Sligo the day your restaurant opens is going to be difficult.

Weddings and airplane travel need checklists. There is not a lot of time to fix things once either of those takes off.

Reactive is running down the hall blaming others for the little things. Reactive behaviors eat efficiency.

As a coach, I am comfortable with entire practices focused on "what if" scenarios. In fact, I love it. I had an assistant coach who hated it and we always had issues. But I was right. We would need to know:

- Overtime rules and play selection

- Last play of the game
    ("Hail Mary," "Hook and Ladder," "Take a Knee")

- Last play at halftime
    (I loved the gimmicks here)

- The two-point safety and all the special rules with it

- Muff versus fumble

- On-sides and fair catch and all the odd American football kicking rules

- Special plays

- Substitutions for injuries
    (Yes, you have to PRACTICE dealing with injury substitutions)

I like to practice these before the game so everyone knows what to do.

Proactive, not reactive.

Winter is coming. Christmas is coming. Thanksgiving, birthdays and anniversaries are always coming.

If you forget the gift, the turkey or the card, it is NOT my fault!

This is the value of being proactive…you don't have to run to the store on Christmas Eve looking for the SuperPokeyGuy-Man5000 figurine.

In leadership, we don't want reactors, nuclear or otherwise. We want thoughtful people with a vision of the future.

When it comes to the next point, "amoeba responsibilities," I need to step back and review a game-changing book.

About the time I was struggling with various principals at the school, Tiffini came home from work with a book, Charles Coonradt's *The Game of Work*. We had run through several principals who lasted only a year or so. My mantra for leadership had become "lead me, follow me or get out of my way."

Coonradt perfectly explained my problem with these school principals:

> *"Another common field of play in business is shaped like an amoeba—a random, globular shape. It describes the employee's understanding of what he or she thinks is expected, and the only problem is that it wiggles and jiggles and changes shape. When something goes wrong that the employee didn't think was his or her responsibility, sure enough, someone points it out as his or her responsibility on the amoeba."*

It happened with budgets. It happened with discipline. It happened with a lot of things and I really began to understand the importance of clear lines of responsibility.

When I work with people, I like to have—no surprise here—checklists that cover their responsibilities. It's why I was such a fan of having chores lists for my children and me as they were growing up.

It helps when someone says, "This is your job." It rarely helps when someone throws a package (ticking) and says, "Now THIS is your job."

That is the opposite of leadership.

Finally, our school hired a good principal. J. Terrence Fitzgerald would soon become one of my mentors and taught me through both example and discussion the two keys to proper leadership:

- Constant assessment
- Constant upgrading

Yes, we started the book with these and, yes, they are crucial.

"Fitz" mastered a leadership style knows as MBWA. MBWA is simply "Management by Walking Around." He was the first principal EVER to show up a football practice. He came to the wrestling room. He visited every classroom, every day. Before, I had academic deans who never, not once, watched me teach.

If something did come up, Fitz could respond. If a teacher or coach was accused by a parent of doing this or that, Fitz's first response was, "Did you speak to the teacher first? If not, please do this immediately."

Then, he dropped the bomb:

"I have been to the class/practice/game and I have never seen this. Did you see this yourself?"

Wisely, Fitz didn't always trust the teenager's story to Mommy and Daddy about the facts. That sentence is a truism. I was at a discipline meeting one time where a mom said, "Little Susie and I have a deal: She promised she would never lie to me."

That still provides me with a good laugh. Folks, teens may, in fact, lie on occasion.

As a strength coach, I wander around. I go to clinics, camps and workshops. I visit gyms. I talk to people. I ask "why." I have had the best coaches of our era correct my techniques. I have done workouts generated by the best training minds in the world.

We buy new equipment for the gym and try it out. We buy books and PDFs and do the programs. Sometimes, these fail so miserably, we still joke about it these years later. Often, we find diamonds.

Well, not very often...

This is constant assessment. Like constant upgrading, it remains at the top of my "Ten Commandments."

"Ignoring perfect" fits with constant assessment. I learned this from Fitz: Pretty good is pretty good. We will always work to be better, but we have to open the doors and let the students in. We have to serve the meal—the family is hungry. It's not going to be perfect.

Constant upgrading, as I review my time with Fitz, can be summed by his frequently used statement: "Don't bring problems, bring solutions."

Something always goes wrong. Always.

I have worked with problem-finders. I worked with a woman who could find a problem in everything. She complained once that our conference would be upset about the events on 9/11. I said I knew this...as my wife had been unable to return from her work in New York City because of the terrorist act. Her follow-up statement was to second guess the hotel choice we made months earlier.

She remains the most clueless person I have ever met and she continues to inspire me to look at the big picture of things.

As we continue this journey through the lessons I have learned as a coach, we keep bouncing into this truth:

Bring solutions.

Don't bring me problems; bring me solutions.

As a fun way to finish this little review of the lessons I learned from school principals, let me finish with an actual un-classified CIA document.

The CIA's Simple Sabotage Field Manual: A Timeless Guide to Subverting Any Organization with "Purposeful Stupidity"
(1944)

Organizations and Conferences

- Insist on doing everything through channels. Never permit shortcuts to be taken in order to expedite decisions.

- Make speeches. Talk as frequently as possible and at great length. Illustrate your points by long anecdotes and accounts of personal experiences.

- When possible, refer all matters to committees, for further study and consideration. Attempt to make the committee as large as possible—never less than five.

- Bring up irrelevant issues as frequently as possible.

- Haggle over precise wordings of communications, minutes, resolutions.

- Refer back to matters decided upon at the last meeting and attempt to re-open the question of the advisability of that decision.

- Advocate caution. Be reasonable and urge your fellow-conferees to be reasonable and avoid haste, which might result in embarrassments or difficulties later on.

Managers

- In making work assignments, always sign out the unimportant jobs first. See that important jobs are assigned to inefficient workers.

- Insist on perfect work in relatively unimportant products; send back for refinishing those that have the least flaw.

- To lower morale and with it, production, be pleasant to inefficient workers; give them undeserved promotions.

- Hold conferences when there is more critical work to be done.

- Multiply the procedures and clearances involved in issuing instructions, pay checks, and so on. See that three people have to approve everything where one would do.

Employees

- Work slowly.

- Contrive as many interruptions to your work as you can.

- Do your work poorly and blame it on bad tools, machinery or equipment. Complain that these things are preventing you from doing your job right.

- Never pass on your skill and experience to a new or less skillful worker.

Source:

http://openculture.com/2015/12/simple-sabotage-field-manual.html

With my hand on my heart and the other on *The Bible,* I swear this is how most organizations work.

I worked at a school that was stumbling blind into insolvency and a member of a key committee held up meetings for three weeks arguing over the titles "Chairman," "Chairperson" or "Chair." I realize now that we may have had an operative in our midst.

At least, this is true of MOST of the organizations I have worked with in my career. I may have to refer my opinion to "further study and consideration."

Chapter 40
Fractals: Seeing the Big Picture

Obviously, the key to great coaching is to see the big picture. The longer I coached, the more I realized that athletic success is great, but it is part of a larger voyage for the athletes. The lessons learned in athletics give a framework for success in life.

Let me offer some obvious lessons:

Showing up
Working alone
Resilience (bouncing!)
Working with others
Sportsmanship and class
The search for mastery

The debate, dance and drama teachers, among others, also teach these great lessons. The key is finding a way to explain that the lessons learned "here" help you in life "there." How we explain this is important.

I take the athlete and look at the big picture of the life and settle on where we want to go. From there, we can narrow this down into a year-long approach and from there sneak into the weekly and daily perspective. Basically, each route, whether this is lifetime, yearly, weekly or daily, is going to look about the same.

The term to use on this is "fractal." A fractal is a never-ending pattern. Fractal patterns are extremely familiar, as nature is full of fractals. For instance, consider trees, rivers, coastlines, mountains, clouds, seashells and hurricanes. A leaf looks like a tree; a small stone looks like a mountain. If done correctly, a training day can look like a career.

Jurassic Park offers us an interesting counter point, or perhaps a warning:

"And that's how things are. A day is like a whole life. You start out doing one thing, but end up doing something else, plan to run an errand, but never get there…And at the end of your life, your whole existence has the same haphazard quality too. Your whole life has the same shape as a single day."
~ **Michael Crichton,** *Jurassic Park*

I think the model of how you explain the journey is very important. Usually people use an arrow going up (Model A):

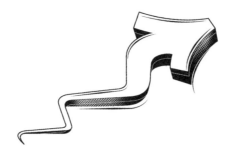

And, generally, that makes sense. A warning: If you view things like this, be prepared for the commandment, "The first step off of a peak is a cliff."

It is a popular way to look at both history and religion. In history, some tend to look at different eras as backward, awful times with an occasional hiccup of glory. Oddly, many religious education people use this image to explain how much better the church is now…*now that I am here!*

The issue with this model is that you start badly and magically improve practically with every rep and session. It ignores the importance of geography and genetics, the "soil" of sports success.

The other common view is an arrow going down (Model B):

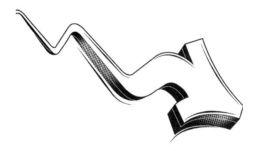

This is "grumpy old man yells at clouds."

You actually hear this a lot as you transition through life and careers: "Back in my day," "People used to know how to drive/cook/live," and the ever-present, "These kids nowadays don't know how to (fill in the blank)."

In my administrative job, I used to deal with a man who complained constantly about how "the Church is going to hell with all the hippie stuff and the women on the altar and the…"

He also took me aside one day and blamed me, among others, for his children leaving the church. I should have used the classic line for parents: "You are probably right; I ruined your child. But you brought her to me with such a head start on it."

He never connected the dots that his model of his church was probably telling his kids that it would be a good idea to jump ship earlier than later.

Programs that go out of their way to tear down athletes to "build them back up" often have huge dropout rates. Some, especially in the military, brag about the dropouts as being a sign that they are doing things right.

Maybe. But, I would argue appropriate preparation and appropriate screening might save us all a lot of time and trouble.

The model I usually use is based on a tree. The soil is the geography and the available resources.

Let me take just a moment to explain the geography of sports: Surfers tend to come from places with oceans and downhill skiers come from mountainous areas. Those are the basics. If you have a fast-twitch kid in Iowa, he wrestles; in Canada, he plays hockey and in Bulgaria, he Olympic lifts.

The seed is your DNA, your genetics. As I often joke, you may want to be an oak or a redwood, but your DNA is all bonsai. If you mix geography and genetics right, you get a superstar.

But this model's great insight is the rings (Model C):

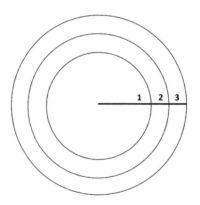

Tree rings are dependent upon the earlier growth. As the tree grows, it builds upon the previous rings.

I see this as the best way to look at sports and life. It was very important that I was raised in South San Francisco, the youngest of six. My parents' DNA gave me some fast twitch and a late puberty. Being the youngest made me always have to catch up. Having my friends hit growth spurts before me made me play catch-up.

One day, I caught up and flew past.

Sitting out in ring three, I realize the importance of the gifts I received in ring one and the road already traveled through ring two. Ideally, I will bear some fruit at the end of this too. For me, the travel and friendships were worth all the work.

Now, there is a fourth model.

Just take pen and scribble all over a piece of paper to build yourself a Model D:

I'm sure you know people who do this model. The Cheshire Cat told Alice, "If you don't know where you are going any road will get you there."

I've met a few people in life who use bumper cars as their North Star, colliding back and forth and back and forth through life. I don't recommend it.

I prefer the tree-ring model. I always try to build upon the foundation, the basics. I like to come back to planks as a strength coach and "Stretch 1–2–3" as a throws coach. We are always building on the beginning.

This quote opens the book *Dune:*

"A beginning is the time for taking the most delicate care that the balances are correct."
~ **Frank Herbert**

This is why I think children should certainly be taught physical education, but they should also play sports. You want the child to develop every physical quality and learn that the lessons learned in basketball carry over to soccer and football and everywhere else.

I was lucky: I played with older kids in multiple sports… daily. I learned to pop back up when I fell and always hustle to the best of my ability. The prize? Most of the time, the prize was yelling "We won!" as you went in for dinner.

Sometimes, the prize was just being asked to play.

With a solid foundation, we can add things. I often struggle understanding this kind of question: "Since all a discus thrower needs are the snatch and farmer walks, is this all throwers should ever do…right from the start?"

I get this question in many forms, but the example is good. The questioner is missing something basic: We need to lay a foundation for the snatch. There is a progression for teaching the snatch. In addition, there are joint, power and strength issues that need to be addressed before the athlete can safely toss more than bodyweight overhead.

It is also important to remember with Model C—the tree rings—that it is certainly fine to go back to the inner rings. Elite athletes can annually use up to weeks of just planking and general carries in their training. It's not regression; it is getting back to the roots…the inner core.

As a coach, fractals give you a vision of today, tomorrow, next year and the next decade. With the tree ring model, we are always building on the basics.

Let's look at how we can do this as a strength coach.

We prefer to plan our daily programs with the big picture in mind. It is based on principles you should know or understand on some level:

1. *Focus on movements, not muscles.*

Ignore biceps, quads or arm day. Stop thinking you are Frankenstein's monster. Training the movements will build your muscles, stretch you back into alignment and bring back joint mobility.

The Fundamental Human Movements

- Push

- Pull

- Hinge

- Squat

- Loaded carries

- The sixth movement
  This is everything else, from rolling to half-kneeling work, to lunges and one arm. It also includes torque, twisting and rotational work.

2. *"If it's important, do it every day. If it isn't, don't do it at all."*

That is a quote attributed to wrestling Olympic Gold Medalist Dan Gable.

If we know the moves, how do we decide when to do them? I argue: every day.

In this vision of training, we will explore the basic movements in nearly every workout. With most athletes, a movement needs repeating far more than most people think. At the elite levels of track and field and Olympic lifting, the total number of full movements is staggering.

3. Repetitions...lots of repetitions.

I can't say it any better than what I learned from a hearing-impaired discus thrower I worked with a few years ago. He had become very good and I asked him his secret.

He took his right middle finger and twisted it over his right index finger and then slapped it into his left palm.

In sign language, that means "repetition."

I have two basic fractal training templates. These reflect the daily, seasonal, yearly and, perhaps, lifetime training cycle. Let's cover the most basic first.

It's based on life.

> *We start off rolling around and crawling.*
> *Then, we get up on one knee.*
> *Then, back to the ground.*
> *We finally rise up and go after it for a while.*
> *We stumble and get back up.*
> *We stumble again and lie back down.*
> *And stay there!*

This is a great template for training.

> *Naked Turkish getups (no weight) and bear crawls*
> *Half-kneeling presses and half-kneeling chops*
> *Bird dogs*
> *Humane burpee: swings followed by goblet squats and pushups—see Appendix Three for details*
> *Mobility movements from six point and half-kneeling*
> *Naked Turkish getups*
> *Savasana (yoga term for laying on the back with calm breathing) or crocodile breathing*

Now, most athletes want to finish with something like "last throw, best throw." Certainly, we all know that saving the best for last is a key to winning championships. So, for athletes, we like to end a workout with a finisher.

This is fractal training: attempting to mimic, at some level, the big picture of the person's goals.

We will use an example for a track and field thrower, but a quick point: Throwers need "continual acceleration" as Ralph Maughan used to emphasize. The key is to finish fast and the implement should come "last and fast."

> *Turkish getups, bear crawls and general easy mobility work.*
> *Slower power work: deadlifts and bench presses*
> *Easy dynamic stretching work*
> *An Olympic lift—snatches or cleans*
> *Hill sprints, sled work or sprints*

There are lots of "big pictures" in life, but a few minutes of looking at the overall goal and stepping back to see if you can mimic it in a daily or monthly training program has great value in setting up success.

Applying an overriding philosophy of strength training has to be put into bite-sized pieces. How do you do "all of this" as you flip through a typical exercise book? There are dozens of variations of minor movements that target muscle groups that can literally be ignored, plus the daily flood of information from what is new and exciting in the fitness field.

Yes, tumbling, foam rolling, sandbags, gymnastics work and all the Olympic sports are great and valuable.

How do you organize it? How do you control it? Moreover, how do we address the daily training session in light of the weekly session with an eye on the lifetime goals of the trainee?

I have found using fractals to shape the daily, weekly and career path to be the easiest way to find clarity in these questions.

Chapter 41
Deprivation—The Great Lesson of Not Having Everything

A memory: Our junior varsity football team bus pulled into a slot next to the stadium. Schools tend to have these massive chain link fences that serve as a perfect place for school buses to unload for games. Sadly, you can see every bit of accumulated trash under the stadium since the last World War. This is all part of the romance of coaching high school.

As the 13 junior varsity football players came off the bus, my assistant coach panicked.

"We don't have any linebackers."

I knew that. We didn't have any running backs either. For those who don't understand American football, basically the issue was this: We were missing some very important players before the game began.

"What are we going to do?"

I love the word "we" when it comes to problems. As I learned as an administrator, I never liked it when people just told me the problems: "Don't bring me problems, bring me solutions."

"What are we going to do without linebackers?"

And running backs.

He seemed to miss that point every time.

I came up with a great idea. Like Barbara Eden from *I Dream of Jeannie* or Elizabeth Montgomery from *Bewitched,* I could either cross my arms and blink or wiggle my nose and WHOOSH…the linebackers (and running backs) would appear.

Let me try that again.

Blink.

Wiggle.

Yup. Still nothing.

Most of the time when I work with young coaches, "we" expect the same thing—magic. It has yet to happen. Listen: We got problems. "Got problems" is simply part of the job description. Solving problems is the key.

Recently, I read that there were international conferences on the biggest single problem in major cities a century ago:

Horse poop.

Oddly, when the automobile took over, the poop problem was eliminated (ha!). Sometimes, problems seem to solve themselves. The airplane industry became safer overnight when pilots adopted checklists. Sometimes little steps solve big problems.

This reminds me of a story I read in *Reader's Digest* as a wee child. A student raised her hand during a presentation and asked a nuclear weapons expert why we don't just get rid of all the nukes. He took his glasses off, wiped his eyes and said, "If it were only that simple."

Sometimes the solutions are simple. Solving things, of course, can paradoxically also be complex.

Actually, I love NOT having everything as a coach.

Let me give you my "big secret." This one is the biggest lesson I ever learned:

Contrarian thinking comes from deprivation!

Let me say it another simpler way:

Deprivation leads to thinking.

I've had issues in my life. I wish I had a blues guitar playing in the background, but, folks, I've had issues in my life.

I basically went without sleep for two weeks when my daughters BOTH had different lung issues. I never missed work and I kept up with everything in my life. I learned a good lesson: Sleep is powerful, but I can keep moving on without it.

As a coach, rarely have my facilities been the best. I coached the discus without a ring and without a field to throw in. NOT having a field made me use a wall. We threw into a wall with balls (ball in a wall!) and soon produced some of the best throwers in high school history.

I trained for an Olympic lifting meet without a place to train. Oh…and I didn't have a bar. I invented some drills and it made me a better coach and a better lifter.

No time? I've been there.

As I started doing Tabata front squats (four minutes of hell), I discovered that this was much harder…maybe better… than traditional squat workouts for me. Recovery would take days, but I can recover working at the desk, cleaning the house or cooking dinner. Measuring rest periods, usually around one minute, became a staple of much of my coaching because I realized how much time we waste in training.

Wishing and hoping is a massive time waster.

I wish I had a drink of water. Isn't that nice to wish?

Wish.

Blink.

Wiggle.

Yup. Still nothing.

If I get up out of my chair, grab a glass and fill it with water, I will discover my wish comes true!

Deprivation makes us think around a problem. I can't wish, blink or wiggle my nose enough to plop down a great facility. As I use my brain, the real magic happens:

I find a solution.

Very often the solution is FAR better than having what everyone else has, or what you *think* everyone else has.

When throwing into a wall, my throwers could get 500 throws in an hour. My competitors had their kids stand in line and all of them took one throw, waited for the rest to throw, then walked out and got the implements. Often, they would get six to 12 throws in an hour.

Five hundred is much more than six. Soon, many schools with great facilities found walls and implemented our methods. We also didn't have a weightroom, so I threw barbells and weights in the back of my beloved pickup and we lifted weights while we threw.

We didn't need a double-blind study to come up with this idea. We didn't have a committee, a newsletter or an email chain. We just did what we could do. It comes down to this:

Deprivation eliminates decisions—a good thing!

Decision comes from the root "to cut or to kill." It is hard to say, "We are NOT going to train on this perfect facility and field because we choose to use this wall." When you don't have things, you don't waste a lot of time deciding. There is no decision!

Decision fatigue is a major issue in the area of fitness and nutrition.

I like to browse used book stores just to see the number of diet books available through the years. If I say there are "thousands of diet books," it is not hyperbole. Put the words "high" or "low" in front of any word like "protein," "carbs" or "fat," and you can find whole sections dedicated to that evil cause of obesity. We can blame milk, bread, meat and eating (fasting is very popular) for fatness or we can adopt the habits of cavemen, Arctic dwellers, Greek farmers or Nordic fishermen.

I get hungry looking at all of this, so I usually go to the bookstore coffee shop and get a cinnamon bun.

That's decision fatigue: The more choices you have to choose from, the more likely you will get exhausted choosing.

I once told my grandchildren I would buy them ONE toy at a local store. They both picked out seven. I said one. The process to watch them go from seven to one probably took years off of my life.

If I gave them an empty box, especially something huge like a refrigerator box, they would have played happily for hours. In my youth, there was nothing better than when one of the neighbors bought a new appliance that came in a big box. We would make it a fort, a meeting house, a super hero club headquarters and play happy for days.

If someone filled it with toys, we probably would have killed each other arguing over them.

This is nothing new. C. Northcote Parkinson argued the same thing in the book, *Parkinson's Law,* the book that changed my thinking forever.

My best coaching and teaching insights almost universally come from deprivation. My best training comes when I have little choice other than to work hard. Put me in a facility with a thousand pieces of high-end equipment and I will probably end up watching TV while walking on a treadmill.

I just described the gym that's half a mile from my home.

I coached at that discus camp in Ohio from 1993 until 2017. We almost shut down in 1994 because of the lack of campers and the relative dangers of everyone throwing metal objects. Fortunately, John Powell went to another clinic and saw the power ball, a medicine ball with a handle. It was safer, and it also allowed us to just focus on technique, especially the feet and lower body, and soon we revolutionized coaching for the young athlete.

Not having safety cages for every thrower or enough room, our "deprivation" led us to a great insight. I now call this style of coaching "contrarian," as it rubs against what most people tend to do and think.

In 1985, I heard world champion and Olympic medalist Bill Koch speak on cross country skiing at a local recreational outlet. As I have often noted, the audience couldn't "hear" him. He was an extraordinary thinker and came up with the skating style of XC skiing.

When asked about training, he replied in simple terms:

"Intervals are the biggest bang for the buck."

"I take my daughters up to the slopes; they take the lift up and I skate up the hill. We then race down.
I repeat that until they are tired."

Bill mixed parenting with training. He focused on what matters. He figured out ways to win. He wasn't stuck on meso-cycles, intermittent bifoculariazation programs…he just found a way to train hard.

Overcoming deprivation, eliminating doing "this and that and this and that and this and that" simplifies and clarifies things. Oddly, we can actively do this in much of our lives; it's sometimes given the name "Contrarian Thinking."

Most of us know contrarian thinking at some level. If you travel a lot, you tend to go to places when the tourists (not meaning *you*) are NOT there. Maybe you might live in an area that allows you to commute opposite the general flow (traffic jam) of the morning and evening rush hour.

In the world of sports, contrarians do things a little different. If it works in sports, an interesting thing happens:

It becomes the norm.

Dick Fosbury attacked the high jump bar "backward" and now every jumper does the Fosbury Flop.

Brian Oldfield (among others) started rotating like a discus thrower in the shot put and now it is far more common than the O'Brien glide. The Parry O'Brien glide, of course, revolutionized the shot before the revolution was revolved by the spin.

When Knute Rockne and Gus Dorais practiced throwing and catching the football as lifeguards in the summer, they came back and defeated the great Army team of 1913. This game made the forward pass the key to winning football games. It stuck.

We could go on in every sport, business and field. Being contrarian is easier, in some ways, than being an inventor or innovator. I often use this quote from Warren Buffet to explain this:

> *"First come the innovators, who see opportunities that others don't and champion new ideas that create genuine value.*
>
> *"Then come the imitators, who copy what the innovators have done. Sometimes they improve on the original idea; often they tarnish it.*
>
> *"Last come the idiots, whose avarice undermines the very innovations they are trying to exploit."*

Contrarians are innovators. Usually, contrarians are not trying to innovate; they are trying to win, maintain or survive. I know Moses got water from a rock, but if you get stranded in a Utah desert, you might want to try Plan B.

I don't know what Plan B is; that's why I always keep a lot of water in my car when I drive in our southwestern deserts.

Oh, that JV football game? We had to be contrarian.

We had to innovate. We simply didn't have any decisions to get decision fatigue.

On defense, we lined up six defensive linemen and said, "Get the quarterback!" We picked five other guys and had them run man-to-man with every eligible receiver. On offense, we threw the ball on every play since we didn't have any running backs…something my assistant coach finally came around to understanding.

We won 52–0.

Chapter 42
The Five Pillars of Coaching

If I can summarize the key to elite coaching and personal training, it would be this:

Ownership.

Your athletes and clients have to OWN the process, the plan. It has to be theirs. It took me years to understand this; I believed people when they told me they wanted to combine elite athletics with academics geared toward medical or law school. I was shocked when I later discovered they were daily drug users or day drinkers...party kids, basically.

I would often stop and ask: "I thought you said..."

"I thought you said..." could be a great coffee mug or t-shirt logo. All too often, the words that come out of people's mouths have little to do with their actions.

It's true: Some parts of my goal-setting toolkit seem odd or weird. You might ask, "Why do I care about what movies or books they like?"

Yet, dialogue, discussion and conversation might be the true keys to establishing the road, the route and the journey to the goal.

Ownership.

This is the first task: to get the person to own the process and then do what needs to be done.

Getting People to Become Actors

I've been told to never watch a medical drama on TV with a doctor in the room. Rarely does real medicine come down to some rare tropical disease and we can only hope that interns don't steal hearts from transplant victims. I'm sure police struggle with cop shows and I hate movies and television shows about teachers.

But, what I hate the most are those idiotic "high five" montages in sports films. You know the kind, a couple of kids from different financial and ethnic backgrounds suddenly put their personal issues aside and start running hills, beaches and fields. They bond through sweat and strain. Then, the HIGH FIVE happens; cue the championship music and the good guys win.

None of that peacocking and posturing really pushes us toward superlative performance. Victory is won in the mundane, the basic and the simple. It is really as fundamental as repeat, repeat, repeat. But, the athletes do need to buy in.

And, to me, this is the secret. Sure, it is as obvious as "buy low; sell high," but it is true. Good coaching stuns you with its power. Yet, it is also subtle.

As a young coach, I fell in love with the Knute Rockne or Vince Lombardi halftime talks. I thought—like the opening scene in *Patton*—that I could stir our force above and beyond their former limits and limitations and we would, dear God as our witness, destroy the forces of evil.

Or, at least, defeat the South Valley Sabercats sophomore badminton team.

I was trying to act like great coaches. In truth, I'm not a good actor. Oddly, taking a course on acting opened up this whole issue for me as a coach.

What happened was, I took an online acting class to improve my presentation skills. I didn't use much of it, but one concept really caught my eye:

Monologue–Dialogue–Soliloquy

A monologue, to understand this concept, is when you talk out loud.

For example, we begin hands-on certifications with a brief introduction from each participant. It can be funny or tedious depending on the group.

"Hi. I'm Dan John. I'm a Virgo. I like long walks on the beach and I hate phony people. My hobbies are skinny skiing and going to bullfights on acid."

Thank you, *Caddyshack.*

Most of the time when I do goal setting, it seems like the client or athlete is reading a monologue from a script:

"I want to lose weight. I want to have a six-pack."

Folks, it's easy to get a six-pack. There are literally three grocery stores within walking distance of my home.

Oh…the other kind? Sorry.

This is the "Not A" kind of goal setting I discussed earlier.

Monologues are fine, but we rarely move the dial ahead with athletes by using just this technique. Dialogues, obviously, are better. We are moving into a discussion now.

I am a believer in the follow-up question. If someone says, "I like to work out," well, I used to let it just stay there.

Now, I follow up:

What do you do when you work out?

"Well, sometimes I, like, get up and maybe walk. Or I go to the gym."

What gym?

"I dunno. I haven't been to one in years."

I learned this first while teaching religious studies. Literally, everyone tells me they practice a faith, a belief or some sort of spirituality. After a follow-up question, I discover most people believe they want a cup of coffee.

As a coach, you need to press people deeper into the statements they make concerning health, fitness, performance and longevity. The follow-up question is the key to dialogue.

But, there is one important next step in the process of getting the person to "own" the goal.

My online acting class taught me this great insight: You want to get the athletes to "overhear" themselves. This is called soliloquy: "An utterance or discourse by a person who is talking to himself or herself or is disregardful of or oblivious to any hearers present."

When athletes tell me they want to be great discus throwers, or whatever, I first press them with deeper follow-up questions. But soon, I want them to listen to themselves.

The first tool is a goal-setting exercise. It's the "waddaya want" question. This is a bit bland, but it opens the door to other things. Most of the time, people have goals that are almost completely unreachable. They have a wish list.

> *I wish I had six-percent bodyfat.*
> *I wish I had a jelly doughnut.*

I can get you the doughnut.

For the athlete or client working on measurable goals, like track and field or reducing the waistline, the wish list goal can be charted on a piece of paper and reasonable steps can be discussed. Most people are shocked when they see the amount of time the goals take to achieve.

For vague goals, I don't really know what to do.

Without a measuring stick, it's tough to figure out a plan.

After the basics of goal setting, I want to encourage the person to buy in to the goal. It seems to help if you can get people to reflect on their life. Autobiography work is excellent, as it opens up the connections that draw people into why they want this goal and not another goal.

I have been introduced to several different methods, but I like to start with the simplest first. The easiest autobiography tools are to list the 10 best movies and books you have watched or read.

Let me share mine.

Books

The Sword in the Stone
The Hobbit
Don Quixote (Book One)
Two Years before the Mast
Hamlet
Hitchhiker's Guide to the Galaxy
Gulliver's Travels
Arnold: The Education of a Bodybuilder
Dune
The Tao of Pooh

Movies

Patton
Star Trek II
Lawrence of Arabia
Star Wars (the original…call it "Star Wars")
Field of Dreams
The Three Musketeers (the Michael York version)
Brigadoon

> *How to Succeed in Business without Really Trying*
> *Moonstruck*
> *Fisher King*

It's a fun discovery and actually easy to do. It's easy to turn this into dialogue:

> *"Why this book?"*
>
> *"Can you tell me more about that movie?"*

But, often people doing the exercise pick up some interesting insights about themselves. I tend to like movies where the characters transform during the adventure—I'm sure I'm not alone here. Understanding that insight helps me plan things far into the future since I know it won't happen overnight.

This assignment comes with a warning: If the person you want to marry hasn't read 10 books, take this under advisement.

It's not a bad idea to do this with favorite musical albums or dining experiences too. Obviously, the audience is the key to how far you can take this assignment. I find the conversation really unpacks the coach-athlete relationship and gives insights that one might not discover for years without this reflective task.

I would also have experienced athletes list their 10 best and 10 worst performances and, perhaps, training ideas or programs. Those 10 best training tools might be all you really need to move forward with the programming.

The drills and the whole idea of soliloquy prepare us for another insight: *Mythos and logos*

Mythos is the *"Why?"* and logos is the *"How?"*

Reps and sets and exercise selection and diet and recovery are the "how."

And, yes, these are important, but more important is the "why" behind things. Truthfully, fat loss clients already know the how: some kind of caloric restriction and probably some kind of exercise. Getting them to go all in with a program needs an answer to the question: "Why?"

Which technique, monologue, dialogue or soliloquy explains mythos or logos better?

Avoid "either/or" here, as some people might show up with a "why" encased in stone. Maybe the goal is to be alive and healthy for their kids or grandkids. Often, it is to rise above a situation such as depressing poverty or pain. The coach needs, once again, a pretty full toolbox to bring the person along.

Getting the people to hear themselves is the key to ongoing improvement in performance. Once the "why" is answered, we can move into the nuts and bolts of things, the "how." As Viktor Frankl taught us: "Those who have a 'why' to live can deal with any 'how.'"

On the coaching journey, like everything else, as I have discovered in life, we tend to go through four phases:

> *Unconscious incompetence—*
> *You don't know what you don't know.*
>
> *Conscious incompetence—*
> *You know what can be done, but you can't do it.*
>
> *Conscious competence—*
> *You think your way through the process.*
>
> *Unconscious competence—*
> *You automatically apply the techniques.*

Young coaches listen to the monologue, nod their heads and start with a warmup. As the weeks move on, the disconnect between an athlete's goals and behaviors will become evident. Soon, the coach will begin to connect the dots with the athlete.

An elite coach will have this as part of the system and these concepts will be applied seamlessly. It will be so effortless, the coach will not even remember there is a process in place. It just becomes part of who we are and what we do.

"What we do."

While taking that acting class, it was interesting to look at the word "actor" and discover that it comes from the same root as "doer." My job is to get you to act—as an athlete, literally one who "contends for a prize," and then to perform until you win the prize. Of course, how you define winning is a huge factor in whether or not you achieve success. I will discuss more on this shortly.

Performance is all about winning. To get from here to there—the very foundation of goal setting—you must have some kind of strategy. It's a plan. It's a program. It's a vision of the route or journey.

And, the vision is bound to be wrong. Plans are often wrong and I'm fine with that.

I live by two great quotes from leaders of the WWII:

> *"You have to be fast on your feet and adaptive*
> *or else a strategy is useless."*
> **~ Charles de Gaulle**

> *"However beautiful the strategy,*
> *you should occasionally look at the results."*
> **~ Winston Churchill**

Preparation is my basic strategy. Preparation is my "secret" to coaching. And, almost universally, preparation is repetition.

Make sure you are repeating the most important tasks for the goal.

Finally, before I hand out advice, I always walk through a three-step process.

First, in many cases, I let other people take over and I stay away. For examples, think of poisonous snake removal, EMTs, trauma surgeons, and lifeguards:

Let the experts work!

Now, certainly I can advise everyone on the basics of not getting into many of life's bad situations with the classic: Don't smoke, learn to fall…wear a seatbelt.

Oh, and don't TRY to be stupid. Watching that how-to video on getting rattlesnakes out of the basement does not make you an expert.

Second, I focus on my mom's advice for most diet and exercise:

"Starches make you fat."

"Go outside and play."

"Are your legs are painted on?"

My mom believed cars were only for going to church or the grocery store.

I make my living with a summary of her advice:

"Eat like an adult. Lift weights and go for a walk!"

Third, when dealing with elite training goals, I always find someone who is:

Elite

Has accomplished the goal

Then, I advise you to do what that person did.

Chapter 43
Measurements

There is a short line in *Think Like a Freak* that made me suddenly realize why I am generally happy. Now, the journey to happiness as a coach is, to quote the boys from Liverpool, "a long and winding road."

But, this line set me free:

Knowing what to measure simplifies life.

As I sit at my desk with my dog occasionally looking up at me when he isn't snoring, I have a vague sense of this hard-to-find quality called "happy."

Like most people, I have achieved goals, traveled to many places and generally had a life worth living. As a coach, this has not always been true.

The issue? It's sometimes hard to know what to measure.

Let's look at how I make my living:

- Strength coach
- Track and field coach
- Fitness consultant (occasional personal trainer)
- Author

How do I know I am doing better as a strength coach? Hmmm. Let me break it down: My people get stronger because they lift more weight!

If load goes up, I did the strength coaching right.

Don't roll your eyes yet; I'm just starting.

Track and field coach? Easy. If the athletes throw farther, jump higher or farther or run fast, we are doing it right.

Personal trainer/fitness consultant/fitness trainer? In my book *Can You Go?*, I give one measurement: waistline. If your client's waistline goes down, you almost universally got it right.

Measuring "author" makes a more difficult calculation.

If you go online and trust the "star" reviews, good luck, my friend, in appraising if a book is good or bad. I have seen people give one-star reviews because their electronic device doesn't work right. Great television shows get reviewed poorly all the time because "I bought the season, but only got one episode." (The, uh, season…um…just started. They will come out every week…one at a time.)

I've seen classic works destroyed by teenage reviewers because: "I was made to read this book and I didn't want to." I saw this in a *Ulysses* review and *The Sword in the Stone.*

Really? You hate *The Sword in the Stone?*

For authors, actors and artists of all kinds, here you go: Measure your success by income. For authors, it's royalties. Mickey Rooney and Burt Reynolds may not be your go-to favorite thespians, but they dominated screen revenue for decades. As kids say, "haters gonna hate," but no matter what you do, in the court of public opinion, some people are going to love your work and others are going to hate it.

In full candor, the late Archbishop George Niederauer once said I was, and I quote, "a diva." His point, and it did hurt, was I tended to only notice the poor or bad evaluations.

When he said this, I tossed my fur boa over my shoulder and stormed out. That's a joke, although many people I know can imagine me doing it.

At one point, I ran a yearly event with up to 1,000 people. I hate evaluations; almost always, they have no value.

"The bathrooms were too cold."

"The bathrooms were too hot."

"There was too much food."

These are actual evaluations from one year. The third one was funny, as we offered a buffet, so "too much food" reflects one's (over)use of the serving spoons.

People actually complained about the toilet paper too. Honestly, one can only do so much.

Which leads us back to my life as an author.

I focus on the royalties. Sometimes, I think, "This is my best work ever," but the book doesn't sell. Now, it might be true: This poor selling book does a great job explaining some key principle in lifting or coaching, but it only applies to the 10 people on the planet who care about that key principle…including me, and I get free copies.

But, if the royalties allow me to lend my yacht to the pilot of my private jet, I know I did something right.

By knowing what to measure, I know my general direction is either going the right way or the wrong way. When things in all areas of my life are going the right way, I tend to be happy.

Oh, I'm sure there is a self-help book that will tell me I should be happy no matter what, but I seem to be happier warm, full, hydrated and surrounded by people I love and who love me.

In my coaching career, I also discovered it is often hard to measure things. American football, one of the true loves of my life, is a great example: You can really play well, improve across the board in all qualities and still get pounded by the opponents. We might have a team filled with future lawyers, doctors and Nobel Prize winners, but we still lost.

And, an undefeated season can also be a horrible experience to endure.

That's tough to explain. I have coached some amazing athletes, but I couldn't turn my back on them. Sometimes, you win the genetic lottery and you are flat-out better.

As a coach, you might have a lot of wins and trophies, but you might be miserable.

"Measuring measurements" is a delicate balance. Statistics are often fraught with issues, as British Prime Minister Benjamin Disraeli said (according to Mark Twain): "There are three kinds of lies: lies, damned lies and statistics."

Years ago, I endured a horrific season of coaching high school football. Frankly, the mix of the personalities of the football staff was bad and we had far too many dads coaching their boys. This is always an issue in the best of times, but in this case, we also had very little talent.

It was that year—and we all have them—when everything just kept going wrong. As we finished our season (we lost every game in our region), one of the coaches mentioned this:

"We have the best pass defense in the region."

What?

"Yeah, look," and he produced some numbers. It was true, nobody threw the ball much on us. But, wait…there might be "the rest of the story."

We were behind in games so fast and by such large margins, the opposition never had to throw the ball. His measurement, "the best pass defense," needed the rest of the story.

I use Jean Fournier and Damian Farrow's book, *7 Things We Don't Know!*, as part of my work for St. Mary's University. I constantly strive to remind my students not to just take measurements, but to study them closely.

My favorite part of the book involves free throw shooting for basketball. There was a study that found that Division One basketball players hit six or seven free throws in a row...ALL THE TIME!

But, they shoot 69% of free throws in games.

Hmmm?

The follow-up was simple. The researcher, Bill Kozar et al, looked at the just the first two free throws in these practice tests. Not shockingly, the basketball players hit 69% of their first two shots in practice.

You don't shoot 10 free throws in a row in a game. You might shoot one or two. That's it.

In personal training, people use the weight scale (notoriously worthless at calculating lean body mass) or dress sizes (this is a fascinating discussion to bring up around wedding and prom season) or, more recently, use photoshopped pictures.

These measurements are, on their best days, worthless.

When trying to figure out what makes an American football team or a rugby team win is really difficult. You have 11 or 15 players on a side. You have a massive field. You have dozens of things happening at once...ALL the time!

If my discus thrower throws 10 feet farther, we are right. If your rugby team loses in a close one...well, good luck finding what really cost the victory.

As we say in American football about the film session after a game: You never look as good or as bad as you thought.

Oddly, after a loss, it is often hard to see where the game was lost on the field. The opportunities to win were...ah, just right there! Watching film after a loss just breaks the heart: We say "coulda/woulda/shoulda" throughout the film session.

Some stats give some clarity. Turnovers in most sports are usually a key, but some turnovers, like tossing the ball deep at the end of a half, don't mean much.

There is a term, MOBP—Missed Opportunity to Make a Big Play—that can really unpack a loss. Literally, you will hear in the film room, "Right there! Right there!"

But, again, that's coulda/woulda/shoulda thinking.

As we've discussed throughout this book, the lessons I learned teaching economics made me a better coach. The lessons I learned pulling together my personal financial security made me a better coach.

Coaching and participating in track and field, the ultimate numbers game (along with competitive swimming), made me a better coach.

If you can measure it, you can improve it.

Chapter 44
Snapacity

As a strength coach, I was lucky to have been young before weightlifting became popular. And, by the way, I mean just that: lucky. I'm pretty sure the whole field changed in the 1970s. I often forget this, but ABC's *Wide World of Sports* invented a celebrity contest called *"Superstars."*

It's fun to watch the old episodes now. You can find them on the internet and often various documentaries will include a few minutes of old footage. I remember a big deal in the early episodes when the producer refused to allow Bob Seagram, the champion pole vaulter, to enter the 100-meter sprint, but allowed O. J. Simpson, an American football player, to compete. Simpson had been on a championship 4x100-meter team for the University of Southern California.

Lifting a weight overhead was one of the contests. In the early events, and it is embarrassing to watch now, the elite athletes struggled (with two spotters assisting a bit too much) with very light weights. When Lou Ferrigno, later *The Hulk,* competed, he pushed barrier up to 290 pounds. The next year, Brian Oldfield took 300 and did it easily for about five repetitions. He later told me he was going to go for 20, but the assistants were "trying to help and messed up the groove."

As the show progressed, everyone got better at lifting. So, I do have to tip the hat to *Superstars* for part of the change in the lifting landscape.

Certainly, we could add Bruce Lee with not only popularizing martial arts, especially with *The Green Hornet,* but he was an important fan of weightlifting for total body training.

Wide World of Sports also took us annually to the Olympic lifting world championships and the quest for the first 500 clean and jerk was must-see television. Vasili Alekseyev, the Soviet lifter, was a true superstar—I had to explain countless times that his huge belly was not part of normal O lifting physiques.

But, the big change came with, first, the documentary based on the book *Pumping Iron.* I saw the movie opening night in San Francisco. A limo pulled up after the film; Tony Martin, Eric Seubert and I were standing there when Arnold came out.

We were the only three to recognize him. He asked me:

"How did you like the movie?"

We talked, shook hands and went our ways. I understand he went on to make movies.

About the same time, he wrote *Arnold: The Education of a Bodybuilder.* Certainly, one could also recognize the impact of the early dance aerobics craze, Jane Fonda and VHS training, but this book, from my seat in history, was the key.

During my first years in college, the weightroom was filled with athletes, people doing rehab, and some oddballs (trust me). After the book came out, the weightroom was filled to overflowing with practically every frat boy at Utah State University.

Since everyone is "elite," they were all doing the six-day-a-week split. I have never seen more quarter-squats in my life.

And since that book, bodybuilding is the mental image people have when you tell them you lift weights. Ask my grandson to "make a muscle" and he will put on a "gun show."

In theology, we call this a "steno symbol." A steno symbol is a word, phrase or symbol that has a single meaning. I'm sitting on a chair. You can probably imagine exactly what I am doing.

If I take that word "chair" and use it like this: "I can't believe how chair she has been to me," you will most likely lean in and turn your ear to me.

Sorry?

Contrast that with the word "bad." When I was young, if I asked how the movie was and you said, "Bad," I would not go. Then, bad meant good. Then, baaaaaaaad meant good. I'm still not sure if a movie is bad or good, but I hope Santa thinks I am nice, not naughty.

All too often, I tell people about O lifting or my career as a strength coach and they "make a muscle."

The funny thing is this: They are right!

And wrong.

Since the book *Arnold: The Education of a Bodybuilder* was published, most people have a mental picture when we say "weightlifting." The audience hears "bodybuilding."

Certainly, the lifting toolkit can do wonders for lean body mass, especially for hypertrophy. But, we can go too far here: When training athletes and people from collision occupations, we must remember that performance is the key.

My worst selling book, *Now What?*, will continue to do poorly because I tell people that health is the optimal interplay of the human organs, fitness is doing a task, longevity is both quality and quantity, and performance is when they call your name and you do something.

I didn't mention ripped abs and barn-door delts.

My mistake.

For performance, you need something else. Since I couldn't find a word to describe it, I invented my own (something I tend to do more and more as I age): Snapacity, pronounced "snap ASS city"). Snapacity is when we combine explosive work (snap) with work capacity training. You see…snapacity.

The road to attaining snapacity obviously involves intelligent training design and time. It involves the weightroom and training field.

But, before we get into the specifics, we need to review something many people miss when it comes to training: What EXACTLY are we trying to build in the weightroom?

Pavel and I wrote *Easy Strength,* in part, to solve the riddle of "what is impact of the strength coach." The ROLE of the strength coach was easy: coach strength.

But the impact?

As I read countless programs throughout my career and tried to decipher the mix of powerlifting, O lifting, bodybuilding, cardio work, yoga, prehab and rehab that seem to have been poured in a blender, pureed, then poured out on paper, I began to wonder: What happened? How did things get so crazy?

As a strength coach, is it my job to do nutritional counseling, meditation work and medical intervention? No. Certainly, I can advise on these issues, but it is not my job. That's not my role: I'm here to teach you to get stronger.

Be sure you read that right: "teach" you to get stronger. Coaches can only do so much.

Now, what is the impact of the strength coach? I used to say, "It depends," but then I worked on solving this riddle.

I used two simple ideas: First, find out how many qualities are needed for the sport. Second, I used another axis for what I summed as the "absolute maximum of human potential."

Qualities for a sport like discus throwing are pretty few: technique and power. I could probably argue for more, but that is the truth.

For fat loss, one could easily suggest two things: caloric restriction of some kind and inefficient exercise.

Contrast these two examples with American football: There are so many physical qualities that I won't waste space naming them all. But, that is just the beginning; a muff and a fumble will look the same to most viewers and fans, but the rules for these two are quite different. I can probably discuss, in depth and detail, a few dozen offensive packages.

That's a lot of stuff to know…a lot of things to coach.

The other axis, absolute maximum of human potential, is hard to understand. As the 100-meter records sneak closer to 9.7 and deadlifters pull over 1,000 pounds, the rest of us mere mortals can be considered strong with 400-pound deadlifts. I was the last deadlifter at a powerlifting meet and pulled 628. Compared to the elites, I'm a D student.

So, I made a quadrant out this idea and got this:

Quadrant One: Basically, this would be children's physical education programs. Lots and lots of things to learn and try, but at a very low level of potential.

Quadrant Two: Collision sports and occupations. Lots of qualities at a very high level of performance. When you walk into an NFL locker room, you will quickly understand this.

Quadrant Three: Most of us live here…even elite track and field athletes (in some cases). An elite thrower is stronger than the bulk of humanity, but pales in comparison to pure strength athletes. Fat loss is QIII.

Quadrant Four: 100-meter sprinters and elite Olympic lifters. Practically only one quality at the highest levels humans can achieve. So much of this depends on geography and genetics: Usain Bolt's national sport is sprinting. If he grew up in West Texas, he might have been an underperforming wide receiver (maybe). Boys growing up in Iowa wrestle; kids in Hawaii surf.

The basics of appropriate strength training can certainly help anyone from any quadrant.

Often, young strength coaches tend to look at the programs of the best and brightest and assume that is what to do with everyone. There is a lot of truth to this, of course, but really most people, even the elite, need foundational training in the beginning and ongoing work with fundamentals as a career progresses.

This "truth" needs to be understood.

I explain this, in my usual adolescent idiocy, with the concept "pull my finger." Don't worry; you are safe. This is just a way to explain the role of strength training.

The role of strength training for the athlete and collision occupation person comes down to the Three Ps:

- *Point*

- *Push*

- *snaP*

Chapter 45
Point, Push, snaP

Point

This is a very simple explanation, but follow along, please. Point your index finger. Now, gently, with the other hand, tug and pull the finger…but resist the tugs and pulls.

Obviously, this is planking. I am a great believer in planking because it teaches the most overlooked concept in correct training: tension.

Teaching people tension is the foundation of strength training. It is far more than just popping on the ground and holding a pushup position plank (PUPP) for a few minutes. To lift massive loads, one must learn to lock down the body, armor up and resist gravity.

In 1970, you remember that I walked over to the Orange Library in South San Francisco and looked on the shelves for books on football and books on getting bigger. This one adventure led me to *The Sword in the Stone*, *Seven Days to Sunday* and Myles Callum's book, *Body Building and Self Defense*.

These three books, without question, changed my life. At the time, Callum's book was the most important. The other two books will have their own stories for another time.

Not long ago, I found the book online and bought it again. I found the following illuminating:

"This method (isometrics/tension) is based on a new theory *[the book was published in 1962]* of muscle growth. German and American scientists and doctors have found that a muscle can grow at only a certain rate. And, according to this theory, it doesn't take as much work as we used to think. If you flex any muscle to its maximum power and contraction, and hold it there for six seconds, once a day, the scientists say, the muscle will grow in strength just as fast as it can grow *[in strength!]*.

"Whether or not this method of muscle tension can ever really replace weight-lifting is still a matter of controversy. **Some scientists say it can; endless repeating of strenuous exercise, they say, 'does not make the strength of a muscle grow any faster.' Weight-lifting, however, may make the size of the muscle grow faster.**"

The italics are my little helpful hints. You see, I read this book nearly 50 years ago, but I continue to relearn this part:

> *"Some scientists say it can; endless repeating of strenuous exercise, they say, 'does not make the strength of a muscle grow any faster.' Weight-lifting, however, may make the size of the muscle grow faster."*

Isometrics, and the whole family of planks, teach tension. In our "pull my finger" model, these teach "point." Teaching tension makes the weightroom safer. Stepping back with 600 pounds in the squat rack is not the time to start discussing politics. You need to brace; you need tense. One of the reasons I emphasize tension so much with new lifters is that tightening up everything from the top of the head to the toes makes them safer.

I have a simple drill I use to teach people who train just body parts (Frankenstein's monster training):

I put a mini-band around the ankles. We put a load in one hand—let's say a 40-pound dumbbell in the right hand—and extend it into the waiter walk position. Then, I have the athlete step to the left, step to the left, step to the left.

If the person understands whole-body tension, the load stays appropriately vertical over the right shoulder. When athletes look like they are going to break in half like a twig in a windstorm…they don't understand whole body tension.

My job is to teach the relationship between tension and relaxation. I went into detail on this in *Now What?*, but essentially, we need to find the proper amount of tension needed for a specific task and practice getting "right there." If you think of the tension dial as one to 10, a 10 would be licking your finger and sticking it in an electrical outlet. A one would be something like a couple of tequilas in a hot tub.

Neither is ideal for sport. A discus thrower needs about a four, a deadlifter needs about a nine, and a football player would slide up and down as the game or even a play unfolds. I can train a discus thrower to understand "four" by doing the Olympic snatch, as they both demand the same level of tension and relaxation.

Pete Giachetti, my high school coach, taught me a great lesson about tension and discus throwing when I was a freshman at Southwood. I asked him to help me with the discus and he gave me a drill:

If the direction of the throw was, for example, at 12:00 o'clock, I got myself in the throwing position and put my hand against a wall at 6:00 o'clock—180 degrees from the target; what we call "3B" in our throwing language. Then, I pulled and stressed and pushed as I tried to tighten my whole body.

For years, I thought this built strength in the throw. Oh, I'm sure it does. But, years later I finally got the concept of why we do tension work, static work…isometric work:

It teaches the nervous system that
"HERE" is where we want to be!

What the isometric craze might have done is teach athletes they were weak at this point HERE—the sticking point. With my front squat, it was 34 inches off the ground. I know this because Dave Turner meticulously reviewed a video to figure it out. Dave convinced me to buy a pair of saw horses and we set them at 34 inches to do a front squat from there.

My first effort was 135 pounds and I struggled. At the time, I was clean and jerking 365. But I was struggling with a front-squat sticking point at 34 inches. Within weeks, I was up to 365 pounds at the sticking point and I never missed another clean in my career. I cleaned 402 pounds at the next meet and missed the jerk behind me.

In hindsight, I was telling my nervous system not to just coast, using momentum through this point. Later, I returned to Coach Giachetti's drill for every issue in the throwing arts. I added "shaking out" the limbs after the isometric movement, bringing the tension level down to an appropriate level.

Then, and here is the key: Do the complete movement.

Oddly, the body "remembers" that position and, as if by magic, we fix the issue with one repetition. One morning at camp in Ohio, we added 10 feet to an experienced collegiate thrower in minutes. His coach turned to him and said:

"This is why we spend the money to come here."

Dave later showed me an article explaining this concept from May 1970 in *Strength and Health:*

"Roman Mielec has been having trouble lately with his knee. He needs leg work badly, but the heavy full squatting necessary for strength irritates his injured knee. Taking a tip from Team Trainer Dick Smith, he has begun working on sticking point squats in the power rack. The lifter figures out his 'sticking point' by doing a

heavy full squat in strict form, while a bystander tells him exactly what point the bar moved the slowest.

"The pins are inserted in the power rack at this point, and the lifter does his squats from this point. This means he is working from his weakest point and the weight he can use is much less, usually approximately the same as his best clean. And this is a top figure, for a single.

"Eight weeks on this exercise will do wonders for anyone having trouble coming up with cleans, and its value for people with knee trouble is unquestioned, as no stress is put on the injured joint."

I have wondered for the past few years if the "secret" of isometrics was actually teaching the nervous system, basically, "Hey, we need to be able to DO THIS HERE!" The tension allows more load over time because the whole system begins to sing together in chorus. This stuff works and works well.

But, you can see that tension/planking/pointing are leading directly to our next P.

Push

I learned typing in 1971. I am a far better typist today than when I pounded the keys on a manual typewriter at Southwood Junior High School. The reason we get better and better at typing is the same reason repetitions are so important in lifting (and practically everything else): Repetition teaches the nervous system. So, when I type, I "push" my fingers to strike the keys and the magic happens.

All too often, that's where most trainers in the weightroom begin and end. Here you go: five sets of five in various exercises on machines and thank you for very much for showing up today.

What makes the push so important in the three Ps of Performance is also the reason most of us fall in love with it:

Lifting weights with appropriate movements, appropriate reps, appropriate repetitions and appropriate load sets the body up for that "miracle" transformation that changes bodies and lives.

When I first learned to *actually* lift, my bodyweight rose from 162 pounds to 202 pounds in four months. The calories in/calories out model can't explain that kind of growth. All those front squats and O lifts with Coach Notmeyer told my body something simple: Grow or die!

I grew.

snaP

The final piece of the three Ps is snaP. Pointing your finger can give directions; pushing your finger can type words on a screen, but to make sound, you snap your fingers. Snapping fingers relies on tension, timing and release. If you use too much tension, nothing is going to happen. If you use too little, it won't make a sound. If you do it right, your snap can be heard across an auditorium.

Throwing, striking and kicking are ways to see this snaP in the real world. snaP should be part of everyone's training.

The three Ps MUST be part of an organized program. There are times for individual work on each, but the best approach is to weave them all together.

Chapter 46
Weaving Together

I have been working on my weightlifting matrix probably since 1970 after reading John McCallum's book, *Keys to Progress*. I have little drawings in my old journals of me attempting to do a full body workout and I put little Xs on the bodyparts I trained. I now believe the body is one piece, but I can understand what I was trying to do. I was attempting to do cover all the muscles.

I should have focused on the movements.

Movement	Planks as a Program	Strength Training *Less than 10 reps* Hypertrophy *15–25 reps*	Anti-Rotation Work	Triads	Olympic Lifts
Push	PUPPs Plank	(Bench) Press Pushup	One-arm Bench Press One-arm Overhead Press		
Pull	Bat Wing	Pullup Row	One-arm TRX Row	Push Press/Jerk	Squat Snatch
Hinge	Glute Bridge with AB Hold	Hip Thrust Rack DLs Goad Bag Swing	**Hill Sprints** **Stadium Steps** Skipping Bounding High Knee Work	Swings LitviSprints/LitviSleds	Clean & Jerk
Squat	Goblet Squats 6-point Rocks	Double KB Front Squat The Full Squat Family	**Bear Hug Carries** Bear Crawls Bear Hug Carries with Monster Walk		
Loaded Carry	Farmer's Walk Horn Walk	Prowler Car Push	One-arm Carries: **Suitcase Carry** Waiter Walk Rack Walk		

There are 37 movements listed in the table and most people quickly learn almost all of them. I see them as progressive. *Progressive Resistance Exercise,* the title of Thomas DeLorme's book that gave us the basic standards of weight training language, needs to be, ummm, progressive.

But, progressive doesn't just mean MORE WEIGHT!

From isometric to ballistic
(no movement to fast movement)

Single movements to compound movements

Equipment choices "progress"
(or regress, if you are old school)

Exercise selection logically evolves
(builds upon success)

Reps and sets progress
(or reduce, if you are using a lot of load)

And, then, yes: load.

To Olympic lift—the movements on the right of the matrix—one needs to be able to march through the Three Ps in a harmonic flow. To jerk, for example, you need to really stay tight, dip, snap, catch the weight and recover. It's snapping plank! Or, a planking snap!

One quick point about the matrix: The exercises in italics are no or minimal equipment movements:

PUPP

Bat wing

Glute bridge/hip thrust

Goblet squat

Farmer's walk/horn walk

Hill sprints

Stadium steps

Bear hug carries

Suitcase carries

For bear hug carries, I often have military operators or American football players pick up a teammate (bear HUG!) and walk away. Yes, it can be that simple.

Let's look at the matrix a bit closer. There is great value in an annual revisiting of this list.

On the far-left column, I label it "Planks as a Program." The push, pull and hinge movements are measured by good old time under tension. It helps to have a trainer insure that you are not just holding the position, but are truly tensing everything in the body. (To learn PUPPs, bat wings or glute bridge, view them at my YouTube channel, dj84123.)

I tell my groups that both the goblet squat and farmer walk are moving planks. My first published article in the field of fitness was about the overhead squat. It took me years to realize the reason this movement helped throwers so much was the moving plank-ness of the lift. Yes, it calls for mobility, flexibility, squat ability and pure strength, but it also keeps changing these qualities every inch of the way down and back up.

I now use planks as a program mixed with Tim Anderson's Original Strength. His resets not only provide a fair amount of mobility and vestibular-system work, but they also get the person to ease off the tension—*to relax.* I have yet to find a simpler method than Tim's for getting people back to where they should be.

Movement	Planks as a Program	Original Strength Performance Resets
Push	PUPPs Plank	Prone Neck Work Bird Dog Family
Pull	Bat Wing	Prone Neck Work Elbow Rolls
Hinge	Glute Bridge with AB Hold	6-point Nods and Rocks Bird Dog Family
Squat	Goblet Squats 6-point Rocks	Prone Neck Work Hip Flexor Stretch/Rolling
Loaded Carry	Farmer's Walk Horn Walk	Crawling and Cross Crawls

The next column is what most of us know: the traditional strength and bodybuilding moves. I have a few suggestions for "most of the time:"

- The total number of reps for the push, pull and squat should always be the same amount. Most people do FAR too many pushes.

- For strength, keep the total reps around 10. That's 3 x 3, 5 x 2, 5–3–2.

- For hypertrophy work, keep the total reps between 15–25. That's 5 x 5, 3 x 8, 3 x 5.

- For hinges, reps will depend on the movement: more for KB work (swings), less for DLs and O lifts.

- For loaded carries: do them.

I don't want to deep dive into this too much, but I am not a big fan of rotation work in the weightroom. It could be my 50-year career as a thrower; 10,000 throws a year (at least) is probably enough rotation work for me.

But, as I hammered this out (ha! I was also a hammer thrower…well, I thought it was funny), I was reminded what I was told by a biomechanist who specializes in throwing: It's not rotation—it's *anti*-rotation that makes the implements go far.

High-level throwing has been described as driving as fast as you can and smashing into a brick wall. Your head snaps forward and…bad things happen. When we throw, we stop HARD and the implement comes around. When teaching linemen to block, we stress "don't get turned." That's anti-rotation work.

We tend to become asymmetrical, so always let the less strong side dictate the reps. If I do two presses with the left arm, I just do two with the right.

I learned this from Taylor Lewis, an up-and-coming strength coach: If I keep improving my strong side, the other side will never catch up.

It's funny to think of this now, but some of my first articles on *t-nation* were about one-arm lifts and a lot of people thought they were crazy. They have become fairly mainstream now.

Strength Training *Less than 10 reps* Hypertrophy *15–25 reps*	Anti-Rotation Work
(Bench) Press Pushup	One-arm Bench Press One-arm Overhead Press
Pullup Row	One-arm TRX Row
Reps for Push, Pull and Squat: Same total Double KB Front Squat The Full Squat Family	**Let the "less strong" side determine the reps**
Five sets of two is strength; three sets of eight is hypertrophy	One-arm Carries: **Suitcase Carry** Waiter Walk Rack Walk

As we move to the right, snaP takes over. We had a discussion not long ago and someone noted that the perfect way to train from "kid to casket" would be:

1. *Ballistics (Olympic lifts, swings, kb snatches), basic plyometrics*

2. *Grinds (powerlifts, general push, pull, hinge, squat)*

3. *Hypertrophy (bodybuilding…with mobility)*

Or, more succinctly, O lift—then powerlift—then body-build. Ballistic work tends to "insist" upon point, push and snaP without have to use words to explain it.

"Perfect" is always a nice word to use when talking about training, isn't it? I was once asked if I could go back in time and change my training. I pointed out that this couldn't happen, but the person asked again.

I said I would have been taller and better looking.

When I look at exercise selection, it really comes down to a discussion of two questions:

Could we do X?

Done correctly, yes.

Should we do X?

It depends.

If you don't have the equipment, the facilities, the abilities and the time to teach something, I would argue you probably don't want your clients and people to do it.

And, frankly, people simply don't need to learn every single thing on the buffet table of training. When it comes to athletes, I find exercise selection to be very simple.

Now, again, let's review the key to just about everything:

I said it would be simple, not easy.

With athletes, I focus on two things in training: snap and work capacity.

Snapacity.

Movement	Planks as a Program	Strength Training *Less than 10 reps* Hypertrophy *15–25 reps*	Anti-Rotation Work	Triads	Olympic Lifts
Push	PUPPs Plank	(Bench) Press Pushup	One-arm Bench Press One-arm Overhead Press		
Pull	Bat Wing	Pullup Row	One-arm TRX Row	Push Press/Jerk	Squat Snatch
Hinge	Glute Bridge with AB Hold	Hip Thrust Rack DLs Goad Bag Swing	Hill Sprints Stadium Steps Skipping Bounding High Knee Work	Swings	Clean & Jerk
Squat	Goblet Squats 6-point Rocks	Double KB Front Squat The Full Squat Family	Bear Hug Carries Bear Crawls Bear Hug Carries with Monster Walk	LitviSprints/LitviSleds	
Loaded Carry	Farmer's Walk Horn Walk	Prowler Car Push	One-arm Carries: Suitcase Carry Waiter Walk Rack Walk		

The two arrows lead us from the hip thrust, rack DL and goat bag swing outward toward the two Olympic lifts. We move from loaded hinging to more and more aggressive explosive movements. These build "snap."

The red boxes are our work capacity movements. Hill sprints revolutionized my coaching in both American football and track and field. They are exhausting, exhilarating and safe.

The red boxes reflect the best of the movements I have found for safely building work capacity. Something as simple as pushing a car a few blocks might forever change the way you think about training.

When I first started doing Highland Games, my overall training and performance improved. Later, through the lens of experience, I realized that HGs made me refocus snapacity.

For training that odd "inner tube" strength needed for so many sports, I use the bear hug carry with mini-bands around the socks to develop anaconda strength. Drive the heels apart and feel the body try to fill in the gaps with internal pressure.

During my workshops, I often include an old Soviet picture: The hammer throwers pick up a partner to practice turns holding his friend bear-hug style. Just imagine the internal pressure!

The concept of snapacity works well with the traditional method of using a bow and arrow image. The bow and arrow is an excellent concept for teaching the throws. When I first learned a correct kettlebell swing, I was amazed that the "hinge/plank" was so similar as in throwing. Quickly, I added appropriate swing work to my thrower and jumper training.

Dr. Stu McGill's insight of the "Hammer and Stone" helped me go even deeper with this concept. Stu is a genius…and a friend. His clarity in training athletes has changed my entire approach to performance. He pounds, and this might be funny in a moment, on twin concepts that make an athlete great:

Hammer

Stone

Hammer is using the hammer. BAM!!! To jump high, you hammer the earth hard and Coach Isaac Newton takes over. Action…REACTION!

Training the hammer is snapacity training. These movements develop the hammer in the weightroom:

Basic skipping, bounding and sprinting

Hill sprints and stadium steps

Swings

Rack deadlifts

The Olympic lifts

But, and this is the great insight of McGill, when you hammer the ground, your body can't sag off and become floppity floopity. Your COLUMN, the area between your knees and neck (I don't like the word "core") must be STONE. If the energy wobbles off in your body like jelly, you lose the pop, the spring, the hop.

For years, I had been circling around this concept of stone. I knew with Quadrant II people—collision sports and collision occupations—we do some exterior callusing, some armor building. It has worked to get football players ready to play football and wrestlers to wrestle.

Anaconda strength movements teach an athlete internal pressure. This internal pressure allows us to throw the hammer and caber or stop an opponent from advancing.

So, I took Stu's insight into Stone to my three As to help develop athletes: armor, anaconda and arrow.

Armor building
The need for exterior stone.

These are the calluses on your hands when you lift. It is the ability of the nose NOT to bleed daily in wrestling practice. It is the ability to handle the stress on your skin.

Anaconda strength
The internal inner tube pressure.

It's the bracing of the body to deal with load—the ability to turn your body into stone from the inside.

Arrow
This is the ability, in an instant, to turn your body into stone.

Blocking in throwing or kicking are great examples—bow and arrow is the classic way to explain stretch-reflex.

You hit hammer, lock down your stone and put your chin on the rim of the basketball hoop.

Armor building can be trained with tumbling and kettlebells.

My favorite easy-to-teach stone movements are:

Bear hug carries

Goblet squats with curls

Double KB cleans and front squats

Suitcase carries, rack walks and waiter walks

Obviously, a foundation in the Three Ps prepares us for the advanced levels of Hammer and Stone.

For the performance athlete, the Three Ps knit together constantly in training and competition. Preparation must reflect the needs for a high level of moving planks, great strength and explosive ability (point, push, snaP).

A coach must have a full toolkit for training both snap and work capacity.

This, of course, leads to snapacity.

Chapter 47
Do It or Diet

A good friend, Amy Stewart Tracy, was telling me something that bothered me: Her nutritionist stated flatly that exercise has almost nothing to do with FAT loss. I tried to counter that argument and realized:

I have been wrong. A long time.

It's true: FAT loss happens in the kitchen. FAT loss happens when you shop, chop, slice and dice.

If you are a personal trainer and you convince all your clients to eat protein and veggies at every meal and drink only water for the next two or three years, you will become the most important name in the fitness industry. Your clients will have unparalleled success in body composition.

And, the exercise we insist upon doing might have little value. *The British Journal of Sports Medicine* says it clearly:

> "…(M)embers of the public are drowned by an unhelpful message about maintaining a 'healthy weight' through calorie counting, and many still wrongly believe that obesity is entirely due to lack of exercise. This false perception is rooted in the Food Industry's Public Relations machinery, which uses tactics chillingly similar to those of big tobacco. The tobacco industry success-

fully stalled government intervention for 50 years starting from when the first links between smoking and lung
cancer were published. This sabotage was achieved using
a 'corporate playbook' of denial, doubt and confusing the
public.

"Coca Cola, who spent $3.3 billion on advertising
in 2013, pushes a message that 'all calories count'; they
associate their products with sport, suggesting it is ok to
consume their drinks as long as you exercise. However
science tells us this is misleading and wrong. It is where
the calories come from that is crucial. Sugar calories promote fat storage and hunger."

https://bjsm.bmj.com/content/49/15/967

Even when you smash evidence in my face, I still think exercise has a role. But, I have the same blinders everyone else has:
I KNOW exercise is "good for you," so it must help in FAT loss.

But, maybe it doesn't.

Certainly, we have gone too far in claiming exercise incin-
erates FAT "right off your body." Now, with various cryotherapy
and cold treatments, we can use extreme cold to melt fat off the
body, so we seem to be going in two directions at once.

At workshops, I spend quality time walking people through
a system of approaching training to help people make better
choices and save the precious drops of self-discipline so they can
focus on better food choices.

Then, about half way through this talk…

The hands go up. I know what the question is going to be;
it's always the same question. It's about FAT loss.

But first, let's rewind and pick up at the beginning of the
talk. I use the system I discussed in *Now What?*, my attempt to
teach people the keys to successful performance.

That last word, performance, is the first of many issues. The key issue can be summed like this: steno symbols. The idea of "steno" is so common, so much a part of our lives, you might not even notice it.

We have all had the experience of hearing about Bob and suddenly become terribly worried, only to discover that the person was talking about ANOTHER Bob...not the one you were thinking about originally.

When I talk about health, longevity, fitness and performance, most people have the preconceived notion that I am talking about this Bob, but, in truth, I am talking about ANOTHER Bob. I'm an O lifter, but people hear "Mr. Universe."

Health—and I use the definition from Phil Maffetone—is the optimal interplay of the organs. If you are disease-free and your blood profile numbers are well lined up, you are basically healthy.

And that's it. Health doesn't mean six-pack abs or slamming over a seven-footer. It means your body is doing its thing...well.

Longevity is an issue of both quality and quantity. Most people focus on a number, like living to 100 years. The longer I see friends and family endure the ravages of life-ending illnesses, the more I realize that quality of life is far more important than the longevity number.

As we often say in grief therapy, there is going to be something on your grave—your name followed by your birth year and the year of your death.

Let's look at mine:

Daniel Arthur David John

1957–2136

And, the key, of course, is that hyphen, the "–" that tells the story of your life. Longevity is both quality and quantity.

Next, I discuss fitness.

"Fit" comes from the Old Nordic word "to knit." I believe strongly that a "fit person" is well knitted. Well knitted in social life, mental health, financial status, and community and personal matters. Fitness is simply the ability to do a task, as we learned from Darwin. If the task is sitting in a chair watching TV, many of us are fit.

Performers perform. The lights come on, your name is called and you perform. It can be a sport, a song, a dance or fill in the blank. Failure is public; success is passing. Tomorrow, someone better is going to be trying to get you knocked off the pedestal.

I have tools to help you. Shark habits—one bite and its gone—deals with everything that comes along that is a binary decision. Off/On, Yes/No. Choose. Check the box.

Then, move on.

I use shark habits in every aspect of life. These are my basics:

> *16 of the same polo shirt*
> *Six pairs of Barbell jeans*
> *Six pairs of Nike Frees*
> *Open an email, answer it.*
> *Open mail, deal with it.*
> *Shopping list/menu*
> *Household chores lists*

Dinner Menu

> *Monday: Steak, salad*
> *Tuesday: Viking enchiladas*
> *Wednesday: Irish jambalaya*
> *Thursday: Breakfast for dinner*
> *Friday: Hang and graze with our friends*
> *Saturday: Open (family meal usually)*
> *Sunday: Whatever was on sale or cool at the store*

Chore List

> *Monday: Dark laundry*
> *Tuesday: White laundry*
> *Wednesday: Bathrooms*
> *Thursday: Garbage*
> *Friday: Nothing special*
> *Saturday: Bedrooms and living room*

I don't spend ANY time thinking about what to wear. It's a black polo and jeans day...every day. While others are sorting through the closet, Bruce, the Shark from *Jaws*, showed up and gave me my outfit. I don't use any brain space to make decisions.

For ongoing things that are important to me, I use pirate maps. This is Pat Flynn's term for a simple idea: Instead of a long, drawn-out discourse, imagine a pirate map.

> *Go to St. John's Island.*
> *Find the white coconut tree and walk five paces west.*
> *Dig down six feet.*
> *Find the buried treasure.*

Done.

For most people, I give them this pirate map:

1. Honor your sleep ritual (make coffee, prep your supps, etc, then sleep)

2. Fast and focus (be grateful and drink coffee!)

   Eliminate (to-do list!)

   Exercise(fundamental human movements; sport training, walking, whatever)

   Eat: Like an adult (protein, veggies, water)

3. Repeat the Three Es.

4. Then, Three Ls:

   Live, laugh, love

My personal goal—to dance at my granddaughter's wedding—involves this pirate map:

1. Sleep ritual: Make coffee for the morning. Supplements. Make tomorrow's to-do list (from Robb Wolf)

2. Wake up and be grateful. (from Pat Flynn)

3. *One Moment Meditation* (app on my iPhone)

4. Daily work on Original Strength and Easy Strength (from Tim Anderson); ruck once a week (from Mike Provost); hypertrophy and 30/30 as appropriate.

5. Eat eight different veggies a day (from Josh Hillis)

6. Live, laugh, love

People are always asking about peaking, planning and programming. I rarely see programs finished, peaks peaked or plans followed. I just stick to pirate maps and let the day-to-day success bring me to where I need to be for my goal.

As I often repeat to my audiences, I use Jim Gaffigan's Mexican food solution for programming:

> *Mexican food's great, but it's essentially all the same ingredients, so there's a way you'd have to deal with all these stupid questions.*
>
> *"What is nachos?"*
>
> *"Nachos? It's tortilla with cheese, meat, and vegetables."*
>
> *"Oh, well then what is a burrito?"*
>
> *"Tortilla with cheese, meat, and vegetables."*
>
> *"Well then what is a tostada?"*

"Tortilla with cheese, meat, and vegetables."

"Well then what i-"

"Look, it's all the same s--! Why don't you say a Spanish word and I'll bring you something."

For you, YES, a VERY special program, just for YOU: push, pull, hinge, squat, loaded carry and something else!

Her? Yes: push, pull, hinge, squat, loaded carry and something else!

Him? Well, of course: push, pull, hinge, squat, loaded carry and something else!

Oddly, this is true in so much of life. I argue that the Four Fs—Finance, Fitness, Food and Friends—all come down to the same "truths:"

Little and often over the long haul

Focus on quality

Foundations first

Master the basics

I use these tools in training for performance. Basically, it works like this:

1. We focus on PERFORMANCE…achieving the goal under the spotlight.

2. Shark habits empty the brain pan of "stuff."

3. Pirate maps, for most athletes, are about five items… at MOST.

4. Programs...well, they are the path toward ONE MOMENT! (Saturday, June 7, 9 am, Seattle)

5. Principles are the focus...the one who masters the principles wins.

"Principle" comes from the root "to take first." In my world, it is very simple. As a throws coach, "Throw far" is the principle. Whatever works, works. We focus on repetitions; we focus on arousal control and we strive for perfect technique and a lot of strength.

For American football, John Heisman taught us to "block, tackle and fall on the ball." It really hasn't changed since he wrote that in 1931.

This is why it is so easy to have my job—to be a strength coach. Basically, these are the principles:

1. Standards—*are you up to the standards?*

2. Gaps—*are you doing push, pull, hinge, squat, loaded carry and sixth movement?*

"Everything else" comes from the actual sport work.

And, then the hands go up...

"Um, what about FAT loss???

We all knew this was coming!

FAT loss is number one...with most people, most conversations. It is the background buzz of this millennium.

Actually, that's not true. Most people only talk about WEIGHT loss. That's why I use all caps talking about FAT loss. I tell people all the time when they ask me about weight loss: Let me cut off your leg.

You WILL lose weight!!!

If you want money in the fitness industry, make FAT loss claims. Sell FAT loss. FAT loss is a mine of pure gold. Chocolate-covered gold.

I repeat this story often: Art De Vany was giving a workshop and, of course, a hand went up: how do you get rid of FAT?

Art De Vany, "Don't get FAT in the first place!"

Fat accumulation is due to too many food choices too many carbs too many calories, and a business industry and body designed to want to eat more…and more…when food is available.

FAT loss happens in the kitchen.

FAT loss is not burpees, lunges or "going for the burn."

De Vany was right. And, the audience wanted to kill him.

Recently, I was at a conference in Norway and the nutritionists trotted out study after study that ruined the day(s). The research is, at best, disheartening. The obesity crisis is just beginning to show the cost in both human life (and lifestyle) and the soaring financial issues.

How do we get rid of FAT? There are three ways to look at it:

First, the "FAT loss happens in the kitchen" position. It is usually stated as: "95% of fat loss is nutritional." This is what my friend Amy learned. And here I actually have a hard time defending exercise…which is what I will be doing in just a moment.

Let me add one thing and this is the truth:

"It's not what you eat, it's what you ATE."

Second, let's just call this our experience—some kind of caloric restriction and inefficient exercise. I agree with most modern nutritionists here: all diets work. Wait, check that. *Adherence* to all diets works.

Next, when it comes to exercise, not being able to float, glide or roll is the key. To get exercise to burn fat is to find those things that are not easy, not smooth. Be as inefficient as possible.

Third, contact Josh Hillis. Here is what he taught me:

1. *Food journal*

2. *Lifting weights up to a standard*

3. *HABITS*

Listen: It's habits. It's always habits. I call them shark habits and pirate maps and everyone thinks I'm joking. I'm telling you—and this might hurt—your habits got you FAT.

Mastering a food journal shows you "It's not what you eat, it's what you ATE."

Lifting weights up to a standard requires repetition.

Everything in life is habits. Knowing the root of the word "habit" might help: It was originally the clothes you wear. I wear a black polo and blue jeans EVERY day. That habit, wearing my habit, makes it easier to follow my other habits.

I make it a habit to make puns in everything I say or write.

When it comes to eating, I always want to answer first:

"Seriously?"

I stand by four words: Eat like an adult!

There, that's enough. For details, eat the following: veggies and lean protein. Drink water.

Train in a fasted state sometimes. Stay hungry after meals sometimes.

That's about it.

So, I came up with a way to help people understand the role of exercise and nutrition:

Do it! and diet

For health, the do-it list is quite short: See you doctor annually, your eye doctor annually and your dentist two to three times a year. I also donate blood and get a mini-physical every time I volunteer.

Diet? Eat like an adult.

Yup. That's it.

For longevity, the do-it list swells a bit. The research—see Bill Guillford's amazing book *Spring Chicken* for details—isn't unbearable:

Do 100 minutes of exercise a week
Do fast…on occasion.
Do wear seat belts and helmets
Do learn to fall and recover

Let me add one "don't" for the do-it:

Don't TRY to be stupid!!!!

Diet seems to be a factor in longevity, but it again comes down to veggies. Eat like an adult. Now, yes, it is true that coffee and red wine might be helpful for longevity, as well as the prescription drug Metformin, but your DNA and life-long habits of good choices are probably more important.

For fitness, be careful of decision fatigue. If you have a task you need to do, find the quickest, most efficient path toward the completion of the task. Ask someone who has done it for feedback and advice. Don't try a million things; stick to the foundations, the basics.

For diet, stick to eating like an adult. Stick to it.

For performance, focus on the principles; literally, "prin" comes from the root for first and "ciple" is from the same root as capture. Principles allow you to "take first."

Find the keys to your task and repeat them, repeat them, repeat them. Diet, by the way, simply doesn't matter, if it doesn't matter. If it does, like physique contests and the like, you better have this dialed in. Sorry…it is that simple.

So, yes, Amy's nutritional coach is right. Put your hands down because no, I don't have an exercise solution for FAT loss. At best, five percent of FAT loss success will come from the gym, pool or track.

For the FAT loss client, there are two truths:

It's not what you are going to eat, it's what you ate.
FAT loss happens in the kitchen.

Except this is NOT true. As little as TWO weeks with less exercise (not none) changed people's system to pre-diabetic conditions. *The New York Times* recently reported this about a fascinating short-term study:

The subjects were healthy adults who normally walked about 10,000 steps a day. For two weeks they had to limit their steps to 2,000, then return to their regular 10,000-step routine.

"The results proved to be consistent if worrisome. The volunteers almost all had developed what the scientists called 'metabolic derangements' during their two weeks of being still. Their blood sugar levels had risen, insulin sensitivity declined, cholesterol profiles became less healthy, and they had lost a little muscle mass in their legs while gaining fat around their abdomens."

"Thankfully, most of these derangements were reversed once the men and women became active again."

"But for unknown reasons, a few of the volunteers did not return to quite the same level of exercise they had engaged in before. They now completed fewer minutes of vigorous activity each week than previously and had some slight but lasting symptoms of insulin resistance, even after two weeks of moving normally."

Folks, "metabolic derangements" might be the best phrase ever. This is why exercise should NOT be shunted to the back alleys of FAT loss. Exercise does so much more than just burn calories.

A follow-up study with just participants over 65 years proved even more frightening:

"Like the adults in the other study, these older volunteers quickly developed worse blood sugar control during their two weeks of barely moving. Insulin resistance climbed. Some developed changes in muscle tissue indicating that they might soon begin to lose muscle mass, and a few had to be removed from the study because they had edged into full-blown Type 2 diabetes after becoming inactive."

I'm not sure it can be clearer: The role of exercise in FAT loss is to save us from metabolic derangements. Exercise is a key to keeping the body's systems from descending into disease.

So, YES!

Yes, exercise plays a MIGHTY role in FAT loss.

If you can remember these two pillars:

Don't get FAT in the first place.

It's not what you eat, it is what you ATE.

And, like many of us, if you do "wake up FAT one day," follow this sane advice:

Find a way of eating that you can stick to for the rest of your life. All diets work; adherence is the key. Find a way of eating that fits your life, your habits and your worldview.

Exercise, as simple as daily walking, is going to keep you from metabolic derangements! I'm not sure there are enough exclamation points to highlight this point.

So, put your hands down, stand up and walk out the door. Find a café 5,000 steps away and order a veggie omelet with a side salad. Depending on the time of day, have coffee or red wine. Enjoy the meal and walk home.

Repeat.

Exercise HAS a role in FAT loss.

Chapter 48
Connecting the Dots

The actual name of one of my favorite books is *The Hobbit or There and Back Again*. The *There and Back Again* part is easy to forget when someone takes a small book and makes it into three over-the-top films.

Many of us seem to return to our original starting point when we do things like strict diets. After a few days of rigorous not eating, it's not uncommon to fall off the wagon and actually end up fatter than when you began.

I was told once:

"Be sure to take a picture on the day you start your first diet...
you will never look that good again!"

The role of the coach is to pick up our passengers (clients and athletes) and, ideally, get them to a destination. We can summarize the job as:

Here to there. A–B.

We draw the line from dot A to dot B.

It's a bit like what Johnny Cash tried to teach us: "I walk the line." In a perfect world, we would always walk from A–B, but we all know better.

I think I can sum coaching as:

The athlete strives to walk from A–B.

The coach madly leaps, dives, sprints, pushes and prods in all directions keeping the athlete striving to walk from A–B.

When you work with elite athletes, the joy of "there" might be a golden moment of their lives. As we discussed, some athletes might also shrug and ask, "Is that all there is?" With most people concerned with fat loss, it would nice to remain "there" forever.

The statistics look grim about that permanent weight loss.

There are times as a coach, teacher and trainer that I feel I just work with failure. Not necessarily "failures," but people who strived for the prize and came up short. Often, those who fail in this goal seem to widely succeed in so many others.

It's a tough lesson to learn, but it is true. I learned this truth the hard way…through failure.

And success. Lessons learned from success are nice. Lessons learned from failure are branded on your heart and soul.

What helps me deal with this contrast of successful failure and failing success is a concept from religious studies. Since I am such a fan of community, this concept resonates with me at my bones. Remember: I invite at least 30 people to Thanksgiving Dinner.

It is two kinds of communities:

Vertical community

Horizontal community

Here is the basic point as I explained it in a blog post:

One of the basic lectures I give in my religious studies classes involves an important concept about community. Everyone seems to appreciate what I call the "horizontal community."

That would be the friends, family, church, group, team, society, brotherhood, sisterhood or whatever you belong to today. It can be as personal as blood relatives or simply bytes in an internet forum.

What most people miss is the vertical community. Most often, the vertical community involves a story and, sadly, most of us forget ours. The vertical community are those people, those events and those tiny connections that knit together at some point and make the sublime to one generation seem obvious to another.

To truly understand the concept of strength and conditioning, one needs to dig deep into their own personal story and personal history.

See Appendix Four for the full text.

Two friends, Chris Long and Jim Markosian, often note that I can't begin a discussion without saying, "In the beginning." With weightlifting, I start with Milo and the story of how he picked up his bull every day as the bull progressively got heavier.

So, I begin with Milo.

Then, I march you through the insights of literally dozens of names who have impacted all of us in so many ways. I like to finish with the names of all those people who continue to embrace and challenge me daily.

I am thankful.

My vertical community certainly includes my coaches, like Dick Notmeyer and Ralph Maughan, but it also includes those authors, gym rats and athletes who shaped our strength community. I don't know all their names, but I appreciate their input. I am thankful.

It also includes my mom and dad. They sacrificed so much for my education. I am thankful.

Not only is my intentional community—my friends at the morning workouts—part of the horizontal community, but so are my family, both near and far.

I also appreciate the people who come to the workshops, sit next to me at conventions and laugh along at the craziness of our fitness field.

I am thankful.

As a coach, I have carried many from A–B.

My communities have carried me.

For those I have carried and for those who carried me: I am thankful.

That is the great lesson of 40 years with a whistle.

Appendices

Appendix One
Free Will

Excerpted from Never Let Go, Chapter One

Free Will and Free Weights

I've said it a million times: There aren't any secrets to training. I would've stood by that too, until the single greatest moment in the history of strength training and fitness happened to me. I finally discovered the secret. I tend to joke about secrets and gimmicks quite a bit. You know what I'm talking about:

- Lose 10 pounds overnight with the diet of the stars!

- Instantly increase your arm size!

- Use psycho power to get women and money!

True, I bought all those products, and I decided to use them all at once. They all worked! I lost my money overnight. Whoops.

No, I'm not talking about a real secret here, the answer to a lot of the crazy issues that plague probably everyone. The funny thing is, I'm serious. There's something you have in short supply that you need to cherish. It's the difference between making your fitness, strength and body composition goals…and not making those goals.

Before I divulge it, let's look at a few examples.

New Year's Eve—A drunk walks over to you, spilling a glass of merlot down your arm and on the Persian rug. "You know what?" he slurs. "Tomorrow I'm laying off the booze, going on Atkins, and I'm going to work out every day, just like I used to. Stopping smoking too. This is probably one of the last times you'll see me smoking."

We all know what's going to happen. Most of us (raise your hands, please) have made a New Year's resolution that didn't exactly work out as we planned:

"I will eat low carb."

"I will work my legs first every workout."

"I will stop looking at inappropriate things on the internet."

What's strange is resolutions are usually good ideas.

Let's be honest, saving the first 10 percent of a paycheck, cutting back on carbs or sweets or whatever, exercising more, or being kinder to humanity are all pretty good things to try to do.

Next example: With my old job I did a lot of prison ministry. Prison is nothing like the movies or television shows, at least in my experience. Sure, there are deep dark bad places in every prison, but most of what I saw wasn't unlike hotels I stayed in while visiting New Jersey and Florida. I sat on a couch once and had a long conversation with a very nice guy without any bars or guards nearby. I later found out he'd killed six people one night...the last just to see someone squirm. He seemed like a wonderful guy.

One of the things people talk about is how buff prisoners are. "Ah, to have the discipline of a multiple offender," you might think.

And there it is. That's the insight I had recently. All of the connections finally linked up, and in a flash...I got it.

306

Got what?

The secret to success in all of our goals.

Don't laugh, don't undervalue, and certainly don't underestimate what I'm about to say. The secret to success is free will.

Free will? Sure, call it what you want: self-discipline, habits, free agency or my personal favorite, no other choice. Now listen, this isn't a religious discussion, but there's a great story that illuminates the concept. By the way, the story is absolutely true. I verified it.

> *There was a very religious man who lived in a flood plain. One year, a big flood hit and he stood on his porch watching the water go by.*
>
> *A neighbor came by driving a motorboat. "Hop on, friend, and I'll take you to safety!"*
>
> *"No, thanks," the pious man said, "The Good Lord above will save me."*
>
> *Later, while sitting on his roof, the sheriff came by in a rowboat. "Here you go, hop in!" he said.*
>
> *"No, thanks. The Good Lord above will save me," the man replied.*
>
> *As the water rose higher, a helicopter dropped a rope ladder down to him and offered him a lift off the top of his home.*
>
> *"No, thanks. The Good Lord above will save me."*
>
> *He drowned. Standing in line waiting to get into heaven, the Good Lord walked by him. The man said, "Why didn't you save me?"*
>
> *The Good Lord answered: "I sent a motorboat, a rowboat, and a helicopter. What did you want?"*

This is a true story and I'm standing by it.

What's the point? We all know we need to take the bull by the horns, pull ourselves up by our bootstraps— add any cliché comment you were told as an adolescent to spur you to get off your computer chair and walk over to the gym and spend the next hour doing nothing but every exercise you hate.

Or, you can keep reading this article and eat some of those chips that are bad for you, but since they come from Hawaii must be pretty good after all, so eat a few more, then sneak over to those websites that we swear we don't look at. Or whatever.

Every great motivational speaker from Napoleon Hill to Earl Nightingale to Anthony Robbins will always dedicate a large amount of time and energy to the concept of self-discipline. My college coach, Ralph Maughan, had a saying for his athletes: Make yourself a slave to good habits.

And you know, to a group of Division One track and field athletes who all have at least a 3.0 GPA, that's a nice bit of advice, worthy of discussion. Of course, that audience was a little different than maybe most of us deal with during a typical day.

So, why does the guy in prison have a better body than you? It's because we have just a little bit of free will. How do I know? People actually research this stuff and then I steal it.

Let me take a quick detour for a second and see if I can explain it.

I shave daily. I recently changed from shaving cream to shaving gel, but I'm going back to cream. Why? Well, with shaving cream, as you get to the bottom of the can, it splutters and spats and spits cream for about a week before it goes absolutely empty. The first time you get shaving cream spit in your eye, you mentally note, "I need to buy more shaving cream." In that week, you have three or four opportunities to get spat on as a reminder to buy more cream.

With gel, you're standing in the shower and you press the button and...nothing. Yesterday, a face full of gel; today you're trying to shave with Dial soap lather and all day your friends comment about your dry, bleeding face. Your coworkers might think you got into another bar fight, like you told them last time.

You see, free will is like shaving gel. It seems you have a one-can allotment and it just runs out without warning.

Researchers did an interesting test on people: Everyone was asked to do a series of complex tests without any chance of success. They timed how long people would try the task before giving up—like maybe a Rubik's cube that had been made impossible to finish.

When the next group came in, they offered everybody cookies. Those who said, "No thanks, watching my diet," or whatever, would quit the impossible task far earlier than those who said, "Whatever, give me a cookie."

Why?

My friends, you basically have about one can of Free Will. It you use it saying no to cookies, you won't have any left for impossible tasks, like quitting smoking or whatever resolution you picked in a carb-induced haze sometime during the holidays.

Sorry. One can.

That's why our friend in prison has a better body than you. When your alarm goes off, do you get up? Why? Could you miss class if you're a student? Maybe. Well, then, getting up out of your toasty bed will eat up some of your free will.

Can you miss work? Sure, but then, you know, something happens, like you miss the Henderson report and the Dingwinglies fall of the Schimshank and whatever the else bad happens to you at work.

Do you have kids? Now we're really talking about losing free will, fast and furious. Children will drink every ounce you have before you send them off to school. Trust me, I don't have any personal choice at all!

Who makes your meals or chooses what place you'll eat? You. There goes some of that decision-making ability.

As decision after decision hits you throughout the week, the reservoir of free will you'll have on hand to spend at the gym begins to fade. When I originally wrote my *Four Minutes to Fat Loss* article, a number of people asked me, "If it's so good, why don't you do it every day?"

My answer was always clouded:

You do it and get back to me.

Why wouldn't I do it every day? To push myself that hard after a long day of commuting kids back and forth to school, choir and volleyball, while the dog is puking next to the broken toilet, while the lady from the reunion wants to know if I can get there early to help hang crepe paper, after I get the truck back from getting new tires, before I mow the lawn, and while the boss still needs that report...I'm happy to hide in the gym.

Lots of us know these workouts. We go into our gym and hide. I call it arm day!

Our buddy in prison? Does he decide when to go to bed? No. Get up? No. Eat three times a day? No choice. Not only no choice on what to eat, but usually our friend doesn't have to do anything to prepare the meal. Quiet time? I don't even know what that is.

Day after day after day, decisions I take for granted are just not a part of the prisoner's life. What does he have control of anyway? His workouts. That whole can of free will—literally bottled up inside of him for days, maybe even weeks, months and years in some cases—can be used for training. And train he does.

You decide on 10 New Year's resolutions?

Here's my unsolicited gambling odds: no chance. If you only make one resolution? Maybe you'll achieve it. It could happen, you know, with the right motivations.

Why am I confident you'll fail? My point: You have only so much in the can of Free Will, and most of us waste the bulk of our self-determination, grit or free choice long before we can muster up the energy to deal with nicotine fits, carb cravings and the three-minute wait to get on the treadmill.

Listen, it's easier to just eat the cookie. I know, I've been there. Hi, I'm Dan and I'm the guy who knows carbs are bad for me, but I eat them anyway so leave me alone in my corner to sob.

How can we save more of the can of free will so we can focus on our workouts or really push that diet? Let's be honest, look at Chris Shugart's Velocity Diet. Just look at it. Pretend for a moment you could do that for a month. Just pretend. I did and immediately came up with 400 events I couldn't bring a protein drink to, even one mixed with flax seeds.

Here are three ideas to help you get more free will out of your can.

Number One

Camp. I'm serious. Each year, I spend up to four weeks in training camps. Somebody wakes me up, somebody makes my meals, somebody else pushes me to work out, somebody else tells me when to put the lights out. You know, I work hard during those weeks.

How can I reinvent camp for my normal life?

A couple of things leap out at me. First, if nutrition is so important and it's my biggest trouble spot, is it possible to sublet my meal planning? One day a week, should I do all the cooking and bag and freeze some meals? Can I hire someone to do all the cooking? Should I buy a lot of pre-made meals? Or, should I just stock all my shelves with really good things…and only eat in appropriate places?

Really, none of these ideas are bad. Not great, but not bad either. In the area of training, we all know what the value of a personal actually is: It's someone making sure you do something in the allotted training time. I'm not ripping on trainers here; I'm just pointing out the single greatest value of a personal trainer is someone else's will replacing your own. That psycho, whistle-blowing high school coach you had might've been on to something.

Number Two

I'm working with a young woman, Edna, who recently did a pretty impressive thing: She quit smoking, lost a lot of body-weight, stopped partying so much and decided to recommit to her lifelong goals. As of this writing, she hasn't smoked in a long time, has lost a lot of weight, and is in the fog of love with a very decent guy.

Her secret? She took on one task at a time, but only with a large community effort behind her. What does that mean? It means she told everybody her goals. I mean that, gentle reader... everybody. Friends, people at parties, coworkers and people in the mall looking for a new microwave all heard the same chorus.

"Hey, I'm quitting smoking, so if I say I need a smoke, tie me down and don't let me smoke 'cause I'm quitting and I'm not going to smoke, so don't let me smoke." Hey, you aren't going to let that person smoke. Leave, yes; smoke, no.

Next, Edna joined Weight Watchers. She goes to the meetings. She talks about things. She talks to other people in Weight Watchers and she lets everybody know she's in Weight Watchers.

I'm telling you, you can save your precious free will by re-cruiting a vast army of people willing to give up their free will to bolster yours. How? Tell them, ask them, beg them for help. Does your family know your goals? Coworkers? Professionals? Mail-man? Start putting it out there.

There was a time in my youth where I could go to a party filled with booze and an assortment of products from Columbia and no one would offer me a share. Why? I was dumb enough to let everyone know I was going after something that drugs and booze would only hinder.

I was joking about the dumb-enough part. I'm proud of those decisions.

Number Three

I don't like this one, but it works: Whittle down your life a little. I've always told my daughters you can measure a good relationship by the way you expand rather than contract. What am I saying? Maybe you do too much.

I'm guilty; I love leaping into things. In fact, it's a rare Fall that I don't have a conflict on a weekend between a Highland Games, flag football or Olympic lifting!

Whittle. I was at a party with a guy recently who told me he couldn't get back into training. Six minutes later he asked me about a list of television shows I'd never watched, and a few I'd never heard of. By God, this guy watched *Joey!*

Whittle that TV habit and the time will appear for training. Don't TiVo a bunch of crap so you can watch it faster without commercials! When I was growing up, we never watched CBS; we didn't get the station where we lived. You know, I never missed a thing. Now, we have 10,000 stations and think there's always something better on another channel.

Whittle. Drunk all weekend and go to work hung-over? Whittle away a little there. Whittle away your workouts too. Why does anybody do the innie and outie thigh machines?

Really, why?

There you go, friends.

Once again, I offer some basic ideas, but the problem isn't so easy. Be very sparing with your little can of self-discipline, free will, or whatever word you want to toss around.

You have three options to help you make better choices:

One

Be proactive and try to find someone or some way to cut back on the options, all those deadly choices and decisions…especially in nutrition and training.

Two

Bring everybody onboard to keep an eye on you. The more personal trainers, mentors, gurus, Yodas, and Gandalfs in your life, the better. Tell everyone you know your goals and watch how much easier it is to stay on track. The crazy lady on the 814 bus might be the one person who stops you from munching on that muffin.

Three

Whittle away at all the extras. Better yet, chop away. I'm not saying disconnect with humanity, but I'd like to see you turn off the television set. Chop. Chop. Chop.

Hey, like the knight in *Indiana Jones and the Last Crusade* said, "Choose wisely."

And not very often.

Appendix Two
Getting Started as a Fitness Writer

Every so often, someone will ask me about writing. Some think it's a gift from the heavens. These people believe some of us are born writers like some of us are born to be seven feet tall.

Height, eye color and the joy of baldness are genetic. I think writing, like most sports techniques, is a skill that takes hours, days and years to just head in the right direction (write direction?).

For me, the process of writing is exactly like preparing for a contest or trying to achieve any other kind of goal.

But first, let's talk about how I got here.

My interest in writing, as everything in life, begins with a story. It was 1970 and the world was a different place. Simon and Garfunkel and The Beatles split the year before, and we hadn't even heard of Watergate yet. It's funny to think that many of the political conservatives were long-haired, dope-smoking revolutionaries back then.

In my house, we had two Vietnam vets (both had been called "baby killers" and "animals" at various times), who were dealing with the injuries of the war. The troubles nationally and internationally brewed in our home, but so did my father's first signs of lung issues and his escalating personal problems.

If you don't mind a moment of cynicism, I just realized I grew up in an ideal breeding ground for an author.

After years of very strict traditional Catholic education, my seventh grade year heralded some changes in education. We still read the Great Books and memorized everything as the pillars of education, but now we had some freedom to explore things a bit. We were given something called an "open writing" assignment.

For those of us in salt and pepper corduroy pants, white shirts and green uniform sweaters, this was stunning. We were allowed to write what we wanted to write about?

So, I wrote a piece about a situation where everything slowly gets colder and darker. The last line explains the reason:

"It turns out, I died five minutes ago."

After reading my paper out loud, my teacher, an Irish nun, said something I have never heard before: a compliment.

"Danny, you are a very good writer."

I had never heard something positive in my life, save for perhaps about my naturally curly hair.

And my only thought was: "If I was a writer, how would I pay for insurance?"

And, sadly, that's the truth.

She may not have been a fortuneteller, but she guessed the future. She was right if you consider that my books sell well, I write for several magazines and I make most of my living as a writer.

Thomas Plummer likes to joke, "Dan John is an overnight success. It just took him 45 years to do it." Sister Eugenia was right; it just took a bit of work and effort to become a born writer.

And, I can pay my insurance.

The foundation of my education is theology, some philosophy and just enough geometry to keep things clear. Each of these fields is based on a simple premise:

Givens.

In theology, if you believe in One God and something bad happens to someone good, you have a whole field of inquiry to study to help you grasp it (theodicy). Now, if your "given" is many gods and one of them doesn't like you, well, that's pretty easy to explain bad things:

That one god who doesn't like you did it!

Geometric proofs—those hated assignments from high school math—are the cornerstone of my writing. It might not always be apparent.

"Given: to prove"

When I coach, I spend a lot of time discussing people's givens. This is why we assess: Hey! This is what you are and what we're working with.

When I coach track and field, your givens are your body, your situation and your personal record. From there, we can look at improving—imProving—your performance.

When I write, I begin with the given: what is established, what do we all know, what do all agree on (basically) and what needs to be improved.

Yes, I begin first with a problem.

When writing fitness articles, the problems tend to swirl around central themes:

We are doing far too much here...
and ignoring the real problem there.

Is there a better way to teach, learn and coach this problem
(generally movements)?

Can we connect and combine things to make things
more efficient or synergistic?

That's the story and the method.

But, the real truth to being a writer is going to be sad for some aspiring authors: It's work.

I arrange my writing as job with a slavish master. Ebenezer Scrooge, before the happy ending, is a good theme for what I imagine.

Tiffini has an early day with her schedule, so we get the alarm before the sun wakes up.

I'm proactive to a fault, so the coffee is always set the night before we go to bed. I like to clear out my basic emails first and, honestly, answering a few questions is a good way to warm up the writing muscles.

One thing that really helps me is a rule I have: I don't eat anything until all the writing for the day is finished. Usually, it takes me about three hours to finish everything and by then, it's 9:30 and my intentional community is at the door. So, I "intermittent fast" daily, but it's just not eating until the work and the workout are finished.

"Not eating" is what I really do and it allows me to focus on the task at hand. I have weekly, monthly and quarterly writing commitments, so I have to get it done. There's nothing wrong with food, but ignoring it seems to make me stay much more focused.

The tradition in most religious communities is "First the fast, then the Feast." I model this daily as I crank out my columns, articles and books.

But, the grind of writing has to be balanced with the joy of reading, watching and learning.

One thing I strongly recommend for writers is continuing education of some kind.

I read a lot in the field of fitness, both online and on paper in the form of books and magazines. This can open some doors for me, of course, but what really helps is reading outside the field.

I mix older works with recent materials fairly seamlessly. It might be my Great Books background, but I find comfort in reading translations like *Gilgamesh, Beowulf* and *The Odyssey*. It's fun to mix a classic with Chad Harbach's *Art of Fielding* or Paul Murray's *Skippy Dies*. I see both of these books marching with the great themes of classics like love, death and the afterlife.

I also pull off the shelf some modern classics too, like *The Once and Future King, Dune, The Godfather* and both *Jurassic Park* books. Again, we see timeless questions and themes that support the big questions like "How many lifts should I do on the One Lift a Day Program."

In addition, I buy classes from The Great Courses. Oddly, studying the great tacticians of history seemed to help me see the difference between achieving a goal and achieving success (it's not the same thing!).

I can listen or watch great professors discuss the Arthurian legends or how to understand wine while I'm doing laundry, prepping dinner or doing any light chores.

The reading and additional coursework lights up my mind. I can suddenly see connections between coaching programs and the issues faced by history's great leaders. Let me just sum up the problem with any leadership position whether it's being a general, a coach or a teacher:

Clarity.

You might think everyone understood what you said.

They didn't.

I often joke that my model of coaching is based on the story of the leader during the French Revolution: "As soon as I find out where my people are going, I will lead them there!"

Most people don't know I had a weekly column in a newspaper for 10 years. Fortunately, the late Jack Shroeder was the proofreader.

After one of my early columns, he came up to my office and sat across from me. He never mentioned that he was the former editor of a major newspaper and that he knew John F. Kennedy.

What Jack wanted to do was make me a better writer. He told me people connect to my work because I talk about people and tell stories. He said, and I didn't get the humor at first, "People like stories and stories about people."

So, I told you my story. I told you how I got here as a writer.

Now, we need to hear yours.

Appendix Three
The Humane Burpee

My favorite kettlebell complex is the humane burpee. Dan Martin gave us this name and I can't think of a better term. You can certainly make this harder or easier, but just do the basic example first.

Be sure to follow the advice about reps on the goblet squat and pushup. We want the reps to descend as we move through the humane burpee, hence the name "humane."

Here you go:

> *15 Swings*
> *5 Goblet squats*
> *5 Pushups*
> *15 Swings*
> *4 Goblet squats*
> *4 Pushups*
> *15 Swings*
> *3 Goblet squats*
> *3 Pushups*
> *15 Swings*
> *2 Goblet squats*

> *2 Pushups*
> *15 Swings*
> *1 Goblet squat*
> *1 Pushup*

That comes out to 75 swings, 15 goblet squats and 15 push-ups. The real exercise seems to be the popping up and down for the pushups. Most of us don't take any rest at all through the workout, but feel free to stop when you need to rest.

To make it harder, just slide the goblet squats and pushups up to 10. 10–8–8–7–6–5–4–3–2–1 gives you 55 total reps and that is plenty of work for a single day....in many cases too much.

I have three other variations that have value.

I'm not sure why this is called "slurpees," but it is:

> *10 or 15 Swings*
> *5 Goblet squats*
> *10 Mountain climbers*
> *(every time the left foot hits is a rep)*

Let the goblet squats descend (5–4–3–2–1). That gives you 50–75 swings, 15 goblet squats and a lot of heart pounding.

"Hornees" are the first of our loaded carries. A horn walk is simply walking around with the 'bell on the chest. It keeps the tension high. So:

> *10 or 15 Swings*
> *5 Goblet squats*
> *Horn walk for an appropriate distance*

Again, let the goblet squats descend (5–4–3–2–1). That gives you 50–75 swings, 15 goblet squats and an interesting feeling in the whole area of muscles that squeeze things together.

Bearpees are great in groups.

10 or 15 Swings

5 Goblet squats

Bear crawl

Again, descend with the goblet squats (5–4–3–2–1).

In groups, you can have the two people be maybe 60 feet apart and they share the same 'bell. You will see a lot of racing here and the participants will quickly learn that they underestimating the crawling.

Appendix Four
The History behind "All of This"

In 1982, I received my master's degree in history. There has certainly been a lot of history since that day, but the discipline of the study of history has served me well.

I remember one of the profs warning us that the name "research" is perfect. "You will find something the very first time you begin a project. Then, you will lose it. It will take you months, maybe years to find it again. That's why we call it RE-search."

I laughed politely, left the classroom and found a few letters that would be the bulk of my thesis. I then couldn't find them again for nine months.

Not only was this true for my studies, but it is true in fitness and sports. My greatest insights have come when I discovered that what I learned the first weeks of lifting and discus throwing continue to be the greatest lessons of my career.

My academic career didn't end in 1982; I went on to study religious education in depth for the next 30-plus years. There are lessons there too. The threads that bind my approach to fitness, health and strength emerge as a tapestry that dates backward centuries and involves dozens of insights from others.

One of the basic lectures I give in my religious studies classes involves an important concept about community. Everyone seems to appreciate what I call the "horizontal community." That would be the friends, family, church, group, team, society, brotherhood, sisterhood or whatever you belong to today. It can be as personal as blood relatives or simply bytes in an internet forum.

What most people miss is the "vertical community." Most often, the vertical community involves a story and, sadly, most of us forget ours. The vertical community are those people, those events and those tiny connections that knit together at some point and make the sublime to one generation seem obvious to another.

To truly understand the concept of strength and conditioning, one needs to go back a long ways.

We can all blame Milo, I guess. Milo was a wrestler and multi-time Olympic champion in the original Games. His good friend was Pythagoras, who made life easier with his idea that, "The sum of the areas of the two squares on the legs (a and b) equals the area of the square on the hypotenuse (c)." Milo also consumed, we are told, a daily amount of 20 pounds of meat, 20 pounds of bread and 18 pints of wine.

But, that is not why we remember Milo. It was his idea to pick up a bull.

The story goes that each day he would walk out to the pasture and pick up a certain calf. The next day, he would repeat this until the bull was fully grown.

That made Milo the father of progressive resistance exercise and it's his fault that many people think that success in strength training is a straight line. I have joked many times with new lifters that if you bench 100 pounds today and only add 10 pounds a week, about a year from now you will bench over 600 pounds. It sure works on paper.

Strongmen have had an interesting role in the development of Western Civilization. We certainly love to see a Beowulf show up when we have an issue with the various Grendels in our basements, but we also know that Little John will be spending more time at the buffet rather than sharpening his shooting skills like Robin Hood. Sampson is going to kill a lot of Philistines, but his understanding of women is going to be dim, at best.

A century ago, the concept of strongman and weightlifting had congealed into the saucy mustached leopard-print wearing circus side-show attraction. With the relatively small Harry Houdini breaking handcuffs, the strongman shows evolved into lifting members of the audience, being pulled or driven over by cars and carts and the various one-arm lifts that seemed to dominate thought. But, how can you figure out who was the true strongest?

With the reawakening of the Olympics in 1896, the Olympic lifts were contested. These would be unrecognizable by today's standards with the clean and press—which was in eliminated in 1972, having the longest tenure in the Games. The one-arm dumbbell lift, lowering the dumbbells, dumbbell curls and one-arm press were all once part of the Games.

At the same time, George Hackenschmidt, a Russian wrestler and early proponent of strength training for sports and general health, began codifying the threads of lifting knowledge into a book, *The Way to Live*.

Hack's influence on the modern world of lifting comes to us in a strange direction. Down in the South Seas in Australia, a man, Percy Cerutty, was changing his life of illness and weakness and adapting his new insights into coaching track and field athletes. Cerutty asked Hack for advice and the interactions between these two knitted together the links from the old "old school" to the modern approach of what I refer to as "easy strength."

Hack outlined weight training into two parts: extensive, which would be a volume (and hypertrophy) approach to training, and intensive, a more load (and, therefore, strength) focused method.

Cerutty adapted and adopted Hack's ideas. I once summed his work:

> *Run up hills.*
>
> *Lift weights.*

Before I was born, he insisted that all athletes do the big five lifts:

1. A deadlift.

2. A form of pressing—Cerutty liked the bench press.

3. An explosive full body move—he liked the heavy dumbbell swing.

4. A form of pulling—Cerutty liked pullups and cheat curls. Cheat curls are like a power clean with a curl grip (power curls) or that bouncing heavy bar curl you see many trainees do.

5. An ab exercise—if deadlifts make you go one way; the ab exercise should strengthen you in the other.

After going heavy on these lifts with two to five sets of two to five (save for swings and abs where the reps go fairly high), you hang from a pullup bar and stretch for a few minutes.

At the same time Hack was corresponding with Cerutty, Dr. Thomas DeLorme and Dr. Arthur Watkins were working with both polio patients and injured soldiers of WWII. In 1945, DeLorme wrote a paper, "Restoration of muscle power by heavy-resistance exercises," published in the *Journal of Bone and Joint Surgery.*

In 300 cases, he found "splendid response in muscle hypertrophy and power, together with symptomatic relief" by following this method of 7–10 sets of 10 reps per set for a total of 70–100 repetitions each workout. The weight would start off light for the first set and then get progressively heavier until a 10RM load was achieved.

Over time, things changed in terms of volume. By 1948 and 1951, the authors noted:

"Further experience has shown this figure to be too high and that in most cases a total of 20 to 30 repetitions is far more satisfactory. Fewer repetitions permit exercise with heavier muscle loads, thereby yielding greater and more rapid muscle hypertrophy."

A series of articles and books followed where they recommend three sets of 10 reps using a progressively heavier weight in the following manner:

Set One—50% of 10 repetition maximum

Set Two—75% of 10 repetition maximum

Set Three—100% of 10 repetition maximum

In this scheme, only the last set is performed to the limit. The first two sets can be considered warm-ups.

In their 1951 book, *Progressive Resistance Exercise*, DeLorme and Watkins state:

"By advocating three sets of exercise of 10 repetitions per set, the likelihood that other combinations might be just as effective is not overlooked...Incredible as it may seem, many athletes have developed great power and yet have never employed more than five repetitions in a single exercise."

I love that last line.

It's easy to miss their audience: injured vets and polio victims.

My mother of Blessed Memory, Aileen Barbara McCloskey John, feared little in her life. She grew up very poor and then things got worse with the Depression. Nearly every man in her life fought in various wars and, admittedly, I did see her cry every day when her sons were in Vietnam. But, nothing frightened her except polio.

Polio was the scourge of youth and destroyer of lives to generations. The causes were thought to be swimming pools, ice cream and open windows.

And, literally overnight, with a series of vaccines, the curse ended. Modern weightlifting's ability to help victims of this disease regain the use of limbs allowed the barbell to become more mainstream in the eyes of many people.

While DeLorme and Watkins were rehabbing vets, Otis Chandler, a young Stanford shot putter and later the editor of the *Los Angeles Times*, began lifting weights to throw the shot farther. He did. He broke one of the longest standing world records and history and drew a line in the sand: If you want to keep up in shot putting, you HAVE to lift. Soon, to compete in any event in track and field, you had no option. You had to lift.

Yet, even 20-plus years later, when I first began to lift, I would hear two things:

"This stuff will make you muscle bound."

"This stuff will turn you homo."

Neither statement withstands the evidence of science or human dignity.

Yet, with polio victims regaining use of their limbs, it was obvious to many that to play in sport, you had to lift. Furthermore, the great Vladimir Janda, the physician and physical therapist, began his great insights into tonic and phasic muscles and his various "crossed syndromes."

It is also important to note is that he, too, was a victim of that terrible disease of the last century, polio. Janda's understanding that stretching (loosening) one muscle and strengthening its opposite would promote better structural integrity than just attacking one side of the equation.

One final thread: In Russia since the 1700s, local men had been testing their mettle against one another by lifting the traditional measure, the one or two pood (36 or 72 pound) kettlebell against one another. This oddly shaped device stayed on the fringe of Russian (and later, Soviet) sport through the modern age. I remember clearly the small black and white pictures of

Soviet athletes tossing, tugging, jumping and juggling these odd cannonballs with handles.

In the West, they were used alongside globe barbells until these are basically disappeared with the advance of the standardized revolving barbell. I have magazines from the 1950s that remind readers not to ignore these important training items. Then, they vanished in a blink.

Until Pavel Tsatsouline emerged on the scene.

Pavel began his coaching in America in an abandoned bank safe. He offered inexpensive community education programs and trained future Navy Special Operators with minimal equipment and lots of knowledge. When John DuCane heard him speak, the two met later for coffee and began publishing books and making kettlebells for America.

In 2004, I met Pavel and he famously told me "how to get stronger:"

"For the next 40 workouts, pick five lifts. Do them every workout. Never miss a rep, in fact, never even get close to struggling. Go as light as you need to go and don't go over 10 reps in a workout for any of the movements. It's going to seem easy. When the weights feel light, add more weight."

It was that simple. It was that easy. I followed the directions exactly and made the best strength gains of my life.

And, for whatever reason, few people have been able to follow those few simple sentences.

Easy Strength and its twin, Even Easier Strength, are the sum of the threads from Hack, Cerutty, deLorme, Watkins, Janda and the Gireveks—the kettlebell enthusiasts.

The reason it seems so contrarian today is another thread of the history of lifting: the bodybuilding and physique world. With Arnold and Jane Fonda pushing volume and the "burn" and rewarding those who want to spend time isolating every muscle, the classic methods of getting stronger with basic movements seemed to be laughable in its simplicity.

Success, honestly, is almost always the simple route. It might not be sexy to follow this approach, it might not have the gonzo, warrior, Spartan or tactical title and tribal tats, but it works.

It's hard to sell boring, but it works.

In my mind, the tradition of strength training supports the vision of reasonableness that I train in the Easy Strength fashion. What's hard to understand is this: It is a system, not just an interesting history lesson.

Appendix Five
Challenges

This is a transcript of a talk I gave a few years ago about using challenges in training.

I get a lot of questions, and they're tough to answer because in our mortal life, not all questions get answered. I'm convinced of that.

I was recently coaching a friend in the discus, and he looked at me and asked, "Why didn't you tell me this before?"

The first thought that crossed my mind was, "I didn't know it before." I thought to myself, "This is how it goes. I've been dealing with the discus since 1971. Here we are a few years later and I'm still doing the same stupid stuff."

The biggest issue I've faced lately is there's this search for perfection—perfection in programming, perfection in exercise and dieting. I think this is what holds back many of our clients from getting involved in exercise and diet programs. Every time we turn on the news, there's some new issue or question.

Recently, my mother-in-law said to me, "I hear fruit makes you fat."

I looked at her, "What?"

She said a friend of hers has a friend who had a friend who

read Tim Ferriss's book, *The 4-Hour Body*. It says you can only eat fruit once a week. Otherwise, fruit makes you fat.

I thought to myself, "No wonder people don't know what to eat." Fruit makes you fat and coffee is bad for you. Coffee is good for you. Wine is good for you. Wine is bad for you. Fish oil is the most important thing to take. Fish oil will kill you. Meat is good. Meat is bad. Eggs are good. Eggs are bad.

How would you ever decide what to do?

This is overriding issue we're dealing with, especially in fitness. I'm willing to say the average person in the world can't sit down and tell you what's in a good diet.

It's even worse in the fitness field because it's extremely difficult to develop a perfect exercise program. We're on the search for a perfect exercise program and the search for perfection is always a problem.

When my young friends ask me for advice, they say, "I want to become a strength coach. What should I major in?"

I want to laugh because they always want to major in exercise physiology, which is great. But I tell them they should probably major in philosophy because philosophy is the best major to have when you're looking at all of this conflicting information.

There's a wonderful thing called Occam's Razor. It's only a few centuries old, but the roots of it are much older. It's a very simple concept. Sometimes it's cut down to this basic point: We have a lot of options. Pick the simplest.

It is a little bit more complex than that, but here's one way to say it, "Among competing things, pick the simplest one."

What's funny is, in life that works out well sometimes. If the simplest decision doesn't work out, you can slowly progress up, as Occam explains. Sometimes we forget that.

Ludwig Wittgenstein, the philosopher I got most of my knowledge from, summarizes it like this:

If a sign is not necessary, then it is meaningless.

I thought about that again and was reminded of the great story from McDonald's where the lady poured hot coffee on herself. You might remember the outrage over it. Why did this woman get so much for that lawsuit?

McDonald's knew the coffee cups they used would fail under the worst conditions. They like to keep their coffee so hot they can serve it, let it sit and it will stay warm. The judge said, "I would like to give her the profit McDonald's makes for one day." It turned out to be, worldwide, McDonald's makes approximately $150 million dollars a day in profit on just coffee sales.

The reason I even bring up that story is every time you buy coffee now, there's a little notation on the cup that says, "It is hot."

Sometimes I think we have so many safety signs that safety signs become meaningless. There's the famous story of people going to the beach. They had all of these signs up by the water that said, "Caution, poisonous jellyfish," and they still had to take 20 tourists out of the water. Twenty tourists who could read all ignored the signs because apparently the poisonous jellyfish wouldn't have bothered them.

Going alongside Occam, of course, is Eubulides. Eubulides had this great insight called Eubulides' Heap—it's a very famous paradox. He's famous for his paradoxes.

Here's the idea of his heap. Over there, you have a heap of sand. Over here, you have a grain of sand. If I take an additional grain of sand and put it with that other grain of sand, I now have two grains of sand. We all look at it and say, "That's not a heap."

The question is, if I can keep taking a single grain at a time, adding it to that little bit of sand, when does it become a heap?

The other paradox involved a bald man.

There's nothing wrong with being bald. If I give the bald man a single hair, is he no longer bald? No. He needs an additional hair. Right? He has two hairs. Now can I say he's not bald? No. Welcome to the great paradox of Eubulides.

My point in saying this is that most people want these either/or concepts in strength, fitness or diet. People want me to look them in the eye and say, "Fish oil must be taken this much every day or you will die."

The next sentence out of my mouth is, "If you ever eat asparagus, you will die." People want that kind of "heap" answer, but it's not appropriate. It's just never right, which is why I spend so much time talking about continuums.

One final paradox of Eubulides,' and it's my personal favorite. It's the way we'll keep the robots down when they finally take over the world—you say to somebody, "Everything I say is a lie." It's the fact that I said it.

Okay, that's the paradox and welcome to it.

I've often felt I've gotten relatively close to a couple of perfect training programs. I do feel that. I had a program I'd done for years, especially when I was extremely busy. It takes about 10 minutes a day. It's called the Transformation Program.

It's based on a very simple concept that had some support at the time. If you did three sets of eight—DeLorme's famous protocol—with exactly one minute of rest, good things were supposed to happen. You were expected to get a growth hormone release. You were anticipated to increase testosterone. It's only 24 repetitions, so it didn't do a lot of damage.

Three sets of eight with one minute of rest one day a week: I would do front squats and overhead squats. Another day in the same week, I did bench press and power curls. The third workout of the week was what I called whip snatches or high-hang snatches, and the other one was clean-grip snatches. That was it—three days a week, only two or three exercises, three sets of eight—and then I would run hills once or twice a week on top of that.

It was a tremendous training program. As busy as I was for a few years, that program kept me throwing the discus and it actually kept me in good shape. Everyone now knows my next sentence: It worked so well I stopped doing it.

When I was probably at my best in my Olympic lifting career, Dave Turner, the Hercules Barbell Club coach, talked to me about something called One Lift a Day—a program that in 1968 almost every heavyweight and super heavyweight in America was doing. I still think for a big non-drug athlete, it's probably the best way to Olympic lift. It's very simple. You do…bump bump ba!…one lift a day.

On Monday, for example, I did snatches. That's all I did. On Tuesday, it was front squats.

Some may think, "I'm going to the gym and all I'm going to do is front squats?" It sounds so easy.

On Wednesday, I did cleans. On Thursday, I took off. On Friday, I did jerks. On Saturday, I always did a light total snatch and clean-and-jerk. Sunday was another off day. This is the program that got my snatch up to 314 pounds and my clean up to 402.

Both of those lifts were low because at the time, I had very spongy Olympic lifting boots. I won't mention the company's name, but they came out with a terrible product. I bought their spongy shoes and I had no idea what the problem was until later. In hindsight, I was a 110-kilo lifter—242 pounds—and I was attempting to clean around 400 pounds.

Those spongy shoes on a soft surface caused me not to be able to move my feet with heavy weights. Whenever the weights got heavy, my technique radically changed. In hindsight, I could've lifted a lot more than those numbers.

Another perfect program I had was the famous 40-Day Workout. Pavel said to me, "Pick five lifts. Do them."

It's interesting to read criticisms of the 40-Day Program.

For example, one person saw one of the programs and said, "Hey, man, you're not squatting." He went on saying these very offensive things to this poor guy doing the program.

My thought was "40 workouts." It takes about eight weeks and you do them five days a week. I've been lifting since 1965. I think it's possible to fill the rest of my life squatting hard and heavy if I take eight weeks aside to master something like the pullup.

I was shocked by how well the 40-Day Program worked. I think you're starting to get a sense of where I'm heading on this.

I have a book and a training program called *Mass Made Simple*. I'm very proud of it. It's a six-week program specifically designed to put on bodyweight. It's designed to get you bigger. It is some upper body movements, complexes and high-repetition squatting. You then spend the next two days trying to recover and getting yourself back on track.

I love the program.

People always ask, "If it's so good, can I keep doing it?" I laugh because it's hard to keep squatting high repetitions beyond six weeks. I always answer, "Oh, YOU can, but the rest of us mortals can't."

Which is it? Which one of those is the perfect program? I gave you four—Transformation, One Lift a Day, the 40-Day Program and Mass Made Simple.

Can you just constantly circuit through those four? You probably could. To repeat something I talk about in my books and something I talk about in every one of my workshops, I want to remind people about the park bench and the bus bench workouts.

The concept of park bench and bus bench comes from Archbishop George Niederauer. He described this with prayers, but it works great with weightlifting too. He said, "There are certain kinds of prayers where you want a result."

I have an injured grandnephew, so we're praying for a result. Let's get him healthy. That would be an example of a bus bench prayer. A bus bench workout is when you do something and you expect a result when you're finished.

Archbishop Niederauer also had what he called the park bench concept. It's funny because both benches are the same, but when you're waiting for a bus, you're expecting the result of a bus arriving.

Put that same bench in a park and you have almost no expectations except to sit down, enjoy the sun for a few minutes and watch a squirrel or two.

In weightlifting, fitness and most sports, we have programs based on both concepts. For the park bench, those workouts I sometimes call "punch the clock" workouts.

Similar to the 40-Day Program, there's no peak. If you feel like going heavy, you go heavy. If you don't feel like it, you don't. It's hard to explain to young people. On One Lift a Day, I was making great progress because I was never beat up. It's a park bench program.

My transformation program is very simple. The idea is to get in the weightroom three days a week, move all of the human body parts, do the fundamental human movements, break a sweat, get your heart rate up, try to add weight if you can…and walk out the door.

The Program Minimum from Pavel, which I like so much, is kettlebells swings and getups. You're probably wondering what the next day is: It's swings and getups.

And again, the next day is swings and getups.

Bus bench programs used to be a lot more popular in the fitness field. You can still find the books, and, like Charles Staley's wonderful line, "Instantly put on one inch in two weeks." Instantly in two weeks always made me laugh, but these are peaking programs.

If I put you on a peaking program and you're getting ready for the Nationals, it would be nice for that bus to come along when it's scheduled. It would be nice for you to do your best that day at the Nationals.

I say this all the time: If you fail on my *Mass Made Simple* program—you eat all of that food and you do all of those squats—and you don't put on any body mass, you can come punch me if you'd like. Bus bench programs are all the "do this" kind of programs. It's all sketched out and you follow the plan.

My interns are now preparing for a kettlebell certification. They're doing Pavel's program called The Rite of Passage. I'll tell you one thing: After you do 75 one-arm clean and presses with both arms and 75 pullups in one day, you should be a bit better with kettlebells. If not, feel free to punch somebody in the mouth. What happens is, most people fall in love with this idea.

"Which one is it, Dan? Should I work on Titanic triceps in two weeks or should I do the Transformation Program? Better yet, should I combine all of them?"

What happens, and you can see it happening—with my background in theology, but this also works well in a lot of other topics—one of the problems is this concept that the lowest kind of thinking for many things is either/or. Personally, I'm a big fan of both/and for almost every answer in life.

I have a funny story I try to keep buried in my memory. I call it the Vacaville Rain Nightmare. I was working as a bartender in college, trying to raise some money. My girlfriend at the time was visiting her sister in Vacaville. She called me at 2:00 o'clock in the morning and said, "If you love me, you'll come visit me in Vacaville."

Vacaville is about a two-hour drive and I had a motorcycle. That wasn't a problem except it was one of those weird northern California storms where the water and the rain started coming sideways off the ocean.

Being young and silly, I got on my motorcycle and drove across several bridges in a rainstorm. When I got there, she was passed-out drunk. She had done what we would now refer to as drunk-dialed me. I learned a great lesson in life that night: Either/or is not a great way to look at life.

I'm a big fan of Covert Bailey's book *Fit or Fat,* so I'm not ripping on it when I say the downside is the title. There have been times in my life where I have been not fit AND fat. There's a picture of me in 1960. I'm three years old and I have a little beer belly. I'm not fit for very much.

A few times in life, I've been fit for the task AND fat...during most of my Highland Games career. We throw a 56-pound weight for distance. We throw a 56-pound weight for height. We throw a 22-pound hammer—that's just a stick with weight. We throw cabers up to 185 pounds. Having a six-pack during those events might put you on your back for life, so I've been fit for the task AND fat.

Years ago, I cut my bodyweight down to 94 kilos—which is 209 pounds—so I could break the state weightlifting record in the 94-kilo class.

Let me tell you from the heart: That day, I was fit and I was also not fat. I was ripped.

It's also possible to be not fat and not fit. When I was in the Middle East, I lost 40 pounds in two weeks because I was able to pick up a little new friend in the drinking water. I might have looked good in some pictures, but I wasn't fit for any task.

I like both/and. I think you need park bench programs AND bus bench programs in your career.

This brings me to one of the basic issues we have throughout life. I talk about this in some of my workshops and it never seems to work well, but I'm going to tell you anyway. There are two things:

There are problems and there are mysteries.

Mysteries are those bizarre things where there's no answer in life. Mysteries are, why does somebody love you and why do you love somebody. Those are probably the most common ones. What happens after you die is a mystery. You can say, "Your body rots," and the person next to you says, "No, no. There are all of these other things that happen."

Mysteries are not what someone in the fitness field needs to worry about. We need to concentrate on problems in fitness.

Listen. I take my keys and throw them in the garbage can. Someone takes that garbage can to the curb. The city guys come by and take that garbage can to the city landfill.

Given enough money, time and effort, we can find those keys. We're going to spend a trillion dollars and have a million volunteers go through all of the landfills, but we'll find them.

That's a problem—not a mystery.

Fat loss is a problem. We all know fat loss. When I was doing a workshop at Chico State, the nutrition professor came in, laughed and said he liked my presentation. The he said, "Oh, we know how to get you to lose 17 pounds in three days. Sure, tie someone to a tree and come back in three days. Statistically, they'll lose 17 pounds."

Weight loss is just a problem. Weight loss is not a mystery.

It's not some substance that's going to be coming from a manufacturer. Let's agree to that.

If you have tight hips, it's not a mystery. It's a problem. We know dozens of ways to loosen up your hips or hamstrings. We know several ways to throw the discus farther. We know a lot of things about a lot of stuff. *These are problems.*

What's great about having problems is they tend to agitate us, which leads us to find solutions. The problem with mysteries is that mysteries agitate us and they lead us to answers, but it's not always the answers where you can sit down and say, "You know? You don't believe me. Write out a list of all the reasons you love somebody. Sit down and give the person that list. Good luck!"

Don't do it. That was a joke. Don't do it because I guarantee if you have 73 things on that list, the person you give it to is going to say, "That's all?"

Welcome to the world of mysteries, my friends.

How do we combine things like park bench programs and bus bench programs for the normal person? I think the essential key to programming is this: The majority of the time—eight to 10 months a year—you should do park bench programs.

You should do these repeatable programs. I've done them many times, but it's difficult for a lot of people to say, "I'm going to do these five movements for the next 40 days—one lift a day." It's a great program. You can keep coming in, taking care of business and continue showing up.

Between the remaining two to four months a year, I think you should do the bus bench kind of programs—becoming ready in six weeks. Look your best on New Year's Day and other eventful holidays—with these quick six- or eight-week boot camp programs, these 90-day programs that are so popular now.

I think that's fine, but what about the rest of your time— both/and? You need to have park bench programs and you need to have bus bench programs.

Recently, I read something where I felt like someone finally got it. I've been doing this interesting little combination of high-repetition swings—300 to 500 swings in a workout—with very minimal pressing, pullups and squats as the rest of the program. Lots of swings and exercises like pullups.

The next day, it's lots of swings and presses.

The following day, it's lots of swings and squats.

It's a very simple program.

The person wrote, "That's interesting, because when it's time for you to gear up for something big, you'll be in the kind of condition you can take off from."

I thought to myself, "You got it right."

Park bench programs build that base. Bus bench programs—clean it up and straighten it out.

You reach for the stars, but when you can't keep reaching. You have to turn around and keep that base going. Challenges are the easiest way for both athletes and non-athletes—maybe you don't want to look great in a bikini even though I strive to.

We'll go through a couple of simple challenges.

One of my favorite challenges is something that has disappeared off the internet. When I first started on the net, back in the late 1990s, we had a group that used to all challenge each other to what was called the 100-rep Challenge.

The first time I tried it, I decided to take the opening lift. I made it my first weightlifting move—165 pounds in the squat snatch—and did it for 100 singles. That's the key in the 100-rep Challenge. You choose a lift and do it 100 times, but all in singles.

I'll tell you something: By the end of the workout, you have absolute clarity about how to do that movement.

The next time, I took 205 pounds and did power cleans with it. That was the easiest one because power cleans aren't very exhausting. Another time, I did clean and jerks with 185 pounds. I think in some ways the hardest one I ever did—because I had just had surgery on that wrist broken—was a 100 singles in the front squat with 255 pounds.

What you can do is have one of these great one-day challenges. You can also do something like a fun run, a 10k or something along those lines.

The second idea for having challenges is what I refer to as, "Sign the check and put it in the mail."

How it works is, you're expecting something is coming up. In my case, it would be like a Highland Games or a weight pentathlon. Maybe it's a triathlon, a 10k or a half-marathon for some of you. Maybe it's one of those two- or three-day bike races. Sign up, put a stamp on the envelope and take it to the post office.

For most people those kinds of challenges do as much good as showing up to the gym three, four or five times a week, week in and week out. It turns up the volume on what you're going to do in your training.

Another idea is something I was recently challenged to do by Chris Shugart from *T-Nation*. He had a very good question. He'd been reading about how a lot of kettlebellers do 10,000 swings and he asked, "How do you do a 10,000-swing challenge?"

Steve Rowe once did 10,000 swings in one day with a 24-kilo kettlebell. That's impressive. Every minute on the minute, he did 25 swings. He rested for the remainder of the minute. Once he got to 1,000, he rested until the hour came around. Ten hours later, he had done 10,000 swings.

You can go ahead and do it that way.

I tried 1,000 swings in a day. I tried 700 swings in a day. What I discovered was 500 swings is a good number for me. The number system I use is simple. I love this idea of getting stronger by doing this repetition sequence: a set of two, a set of three, a set of five—all with the same weight. You just keep greasing that 2–3–5, 2–3–5, 2–3–5.

For hypertrophy, I like its friend—2–3–5–10, 2–3–5–10, 2–3–5–10. If you do five groups of 2–3–5–10, you've done 100 repetitions. We've done that a number of times in our training. It's stunning how it feels to have done 100 repetitions in any movement at all.

I took that number scheme and multiplied it by five. What we did for our 10,000-swing challenge was a set of 10, a set of 15, a set of 25 and a set of 50. If you do that five times, that's 500 swings. It's a very simple workout, and in a 20-day period, we got 10,000 swings done.

What most people noticed during the 20-day period was that their hamstrings loosened up quite a bit. Their posture improved. Some people said they actually noticed their waistlines diminished. I noticed that quite a bit. We also tied in one extra thing, which may or may not work for you, fasting.

We all did intermittent fasting and the reason is, we decided to work out at 9 o'clock in the morning. It's hard to do 500 swings with anything in your stomach. You only have a cup of coffee or two. Do 500 swings, maybe some pullups or something else. It doesn't matter. Then after that, you can go eat.

Ah! Magically, we're intermittently fasting.

The fourth idea about challenges is something I stole directly from Clarence Bass. Just about any artist or movie star will say the same thing: It's the annual photo shoot. There's great value in it. It might be as easy as making yourself beautiful in a bikini once a year. For example, every year on September first, you pay a photographer to take pictures of you in a swimsuit.

Every year you focus on "That's when I'll do it," so that will be your bus bench. It might take you two months to get into the best shape of your life. It might take somebody else three months or somebody else four months, but here's the great gift from doing this: Every year, you're going to figure out smarter and better ways to get yourself in that condition.

Those are four challenges that allow you to knit together both a park bench and a bus bench approach for those who don't have competitions. For the rest of us, the Nationals and the State Meet are coming up, folks.

This is all great. Challenges are one side of the coin, but there's another side I want to talk about.

I have this great belief that deprivation builds capacity.

I work with military members. These people often go days without food and sleep—particularly those who go through advanced schools, advanced certifications and advanced training. They are also sometimes at the limit of their emotional, mental and physical abilities. Once they get a couple of night's sleep, a couple hours of R&R and some food in them—the next time they do something, they're twice as good as where they were before.

Nassim Taleb, in his book *Antifragile,* has a very interesting line. He says, "While generals might fight the last battle and prepare for the last battle, the human body attempts to outfight the next great challenge."

If you survive cholera, your body's response is to survive something even bigger than cholera the next time. The body expands much larger to deprivation than it does to anything else.

This is one of my thoughts about why there was such great discus throwing in the 1960s. There were these little pockets of superlative performance at different places. You go back and you hear about their lifestyles. In the Greatest Generation, we're talking about Mom and Dad. They didn't fast when they were growing up. They simply had no food. Because they had deprivation, they were able to expand all of their qualities of life.

I always joke on this next part; I call it my Charles Dickens life. I've had a good life. I can't complain too much, so it's hard for me to come up with good examples about me ever being deprived.

One of my thoughts is when you have a good case of the stomach flu. I mean a great case of the stomach flu where you literally have your forehead on the toilet bowl just to cool off and you vomit out everything. You begin to wish you could just have a delicious glass of water. Water tastes so good. It touches your lips. You start to think, "Oh, it's so great," but if it's a great stomach flu, you vomit it right back out. The stomach flu teaches you how delicious water is.

When I first went to college, I had a hard time getting to sleep at night because the dorms at Utah State were so loud. The roommates above me believed the song *Heard It in a Love Song* had to be played as loudly as possible from about 11:00 o'clock until 3:00 o'clock in the morning—every night. These guys, who didn't get their bachelor's degrees after eight years of college, certainly had a great time, but they weren't Division One athletes.

Once I graduated from Utah State, I got a job at a cheese factory. My shift was 10:00 o'clock at night until 6:30 in the morning. Okay, great, but I was also getting my master's degree and had classes in the morning. I obviously didn't think that through.

So I taught myself to fall asleep anytime, anywhere and in any situation. I would leave class, get to the next class early and fall asleep in the chair. The professor would arrive and I would wake up, take notes and fall back asleep. This was amazing—being deprived of sleep taught me how to sleep better. I was once told one of the cures for insomnia is to actively not sleep because depriving someone of sleep teaches them how to sleep.

Another example from my lifting career was I had that great training facility at the Upper Limit Gym here in Murray, Utah. There were platforms as far as you could see. There were bumper plates everywhere, and racks and chains. There was a sprinting pad. There were elite athletes everywhere.

Like all great stories, you can guess the rest—the gym closed. All I had to train with was 165 pounds of weight, so I taught myself how to train as a good Olympic lifter with only 165 pounds. Being deprived of racks, platforms and bumper plates taught me to lift in a smarter way.

When I was at Utah State, I had teammates who were Vietnam veterans. I regularly complained about these brown-bag lunches we had to eat on the way to the track meets on these 14-hour bus rides. We got a brown bag with a sandwich, an apple and a cookie. One time, one of our guys, a steeple-chaser named Mike Kelly, said when he was in the service, one time he went without food for almost a week. They had to eat things that moved along the ground.

After that, I enjoyed my brown-bag food.

Deprivation leads to increased capacity.

In all of the religious traditions, there's a custom that rings a bell for me—first the fast, then the feast. This ties into my thoughts on elimination in exercise and eating. There's no question about that, but I also think somehow not having something for a while sometimes causes you to like it even more.

Dan Cantore, the great American Olympic lifter, went to the 1976 Olympics. When he came home, Eric Seubert and I asked him if we could get some gear that had USA on it. I'll never forget what Dan told me. He said, "Trust me, if you work long enough and hard enough to earn it, you'll never let it go."

He was trying to explain, nicely, that "You fast...and then you feast."

I thought it was an insightful point.

The problem we run into here is when I talk about fasting or deprivation, people are always saying, "But, Dan, you're the one who pushes breakfast all the time." "Dan, you're the guy who pushes protein powders between meals." "Dan, you're the guy who pushes peanut butter and jelly sandwiches during workouts."

True, true and true.

Let me quote Oscar Wilde for you: The test of a first-rate intelligence is the ability to hold two opposing ideas in the mind at the same time and still retain the ability to function.

I have to agree with Oscar here. It's okay for me to have conflicting ideas in my head because so much of training, fitness and health is in understanding that concept.

There's a time to fast and a time to feast.

There's a time for park bench training and a time for bus bench training. There's a time to challenge yourself. There's a time to just pat yourself on the back and think, "Ah, this is just enough." Nothing I'm saying is new and I think you know that.

Hippocrates, somewhere around 471 BC, said something everyone who says they invented intermittent fasting should remind themselves about daily. "Obese people and those desiring to lose weight should perform hard work before food."

That's intermittent fasting. That's my Three Es idea—exercise, eat and eliminate. That's everything.

The idea I'm trying to get across today is very simple: You're never going to find a perfect program. You're probably never going to find a perfect diet. What you need to start doing is embrace the concept of both/and. There's a time to rejoice and a time to cry. There's a time to leap for joy and a time to comfort those without joy.

Those of us in the fitness, health and diet fields need to constantly remind everyone there are going to be times where you're just going to stuff yourself full. I call it Thanksgiving or my daughter's wedding. There are going to be times you should back off of the food.

"Both" and "and" are important. There's a time to train as hard as you physically can and leave no stone unturned, but there's also a time to just show up and enjoy the process.

The search for perfection isn't the problem. It's a mystery.

Appendix 6
Don't Fear the Obvious

Excerpted from Now What?, Chapter One

I've been lucky. I have had the opportunity to train, visit and party with excellent coaches, outstanding athletes and training partners. To find the keys to progress and success. I like to talk with people who have walked the walk before me.

Sometimes, the answer is to do the opposite of what everyone else is doing.

Years ago, Bill Koch lectured at the Salt Lake City REI, where he discussed "inventing" a form of cross-country skiing that completely changed the sport. He skated past his competitors, and the sport morphed on the spot. He also trained differently from everyone else, using his focus on hard intervals versus junk long-distance training.

I call this a contrarian approach, and I love it. There's an ebook, which you can grab for free from *danjohn.net*, about discus throwing that discusses how I approach coaching the event by *not* throwing the discus. Now *that* is the definition of contrarian.

And, I love it. I love it.

But, being contrarian is nearly worthless in most areas of life. Generally, the answer to most of our questions will be fairly straightforward. The answer is boring. The answer is obvious.

Steven D. Levitt and Stephen J. Dubner have a series of books they call *Freakonomics.* These are fascinating books, and some readers find things that make them want to say and do horrible things to the authors. But, like my professor used to tell us in my college econ class, there is not a lot of "nice" in economics.

Three points leaped off the pages as I read *Freakonomics.* It was at that moment that I realized that economics, in addition to geometry, might be the two best fields of study for a coach.

The three points:

- *Knowing what to measure simplifies life.*

- *Conventional wisdom is usually wrong.*

- *Fear of the obvious—Don't be afraid to do the obvious!*

I would like to apologize to the authors for taking such an excellent book and summing it up so pithily.

Knowing What to Measure Simplifies Life

One of the reasons I enjoy coaching track and field is that there is almost no judging. No one votes on a winner. There is neither a swimsuit contest nor a Q and A after the event to help the judges decide.

It's distance and it's time. The victor jumps or throws the farthest. In the races, the winner is the first across the finish line. It's pretty simple stuff.

When judges are involved, universally we boo the decision.

Track and field coaches know what to measure. I was at an event and a woman told me she high jumped in high school. I asked about her best. The number was impressive and we talked about how she went to a major regional championship and even considered competing past college.

The husband asked, "How did you know she was good?"

She jumped "this high."

It's pretty simple: Knowing what to measure lets you know what is working or not working—good or bad, excellent or poor. I knew she was very good because her mark was very good.

Strength coaches should stick to load. Certainly, mastery of movements and solid techniques are important, but load is how we measure things.

With the human body being such an amazing, adaptable thing, measuring weight on the scale is rarely a good idea. You learn nothing about lean body mass from stepping on the scale.

The waistline measurement is a key for the fitness trainer. Almost always, when the waistline measurement goes down, good things are happening with fat loss. Yes, you can buy and use very expensive machines to determine bodyfat percentages, but the waistline measurement usually does the same job far cheaper.

So:

> *Track coaches measure time and distance.*
> *Strength coaches measure load.*
> *Personal trainers measure waistlines.*

You might be reading this and wondering: What should I measure?

This is where the rest of the discussion will lead us. Sometimes in team sports, what to measure demands some thought. But for longevity, you could simply measure quality years of life.

Find something to measure. Measure it. Apply practice and programming. Measure again.

Then, assess to determine whether it's a good measurement!

Conventional Wisdom is Usually Wrong

One of the more annoying habits of modern parents is to come to practice and ask if the kids are doing cardio. Technically, if hearts are beating, the kids are doing cardio.

I have a new answer: "Well, today we are focusing on the lymphatic system."

That shuts everyone up, as most people only have a vague notion of this important system, as opposed to the "unimportant systems" that keep us alive, and we can continue running 400-meter repeats.

Conventional wisdom in strength and conditioning seems to be this:

- There is a need for an arm day, but few understand the need for a leg day or back day.

- Mindless aerobic work leads to mastery in sports through sweating.

- Core or lots of ab crunches improves athletic ability.

- Warming up and then cooling down later are crucial to performance.

- It is an absolute must for the athlete to look the part, both physically and materially, with proper expensive gear.

None of these are true.

In fact, none of these are even that important in the big picture, but I sure like how well outfitted the athletes of the current generation are when they show up to practice. They might not be able to run a lap or do a pullup, but, wow, do they look good in their matching apparel.

Fads tend to dominate the fitness world. Jogging, yoga, aerobics, step aerobics, Jazzercize, Nautilus and all the rest of the workouts that shall not be named dominate training, fitness and fat loss until we all come to realize these options simply don't work.

That's a problem: We start doing something that is really hard, makes us sweaty and maybe makes us puke but rarely delivers the benefits promised.

But, these methods *have* to work! The people on the commercial got great results!

And…that is the issue with conventional wisdom: It's based on commercials, popular magazines and hearsay. Conventional wisdom tends to be so right sometimes and so wrong at other times.

The problem with conventional wisdom is that there is no measurement. Next week in the hair salon, there will be a new magazine; the TV doctor will find a new herb, and someone with shinier pants will be selling a new program.

Fear of the Obvious

I have based my life on trusting the obvious answers first. My overview of being a track and field coach is:

> *Throwers throw.*
> *Jumpers jump.*
> *Hurdlers hurdle.*
> *Sprinters sprint.*

If you can prove to me that anything works beyond this, I am all ears. But, until that day, you can coach a teen to the finals of the state meet using these simple truths.

I know. These are obvious.

Lift weights to get stronger. Fast to lose bodyfat. Stretch to get flexible. Read a lot to be well read.

Obvious. I wish I could sell it to you.

Most of us have an odd fear of the obvious. Somehow it isn't sexy enough. It's not flashy enough.

But, it works. The answers to most of life's questions are obvious. And we all seem to hate this. We all seem to fear this. Most of what works in life is so obvious, we refuse to put our arms around it and apply it.

Percy Cerutty

Percy Cerutty is one of my coaching heroes.

I was struggling as a throws coach when I went "all in" and signed up, as a camper, to the John Powell Discus Camp at Dennison University in Granville, Ohio. During one of our rare hours off, I walked into the library and went to the sports section, where I found one of Cerutty's books…a rare find in 1993.

His insights changed my career. From his work, I developed *Easy Strength*, while adding more medicine ball games, more gymnastics and an understanding that the athlete needs to use imagination to become elite.

He emphasized "thinking" before training. Famously:

> *"While work does do things,*
> *it's intelligent work that does superior things."*

Intelligent work.

Growing up, there was a phrase used for everything in life: *Look before you leap.* A few minutes of planning trumps years of rehab from lack of planning.

Intelligent work means using your brain before you rely on pain. As I often tell people: You might have one more injury, but do you have one more recovery?

You can run with this as far as you want:

- You might have one more offseason, but do you have one more season?

- You might have one more hard workout, but do you have one more recovery?

- You might have one more "hold my beer and watch this," but do you have one more chance of escaping the alligator's jaws?

Hard work does amazing things. Intelligent work does even better things.

Intelligent Work...Intelligent Coaching

Once we embrace the idea that intelligent work trumps... well, whatever is the opposite of intelligent work—we soon understand that intelligent coaching is the best thing coaches can do.

The value of using the brain first means several things:

- More efficient technique

- Injury avoidance

- Faster recovery
  (injury avoidance...*is this redundant?*)

- Faster...longer...stronger...better...any other word with "er" at the end

- Longer "youth"

- Better performance

I can always tell when people have been well coached. Their technique seems to save energy. Their approach is simple. The execution seems flawless. There isn't a lot of wasted energy. As we say in sports: Nothing "bleeds out."

Including the athlete!

Learning from the One-percenters

Years ago, I sat in an audience and listened as two rabid speakers assailed each other's positions, character, moral code and parentage. Finally, a third speaker was allowed a moment. He paused and said:

"I represent the radical middle. I reflect what 98% of the population believes about (this topic). We can learn from the one percent on both sides, but the rest of us need to have our voices heard."

Radical middle. The one-percenters.

The concepts changed my political thinking, but more important to this discussion, the concepts changed my coaching.

I tell my young interns—and all my audiences—this simple wish: I wish all of the fitness trainers and coaches would help an underserved community. There are plenty of people who need help. Help them.

A coach I spend time with, Taylor Lewis, works with the two most famous professional baseball players in the sport. If I said their names, you would know them, but I won't. Taylor then hops in his car and heads off to help people with cystic fibrosis. When Taylor talks, you should listen.

Why?

When Taylor says something works, it's because it works with the elite of the elite of sport and also with people struggling every day to do the basics of life…like breathing. Trust me, if something Taylor does works to improve the best MLB players in history *and* helps people struggling with CF, it's going to work for the rest of us, too.

In addition to elite athletes, I also work with people who have multiple sclerosis. Thomas DeLorme worked with injured WWII vets…and polio victims. Most of the great insights in training come when we test both ends of the spectrum: the underserved and struggling, and the top of the performance pile.

Taylor always calls his clients with CF athletes because they strive, as the original definition of "athlete" reminds us, for the prize. For people with any physical (or mental or…) issues, the prize is quality of life.

My book *Can You Go?* attempted to find a simple way to assess the general population—these are the people I call "everybody else." These are the 98 percent who need to address one or more of these three issues:

- *Body composition*

- *Strength*

- *Mobility*

The 1–2–3–4 Assessment in *Can You Go?* gives a general idea of where the typical client needs to focus for a few weeks. The client's actual goal is secondary, as the focus is not on what the client *wants,* but on what the client *needs.*

It always sounds harsh, but more often than not, most clients truly don't know the answer to the question, "What's your goal?" Most people spout off vague concepts like "lose weight" that don't even make sense in the big picture of health, fitness and longevity.

Oh, you want to lose weight? Cut off a leg.

Now, if you want to change lean body mass in a positive direction, we have a different discussion.

Can You Go? was based on a three-word assessment I use for active athletes: *Can You Go?* If not, let's go home…the day, season or career is over.

The assessment for performance sports is simple: Here you are! Life as an athlete is a study in the *pure present.*

Like actors and most entertainers, athletes live in the pure present. The active athlete is only as good as the last performance, the last competition or the last mark. The assessment is simple: *The last time under the spotlights is who you are right now.*

Your goal is still your goal. The journey from "here we are right now" to the goal has usually been walked before…perhaps even by you.

Generally, for active athletes I recommend 20% of their training time be spent in the weightroom getting stronger with something simple like *Easy Strength*. The other 80% of the time should be spent practicing the sport.

But, mindlessly doing the sport will have little impact on performance. Performers need to rehearse *the problems* associated with performance. This could be rain, cold and snow, but it can also be endlessly waiting around, silly last-minute officiating gaffes, or attempts by others to unnerve you.

We can all learn from the performance athlete and the performer on stage or screen. We need to prep for this with checklists, planning and sharing experiences.

But, we also need to practice the appropriate physical tension, mental arousal and proper heart rate.

The tools of arousal control made my parenting skills better, as I learned not to shoot up to the fifth floor when my daughters "push my buttons." There are moments in life, like walking those daughters down the aisle in their weddings, where being able to control the heart rate, physical tension and mental arousal are all very good things.

I want to introduce you to how I look at this. I can support anyone's goals through four basic mental sets:

- *Shark habits*

- *Pirate maps*

- *Peaking, planning and programming*

- *Principles*

These four points will weave together and interact, depending on the specific issues of the day, week, month or year.

In addition, there are four interacting terms that deserve clarity in the field of fitness and health:

- *Health*

- *Longevity*

- *Fitness*

- *Performance*

Health, according to Phil Maffetone, is "the optimal interplay of the human organs." We determine health with blood tests, annual screenings and medical checkups.

That's it. There are far too many stories of athletes in the prime of their careers dropping dead due to some unseen health issue. We need to measure health.

Longevity is an issue of both quality and quantity. Robb Wolf once summed it up very well: Live long, drop dead. Certainly, we are living longer lives, but are we living better lives? This quickly becomes an ethical question; still, we need to insure the quality of life, too.

Fitness is simply the ability to do a task. That's it. You don't need six-pack abs to toss a caber; in fact, being too lean might make it more difficult. If the task is a marathon and you complete it, you are simply fit for the task of running more than 26 miles. That might, by the way, impact your health and longevity to do a fitness task!

Performance comes the instant your name is called—the spotlight shines on your face and you must perform.

Performance is the key to sports, acting, dancing, music and musical theater. It probably helps politicians, teachers and anyone else who needs to persuade an audience.

To perform is the master quality for success in sports and the arts. Much can be learned from performance, even for those who never want to be on the stage.

There is one other thing to consider: Some of the best things you can do for health, longevity, fitness or performance might have to be done only once...or, at most, a few times. There are other concepts that might be ongoing.

Index
of People Referenced

About the Author

"Music is essentially 12 notes between any octave—twelve notes, and the octave repeats. It's the same story told over and over, forever. All any artist can offer the world is how they see those 12 notes. That's it."
~ **Bobby Maine,** *A Star is Born*

I love music. Music has the power to rile me up and calm me down. I see it as an analogy for life.

I had to do the math on this, because the last time I checked, the white keys on a piano add up to eight notes before it repeats. ABCDEFG. ABCDEFG.

As Dan often points out, sometimes I miss the important notes—the minor chords, the major lifts.

Dan John does not.

Having spent more than 30 years observing the man with the whistle, I can attest to the fact that Dan will never look past the minor chords.

The high school baseball phenom who didn't make the cut and, begrudgingly, decided to throw the shot put.

And won the state championship.

And went on to throw for a storied NCAA program. And whose wedding we will attend later this year. Minor chord.

It also includes watching a father coach his daughters.

Dan's proudest, weepiest moments (we all know the man cries), were watching Kelly and Lindsay marching out to the ring as a senior and a sophomore. And, again, watching Lindsay, literally, pull it out of her ass, on the last shot put throw of her high school career.

Last throw, best throw. State championship. Major lifts.

Twelve notes and the octave repeats. It's the same story told over and over.

The workshop audiences vary. The faces in the gym change. But the coach does not. Dan won't ever put down the whistle. And he will continue to push the humans he interacts with to make a difference.

Tiffini John